CROWDSOURCING

JEFF HOWE is a contributing editor at *Wired*, where he covers the entertainment industry among other subjects. Before coming to *Wired* he was a senior editor at Inside.com and a writer at the *Village Voice*. In his fifteen years as a journalist he has travelled around the world working on stories ranging from the impending water crisis in Central Asia to the implications of gene patenting. He has written for *US News & World Report*, The *Washington Post*, *Mother Jones* and numerous other publications. He lives in Brooklyn with his wife and daughter.

CROWDSOURCING

HOW THE **POWER OF THE CROWD**
IS DRIVING THE FUTURE OF BUSINESS

JEFF HOWE

BUSINESS
BOOKS

Published by Random House Business Books 2009

2 4 6 8 10 9 7 5 3 1

Copyright © Jeff Howe 2008

Jeff Howe has asserted his right under the Copyright, Designs
and Patents Act, 1988, to be identified as the author of this work

First published in the United States in 2008 by Crown Business,
an imprint of The Crown Publishing Group,
a division of Random House Inc., New York

First published in Great Britain in 2009 by
Random House Business Books
Random House, 20 Vauxhall Bridge Road,
London SW1V 2SA

www.rbooks.co.uk

Addresses for companies within The Random House Group Limited can
be found at: www.randomhouse.co.uk/offices.htm

The Random House Group Limited Reg. No. 954009

A CIP catalogue record for this book
is available from the British Library

ISBN 9781905211159

The Random House Group Limited supports The Forest Stewardship
Council (FSC), the leading international forest certification organisation.
All our titles that are printed on Greenpeace approved FSC certified
paper carry the FSC logo. Our paper procurement policy can be found at
www.rbooks.co.uk/environment

Mixed Sources
Product group from well-managed
forests and other controlled sources
www.fsc.org Cert no. TT-COC-2139
© 1996 Forest Stewardship Council

Printed and bound in Great Britain by
CPI Bookmarque, Croydon, CR0 4TD

To Alysia and our very small crowd

CONTENTS

INTRODUCTION

The Dawn of the Human Network

The Jakes didn't set out to democratize the world of graphic design; they just wanted to make cool T-shirts. In 2000, Jake Nickell and Jacob DeHart, as they're more formally known, were college dropouts living in Chicago, though neither had found much work putting his abbreviated educations to use. Both were avid members of a burgeoning subculture that treated the lowly T-shirt as a canvas for visual flights of fancy. So when they met after entering an online T-shirt design competition, they already had a lot in common. For starters, both thought it would be a good idea to start their own design competition. But instead of using a jury, they would let the designers themselves pick the winner. That November a company was born—the product of equal parts youthful idealism and liberal doses of beer.

The pair launched Threadless.com a few months later with a business plan that was still in the cocktail-napkin stage: People would submit designs for a cool T-shirt. Users would vote on which one was best. The winner would get free T-shirts bearing his or her winning design, and everyone else would get to buy the shirt. At first the Two Jakes, as people called them, ran Threadless from Nickell's bedroom. But the company grew. And grew. And grew yet more. People liked voting on T-shirts, and the designs were less staid and less formulaically hip than those sold by Urban Outfitters or Old Navy. The winning designs started appearing on hit TV shows and on the backs of hip-hop artists. The company has nearly doubled its revenue every year since. Threadless currently receives some one thousand designs each week, which are voted on by the Threadless community, now six hundred thousand strong. The company then selects nine shirts from the top hundred to print. Each design sells out— hardly surprising given the fact Threadless has a fine-tuned sense of consumer demand before they ever send the design to the printer.

Design by democracy, as it happens, isn't bad for the bottom line. Threadless generated $17 million in revenues in 2006 (the last year for which it has released sales figures) and by all accounts has continued its rapid rate of growth. Threadless currently sells an average of ninety thousand T-shirts a month, and the company boasts "incredible profit margins," according to Jeffrey Kalmikoff, its chief creative officer. Threadless spends $5 to produce a shirt that sells for between $12 and $25. They don't need advertising or marketing budgets, as the community performs those functions admirably: designers spread the word as they try to persuade friends to vote for their designs, and Threadless rewards the community with store credit every time someone submits a photo of themselves wearing a Threadless shirt (worth $1.50) or refers a friend who buys a shirt (worth $3).

Meanwhile, the cost of the designs themselves isn't

much more than a line item. DeHart and Nickell have increased the bounty paid to winning designers to $2,000 in cash and a $500 gift certificate, but this still amounts to only $1 million per year, a fraction of the company's gross income, and Threadless keeps all the intellectual property.

But as any number of winners will happily volunteer, it's not about the money. It's about cred, or, to give that a more theoretical cast, it's about the emerging reputation economy, where people work late into the night on one creative endeavor or another in the hope that their community—be it fellow designers, scientists, or computer hackers—acknowledge their contribution in the form of kudos and, just maybe, some measure of fame. Threadless's best sellers (such as "Communist Party," a red shirt featuring Karl Marx wearing a lampshade on his head) are on regular view at coffee shops and nightclubs from London to Los Angeles.

The Jakes now enjoy a certain degree of notoriety themselves. Nickell and DeHart have become heroes among the do-it-yourself designer set, and even have given lectures to MBA students at MIT's Sloan School of Management. Aspiring executives spent much of the time explaining all the basic business tenets the Jakes had broken in building Threadless. Good thing they weren't there when Nickell and DeHart were first launching their company. Nickell and DeHart are smart enough to know a good idea when they stumble on it. They created a parent company, skinnyCorp, which includes not just Threadless but a spin-off division that takes a similarly democratic approach to the creation of everything from sweaters to tote bags to bed linens. "Next we're thinking of doing housewares," says Nickell.

An Accidental Economy

In late 2005, the Pew Internet & American Life Project released a paper called "Teen Content Creators and Consumers." The study, which consisted of interviews with more than eleven hundred Americans between the ages of twelve and seventeen, drew little attention when it was published, but the findings were extraordinary: there were more teens creating content for the Internet than there were teens merely consuming it. At the time it was commonly assumed that television had created a generation of consumers characterized by unprecedented passivity. Yet now it seemed the very opposite was the case. In his book *The Third Wave* the futurist Alvin Toffler predicted that consumers would come to exercise much more control over the creation of the products they consumed, becoming, in a word, "prosumers." In 1980, the year Toffler published his book, this seemed like mere fodder for bad science-fiction novels. From the perspective of 2005, it seemed stunningly prescient.

Pew's conclusions confirmed my own recent experience. A few months before the study was released I had been hopscotching across the country attending concerts on the Warped Tour, a carniesque collection of punk bands and the hangers-on that followed them from town to town. I was writing about the social networking site MySpace, which was known—to the degree it was known at all—as a grassroots-marketing venue for Emo bands, off-color comedians, and Gen Y models. In the hours I spent with the performers and their fans, I noticed that very few defined themselves as musicians, artists, or any other such label. The singers were publishing books of poetry; drummers were budding video directors; and the roadies doubled as record producers. Everything—even one musician's pencil portraits—was posted to the Internet with minimal attention to production quality. These were what Marc Prensky, a game designer and educator, calls the "digital natives." The rapidly falling cost of the tools needed to produce entertainment—from editing software to digital video cameras—combined with free distribution networks over the Web, had produced a subculture unlike anything previously encountered: a country within a country quite capable of entertaining itself.

Next I heard about the Converse Gallery ad campaign, in which the shoemaker's ad agency solicited twenty-four-second spots from anyone capable of wielding a camcorder. The shorts had to somehow convey a passion for Chuck Taylors, but that was it. You didn't even have to show the shoe. The best of the spots were very, very good—electric with inventive energy, yet grainy enough to look authentic, as indeed they were. Within three weeks the company had received seven hundred fifty submissions, a number that climbed into the thousands before Converse discontinued the campaign in early 2007. It was viewed as a smashing success by both the company and the advertising industry, as well as a seminal example of what is now called user-generated content.

This was the new new media: content created by amateurs. A little research revealed that amateurs were making unprecedented contributions to the sciences as well, and it became clear that to regard a kid making his own Converse ad as qualitatively different from a weekend chemist trying to invent a new form of organic fertilizer would be to misapprehend the forces at work. The same dynamics—cheap production costs, a surplus of underemployed talent and creativity, and the rise of online communities composed of like-minded enthusiasts—were at work. Clearly a nascent revolution was afoot, one that would have a deep impact on chemistry, advertising, and a great many other fields to boot. In June 2006, I published a story in *Wired* magazine giving that revolution a name: crowdsourcing. If anything, I underestimated the speed with which crowdsourcing could come to shape our culture and economy, and the breadth of those effects. As it happens, not just digital natives, but also digital immigrants (whom we might define as anyone who still gets their news from a newspaper) would soon be writing book reviews, selling their own photographs, creating new uses for Google maps, and, yes, even designing T-shirts.

As I've continued to follow the trend, I've learned a great deal about what makes it tick. If it's not already clear, Threadless isn't really in the T-shirt business. It sells community. "When I read that there was a site where you could send in designs and get feedback, I instantly thought, this is really cool," says Ross Zeitz, a twenty-seven-year-old Threadless designer who was hired to help run the community after his designs won a record-breaking eight times. "Now I talk to other designers, and they're motivated by the same things I was. It's addictive, especially if you're at a design school or some corporate gig, where you're operating under strict guidelines," says Zeitz. The only restriction at Threadless, by contrast, is that the design has to fit onto a T-shirt.

Threadless, its founders have noted, is a business only by accident. None of the Threadless founders set out to "maximize profits" or "exploit the efficiencies created by the Internet." They just wanted to make a cool website where people who liked the stuff they liked would feel at home. In succeeding at this modest goal, they wound up creating a whole new way of doing business.

Around the same time that the Jakes were stumbling into their business, Bruce Livingstone was stumbling into his. A Web designer, entrepreneur, and former punk rock musician, in 2000 Livingstone set up a site where he and other designers he knew could share each other's photographs. This way they could avoid paying for stock photographs—which generally ran several hundred dollars apiece—and could improve their skills at the same time. A community of mostly amateur photographers grew up around the site, which he called iStockphoto. Soon Livingstone started charging a nominal fee—twenty-five cents—for each image. Part of the money went to him; part to the photographer. Because they weren't making a living off the proceeds, it was all gravy. Business was good, and then it got even better. iStockphoto was undercutting the big stock-photo agencies by 99 percent, and was fostering a vibrant community of creative types at the same time. Livingstone radically upset the insular world of stock photography. The stock image—which is nothing more than a preexisting photograph licensed for reuse—is the little white lie of publishing. That image of a beatific mother nursing her infant in a woman's magazine? Stock. Those well-groomed, racially diverse executives on the cover of the Merrill Lynch prospectus? You might recognize them as the well-groomed, racially diverse insurance agents from, say, a brochure from Allstate.

Recognizing that iStock's growth came at the expense of its own business, in 2006, Getty Images bought Livingstone's company for $50 million. It was a smart buy: iStockphoto sold 18 million photographs, illustrations, and videos, earning Getty $72 million. Investment bank Goldman Sachs estimates that iStock's revenues will increase to \$262 million by 2012. Meanwhile, Getty expects its traditional stock offerings to enter a steep decline in that same period.

Threadless and iStockphoto aren't novelty acts. They are part of the first wave of a business and cultural revolution that will change how we think about the Internet, commerce, and, most important, ourselves. Over the past several years people from around the world have begun exhibiting an almost totally unprecedented social behavior: they are coming together to perform tasks, usually for little or no money, that were once the sole province of employees. This phenomenon is sweeping through industries ranging from professional photography to journalism to the sciences.

Crowdsourcing had its genesis in the open source movement in software. The development of the Linux operating system proved that a community of like-minded peers was capable of creating a better product than a corporate behemoth like Microsoft. Open source revealed a fundamental truth about humans that had gone largely unnoticed until the connectivity of the Internet brought it into high relief: labor can often be organized more efficiently in the context of community than it can in the context of a corporation. The best person to do a job is the one who most wants to do that job; and the best people to evaluate their performance are their friends and peers who, by the way, will enthusiastically pitch in to improve the final product, simply for the sheer pleasure of helping one another and creating something beautiful from which they all will benefit.

There's nothing theoretical about this. Open source efforts haven't merely equaled the best efforts of some of the largest corporations in the world; they have exceeded them, which explains why IBM has pumped a billion dollars into open source development. Analysts at IBM know that open source produces results. From the Linux operating system to Apache server software to the Firefox Web browser, much of the infrastructure of the information economy was built by teams of self-organized volunteers. And now that model of production is rapidly migrating to fields far and wide.

This migration isn't made up of just design students, shutterbugs, and programmers. Crowdsourcing has profoundly influenced the way even Fortune 100 companies like Procter & Gamble do business. Until recently, P&G's corporate culture was notoriously secretive and insular: if it wasn't invented in-house, then it didn't exist. That worked fine for the first 163 years of P&G's history, but by mid-2000 the company's growth had slowed and its ability to innovate and create new products had stagnated. In the six months between January and June of that year, its stock lost 50 percent of its value, wiping out $75 billion in market capitalization.

The board responded by bringing in A. G. Lafley as CEO with a mandate to right the listing ship. The former head of P&G's global beauty care division, Lafley issued an ambitious challenge to his employees: Open up. Tear down the internal walls that separated sales from R&D and engineering from marketing, as well as the walls that separated P&G from its suppliers, retailers, and customers. When Lafley took over, only 15 percent of its new products and innovations originated outside the company. Lafley created an initiative called "Connect and Develop," with the goal of raising that figure to 50 percent by 2007.

P&G has now exceeded that mark, an accomplishment largely built on one of the more compelling turnarounds in corporate history. Lafley writes in a book about his experiences leading P&G, entitled *The Game-Changer*: "P&G has about 8,500 researchers; and we figured there are another 1.5 million similar researchers with pertinent areas of expertise. Why not pick their brains?" To reach them the company has either created or partnered with what Lafley calls "Internet-based engines" capable of tapping the collective brainpower of scientists around the world. In order to leverage the expertise of retired scientists from P&G as well as from other companies, Lafley helped create YourEncore, a website through which these scientists can work part-time on projects posted by companies such as P&G. Recognizing that vital intellectual capital is increasingly found overseas, from Eastern Europe to China and India, P&G also uses a network of 140,000 scientists called InnoCentive. When the in-house R&D staff gets stumped, it can post the problem to InnoCentive's website. If one of InnoCentive's scientists can come up with the solution, P&G pays them a reward (and keeps the intellectual property). P&G has realized that tens of thousands of talented scientists are willing to put in the time and effort in their own jerry-built labs for the satisfaction of solving a puzzle and coming up with a practical solution—and, not unimportantly, of earning additional cash. The value of Lafley's strategy can be seen in the sustained growth in both P&G's revenue and its profitability. Since Lafley took over the company, its stock price has surpassed its former highs and net profits tripled to $10 billion in 2007. The Connect and Develop initiative has also led to some of P&G's most innovative products, including the now-ubiquitous Swiffer, among others.

Despite their obvious differences, Threadless, iStockphoto, and P&G all have one thing in common. They embody a central truth that was first articulated by Bill Joy, cofounder of Sun Microsystems. "No matter who you are," Joy once said, "most of the smartest people work for someone else." That, in a nutshell, is what this whole book is about. Given the right set of conditions, the crowd will almost always outperform any number of employees—a fact that companies are becoming aware of and are increasingly attempting to exploit.

A Revolution of Many Small Parts

While crowdsourcing is intertwined with the Internet, it is not at its essence about technology. Technology itself consists of wires, chips, and abstruse operating manuals. Worse yet for a writer, it's boring. Far more important and interesting are the human behaviors technology engenders, especially the potential of the Internet to weave the mass of humanity together into a thriving, infinitely powerful organism. It is the rise of the network that allows us to exploit a fact of human labor that long predates the Internet: the ability to divvy up an overwhelming task—such as the writing of an exhaustive encyclopedia—into small enough chunks that completing it becomes not only feasible, but fun.

We can see this principle at work in, of all things, the search for alien life-forms. The University of California at Berkeley has been looking for aliens for nearly thirty years. Berkeley's SETI (Search for Extraterrestrial Intelligence) project scans data gathered by large radio telescopes such as the massive Arecibo observatory in Puerto Rico (made famous by the 1997 Matthew McConaughey and Jodie Foster movie *Contact*). Radio waves constantly bombard Earth's atmosphere. By recording and analyzing them scientists hope to identify anomalies—signals amid the noise—that would betray the presence of intelligent life on other planets. Rush Limbaugh, in other words, could have an extraterrestrial counterpart, and if we listen hard enough we might be able to hear him.

Berkeley had been using powerful computers to analyze all that data. Then in 1997 a handful of astronomers and computer scientists proposed a novel solution: Recruit the public to donate computer time to the task. Volunteers would download a simple screen saver, which would kick into gear whenever the user stopped using his or her machine. Once a computer finished scanning a chunk of data, it would automatically send it back to a central server, which would then give the computer a new chunk to work on. The project was called SETI@home, and it launched in May 1999 with what seemed like an ambitious goal: get one hundred thousand people to help.

That turned out to be a very modest target. By 2005, 5.2 million users had downloaded the SETI@home screen saver, logging nearly three million years of computing time. The *Guinness Book of World Records* recognizes it as "the largest computation in history." While SETI@home has failed to find any proof of extraterrestrial life, it has conclusively succeeded in proving that the many can work together to outperform the few. Distributed computing—the term for a network of numerous computers working on a single task—is now being applied to a wide range of computationally intensive problems, from simulating how proteins assemble inside the human body to running climate prediction models.

SETI@home and distributed computing illustrate the immense power of networks. Who would have predicted that the most powerful supercomputers would reside not in an institutional laboratory, but in our own homes and cubicles? SETI@home harnesses the "spare cycles," or excess capacity of individual computers. Crowdsourcing operates on the same principle, except that it uses the network to harness individual people's spare cycles—the time and energy left over after we've fulfilled our obligations to employers and family.

However, unlike the distributed computing model—which was consciously conceived by a group of academics—crowdsourcing emerged organically. It was not the product of an economist or management consultant or marketing guru. It arose instead out of the uncoordinated actions of thousands of people, who were doing things that people like to do, especially in the companionship of other people. The Internet provided a way for them to pursue their interests—photography, fan fiction, organic chemistry, politics, comedy, ornithology, anime, T-shirt design, classic video games, atonal musical composition, amateur pornography—together. In doing so, these people incidentally created information, a commodity of no little value in an information economy.

Around the time the Internet was first making its way into mainstream culture, *The New Yorker* ran a now famous cartoon: a dog sitting in front of a PC says to his canine companion, "On the Internet, nobody knows you're a dog." With crowdsourcing, nobody knows you don't hold a degree in organic chemistry or that you've never shot photographs professionally or that you've never taken a design class in your life. Crowdsourcing has the capacity to form a sort of perfect meritocracy. Gone are pedigree, race, gender, age, and qualification. What remains is the quality of the work itself. In stripping away all considerations outside quality, crowdsourcing operates under the most optimistic of assumptions: that each one of us possesses a far broader, more complex range of talents than we can currently express within current economic structures. In this sense crowdsourcing is the antithesis of Fordism, the assembly-line mentality that dominated the industrial age. Crowdsourcing turns on the presumption that we are all creators—artists, scientists, architects, and designers, in any combination or order. It holds the promise to unleash the latent potential of the individual to excel at more than one vocation, and to explore new avenues for creative expression. Indeed, it contains the potential—or alternately, the threat—of rendering the idea of a vocation itself an industrial-age artifact.

Crowdsourcing capitalizes on the deeply social nature of the human species. Contrary to the foreboding, dystopian vision that the Internet serves primarily to isolate people from each other, crowdsourcing uses technology to foster unprecedented levels of collaboration and meaningful exchanges between people from every imaginable background in every imaginable geographical location. Online communities are at the heart of crowdsourcing, providing a context and a structure within which the "work" takes place. People form lasting friendships through iStockphoto and Threadless; they also enrich everyone's experience by critiquing one another's work and teaching what they know to less experienced contributors. Crowdsourcing engenders another form of collaboration as well, between companies and customers. Toffler was right: people don't want to consume passively; they'd rather participate in the development and creation of products meaningful to them. Crowdsourcing is just one manifestation of a larger trend toward greater democratization in commerce. Governments have slowly moved toward democracy; the enormous promiscuity of information facilitated by the Internet is catalyzing the same movement in business, enabling a movement toward decentralization that has begun to sweep across every imaginable industry.

Crowdsourcing has revealed that, contrary to conventional wisdom, humans do not always behave in predictably self-interested patterns. People typically contribute to crowdsourcing projects for little or no money, laboring tirelessly despite the absence of financial reward. This behavior seems illogical viewed through the lens of conventional economics, but rewards can't always be measured by the dollar or the euro. A study conducted by MIT examined why highly skilled programmers would donate their time to open source software projects. The results revealed that the programmers were driven to contribute for a complex web of motivations, including a desire to create something from which the larger community would benefit as well as the sheer joy of practicing a craft at which they excel. People are inspired to contribute to crowdsourcing endeavors for similar motivations, though financial incentives also play a role, especially when the contributors hail from developing countries. People derive enormous pleasure from cultivating their talents and from passing on what they've learned to others. Collaboration, in the context of crowdsourcing, is its own reward.

This doesn't mean that the companies employing crowdsourcing get a free ride. Those that view the crowd as a cheap labor force are doomed to fail. What unites all successful crowdsourcing efforts is a deep commitment to the community. This entails much more than lip service and requires a drastic shift in the mind-set of a traditional corporation. The crowd wants to feel a sense of ownership over its creations, and is keenly aware when it is being exploited. The company, in this context, is just one more member of the community and you don't have to watch *Survivor* to know that people who act duplicitously are kicked off the island.

Crowdsourcing paints a flattering portrait of the human race. We are more intelligent, more creative, and more talented than we tend to give ourselves credit for. I've seen cases in which electricians solve complex industrial chemistry problems, and forklift operators show a knack for investing in the stock market. Crowdsourcing, with its uncanny tendency to draw gifted people from the most unlikely nooks and crannies, is like an immense talent-finding mechanism. We see this on YouTube, in which budding comedians and filmmakers have been able to secure first a cult audience, then industry contacts and finally paying gigs and mainstream recognition. But more than simply identifying diamonds in the rough, crowdsourcing also cultivates and nurtures that talent. In this way, crowdsourcing adds to our culture's general store of intellectual capital.

Crowdsourcing has generally been embraced as a positive development. It's been hailed as a potentially vital force in politics and governance, and has even made its way to the virtual seminary, with theologians speculating that it could facilitate more meaningful collaboration between congregations and their religious leaders. But as with any sweeping cultural and economic change, crowdsourcing's beneficial effects will be tempered by upheaval and disruption. Crowdsourcing represents a radical shift in how many industries—especially those trafficking in information—do their work, so it's no wonder that some view it as more of a curse than a blessing. As the phenomenon grows in scope and power, more and more vocations have come under threat. Companies are moving their tech support functions over to user forums, where volunteers happily offer to walk newbies through basic troubleshooting exercises. In journalism, the BBC, Gannett, and Reuters have all started to crowdsource such essential work as investigating government malfeasance or reporting on local events that have always been the province of trained journalists. Such moves are widely feared to be a prelude to layoffs and staff reductions. In the case of stock images, the crowd has already put traditional photographers out of work.

Likewise, crowdsourcing accelerates the globalization of labor and the economic dislocation that we see in outsourcing. Like the Internet through which it operates, crowdsourcing recognizes no boundaries. The network doesn't care if you're down the block, downstate, or down under—if you can perform the service, design the product, or solve the problem, you've got the job. The earth, it turns out, is flatter than anyone ever imagined. Crowdsourcing is already causing money to flow from the developed world to countries like India or Russia (to name but two), with their overqualified but underemployed professional classes. So is crowdsourcing the new outsourcing? Not quite, but it does take advantage of the same disparities between developed and developing economies. Finally, there are the understandable concerns that crowdsourcing is fostering a cultural mediocrity: Could crowdsourcing really ever yield a Shakespeare play, Beatles song, or Picasso painting? The answer, I believe, is an unequivocal yes, but such masterpieces are unlikely to emerge in the ways we expect them to, or from the usual quarters.

The book is roughly divided into the past, present, and future. In the first four chapters I argue that four fundamental developments—a renaissance of amateurism, the emergence of the open source software movement, the increasing availability of the tools of production, and finally the rise of vibrant online communities organized according to people's interests—have made crowdsourcing not only possible, but inevitable.

The subsequent five chapters are devoted to the present—how crowdsourcing is manifesting at this current moment in history. Crowdsourcing is just a rubric for a wide range of activities. Its adaptability is what makes it pervasive and powerful. But this very flexibility makes the task of defining and categorizing crowdsourcing a challenge. When twenty-eight thousand strangers use the Web to pool their pocket change to purchase the ailing British football club Ebbsfleet United, is that crowdsourcing? What about when the decisions of thousands of mock investors are aggregated to guide a very real mutual fund? The answer is yes on both counts, but they constitute two very different applications.

In order to make sense of such disparities, I try to establish a basic taxonomy of crowdsourcing. Chapters 5 and 6 are focused on how we are using collective intelligence to predict the future and solve otherwise intractable problems. Chapter 7 explores the crowd's creative energies, and how that considerable resource is changing the way everything from journalism to language translation to entertainment is being produced. Chapter 8 examines the crowd's uncanny ability to filter and organize that vast repository of information that is the World Wide Web. Chapter 9 looks at how the crowd's collective pocketbook is being used to create new ways of financing everything from micro-credit organizations to would-be rock stars. Chapter 10 provides a glimpse into how today's teens—who certainly don't need to read a book to tell them what crowdsourcing is all about—will change the nature of work and creativity.

What we are seeing with crowdsourcing is the phenomenon of creative destruction happening in near real time. Social and economic changes such as the move from manufacturing to services took place over decades. But the pace of change has accelerated alongside the light-speed pace of innovation, and the consequential transformations are rapidly becoming a part of our daily lives, as anyone with a teenager in the house can attest. What we may well see in the not distant future are people experiencing crowdsourcing as a fish does water—the stuff we swim in day after day. Although we're unlikely to see, say, UPS put it to use in the shipping of freight, we could well see that company use crowdsourcing to divine new logistical solutions or design a more compelling corporate identity.

The short-term growing pains that will surely accompany such a transition will be outweighed, I believe, by the long-term benefits of a flattened environment in which we will all become valuable contributors. Crowdsourcing has the potential to correct a long-standing human conundrum. The amount of knowledge and talent dispersed among the numerous members of our species has always vastly outstripped our capacity to harness those invaluable quantities. Instead, it withers on the vine for want of an outlet. Crowdsourcing is the mechanism by which such talent and knowledge is matched to those in need of it. It poses a tantalizing question: What if the solutions to our greatest problems weren't waiting to be conceived, but already existed somewhere, just waiting to be found, in the warp and weave of this vibrant human network?

SECTION I

How We Got Here

1

THE RISE OF THE AMATEUR

Fueling the Crowdsourcing Engine

There is a shadow labor force in America. These people toil away cheerfully at tasks ranging from raising heirloom vegetables to making after-market "mods" for their cars to translating obscure nineteenth-century French novels into English. These are the amateurs—the hobbyists and enthusiasts long judged to possess more passion than talent. That is no longer a fair, or even accurate appraisal. Increasingly skilled and capable of organized, sophisticated collaboration, amateurs are competing successfully with professionals in fields ranging from computer programming to journalism to the sciences. The energy and devotion of the amateur comprises the fuel for the crowdsourcing engine.

Quantities of both energy and devotion can be found in ample supply at the PLUG Independent Music Awards. PLUG is like the Grammy Awards, in that both are annual ceremonies held to honor the finest musical accomplishments of the year. PLUG is unlike the Grammys in every other respect. The Grammys are attended by hundreds of the music industry's leading lights; PLUG is attended by a few hundred unshaven hipsters from downtown Manhattan. The Grammys are televised across the nation; PLUG *would* be webcast over the Internet if the organizers could ever get the technology worked out in time. The Grammys draw a cavalcade of stars and give the winners a gilded gramophone to honor their achievement. PLUG winners may not even know they've been nominated, and they don't receive anything even if they do show up.

It goes without saying that PLUG doesn't take itself too seriously. The ceremony radiates ramshackle detachment, and it's difficult to say if anyone—from the musicians to the performers to the backstage technical crew—could be labeled a professional. In fact, PLUG doesn't have one full-time employee. This is, of course, its appeal. The audience laughs and cheers at every technical malfunction. In the PLUG bizarro world—the orbit of which falls well within today's pop cultural universe—low production values trump slickness every time.

I attended my first PLUG in February 2007. I didn't come for the ceremony, such as it is, but to observe the twenty-two amateur photographers the organizers chose to shoot the event. For their part, the photographers agreed not to charge for their time. They work for iStockphoto, which markets and sells images created by some fifty thousand photographers, nearly all of them amateurs. This company has taken advantage of an imbalance that's emerged in the digital economy: compelling, high-resolution images have become ubiquitous, yet professional photo agencies were still treating them like a scarce resource. iStock crowdsourced their product, undercut their competitors, and made a killing in the process.

The iStock photographers fit right in: they were

jammed into a reserved area just in front of the stage and if not for the all-access passes dangling from their necks would have been indistinguishable from the fans. This is appropriate; PLUG is essentially a festival displaying the moxie and talent of the crowd, be it expressed in music or images or the barbershop quartet that takes the stage between each award. PLUG celebrates everything that's best about amateurism: authenticity, spirit, passion, and, perhaps most of all, a well-developed sense of humor about its own humble place in the world. At one point in the green room I complimented one of the founders, Gerry Hart, on having pulled off the show at all. "Well," he said, "we knew we'd never do it right, so we figured we'd do it wrong."

I wanted to get to know iStock's unusual workforce firsthand, so between performances I cornered one of the photographers, Nick Monu. Monu looks young enough to be shooting the awards for a high school newspaper, and in fact he's only twenty-two. Tall, handsome, and intelligent, Monu has the sort of easy smile that could lead to a lucrative career selling securities, or cars, or expensive homes. From looking at him you'd never guess he represents the greatest threat to professional photography since the Kodak Instamatic started putting portrait photographers out of business.

Monu wants to be a doctor, for all the reasons people still admire that profession, and is enrolled in his second year of medical school at Brown University. Born in his mother's hometown, Kiev, he grew up in Lagos and went to high school in upstate New York. He spent much of his childhood watching his mother and father, a pediatrician and cardiologist respectively, tending to the impoverished in various Third World clinics. But Monu's mother also made her two sons study art. "We both had to take piano and drawing lessons. My mom was really serious about that." Monu took to drawing early, and when he got to high school he started taking photographs. "I'd been doing these photo-realist paintings, so I bought a digital camera in order to project the images onto the canvas." Soon he realized he liked taking pictures more than he liked painting them, and Monu pursued photography with the enthusiasm that has infected shutterbugs ever since it was introduced to the masses by George Eastman—who started as an amateur photographer himself.

If this were 1985, 1995, or even 2001, that's all taking pictures would be to Monu: a hobby. Instead, photography is putting Monu through medical school, with a whole lot of spending money to spare. "I made ten thousand dollars last month," he admitted sheepishly, as if he's committed some minor indiscretion. Not that financial success has gone to his head. "I don't see why I can't practice medicine and shoot photos at the same time."

Monu has an exclusive contract to shoot for iStockphoto, and he has come to the award ceremony at the invitation of Bruce Livingstone, iStock's thirty-seven-year-old CEO, who has been able to secure the exclusive rights for his photographers to shoot the PLUG awards for the excellent reason that he helped start them. In 2001 Livingstone and Gerry Hart, an old friend from his punk rock days, decided to turn their love for mixed tapes into an awards show. "It was really born of a disdain for the MTV awards and every other awards ceremony," Livingstone said while we sat in the green room talking to Hart and a few of the musicians. But eventually I meandered back down to the main floor to watch the action. I've covered music for years, often in tandem with a photographer. Rock photographers and writers tend to gravitate to their calling for the same reason: a devotion to the music. Then the calling becomes a career, and at some point a job. The beer-sticky floors lose their appeal, and bands blend into one another. The professional music journalist assumes a posture of studied detachment. They can usually be spotted in the crowd as the ones not bobbing their heads or tapping their feet, but writing in a notebook with a vague smirk on their faces.

Monu and the other iStockers, then, provide a study in contrast. By the end of the closing act, a mop-headed photographer named Louis had cast his equipment bag to the floor and begun banging his head in rhythm to the music. He held his camera above his head and started taking exposures blindly, carelessly, joyfully. He looked at me, grinned, and hoisted his index and pinkie fingers into devil horns, the universal sign of rock 'n' roll abandon.

The Amateur Renaissance

When a photographer makes $10,000 a month from something he considers a hobby, it's probably time to redefine the term "amateur." Very few iStock contributors make anything close to what Monu makes; only 4 percent of them claim "photographer" as their chief occupation, according to one study of the iStock workforce. The IRS defines a professional photographer as one who makes more than $5,000 from the sale of his or her photographs, which might be news to Monu, who has no plans to sacrifice his ambitions in medicine for a career in photography.

Relying on financial income to draw distinctions

between professional and nonprofessional is a good rule of thumb if you prepare tax returns for a living. But if you're looking at crowdsourcing, it only produces confusion. What is evident in crowdsourcing is that people with highly diverse skills and professional backgrounds are drawn to participate. While very few iStock contributors are professional photographers, more than half have had at least one year of formal schooling in "art, design, photography, or related creative disciplines."

In an era of Internet-enabled mass participation, we clearly need a more flexible definition of "amateur." If a chemist with no prior training in biomedicine makes a key advance in the search for a cure for Lou Gehrig's disease, do we say she's an amateur? Surely not in the same sense I would be if I started performing stand-up comedy. In their book *The Pro-Am Revolution: How Enthusiasts Are Changing Our Economy and Society,* Charles Leadbeater and Paul Miller argue that the quantity and quality of amateur efforts has increased so greatly in recent years that we need a third designation altogether: "the Pro-Am— amateurs who work to professional standards." In the twentieth century, they write, "amateurism came to be a term of derision," while "professionalism was a mark of seriousness and high standards." By looking at examples from sports, acting, gardening, and other fields, they propose that a new breed of amateur has emerged: "The Pro-Ams are knowledgeable, educated, committed, and networked." I'll make a slightly different argument: we need to understand that amateurism is less a designation than it is a spectrum.

Crowdsourcing efforts generally attract people both with and without professional credentials. Further complicating matters, some projects pay their contributors (iStock) and some do not (Wikipedia). There are, however, two shared attributes among almost all crowdsourcing projects: participants are not primarily motivated by money, and they're donating their leisure hours to the cause. That is, they're contributing their excess capacity, or "spare cycles," to indulge in something they love to do.

It's no accident that crowdsourcing is emerging during a renaissance of amateur activity all around the world. A confluence of factors contributed to this sudden creative abundance. An exponential rise in education has coincided with the emergence of the greatest mechanism for distributing knowledge the world has ever seen: the Internet. But this diversely talented, highly skilled workforce must toil away in a labor market that requires ever-greater degrees of specialization. This leaves people feeling overeducated and underfulfilled, with job satisfaction rates reaching all-time lows. Is it any wonder they're seeking more meaningful work outside the confines of the workplace?

Evidence of this is nowhere so obvious as on the Web. Obviously this technology has transformed the way we work and the way we shop, but it's also transformed the way we play. The time we once devoted to pastimes such as bowling or bridge is increasingly being spent producing information—writing a blog, writing reviews on a food site such as Chowhound.com, or adding to the message boards on Lost.com, a website devoted to ABC's hit TV show. The owners of these sites—which bring in money through ad revenue—have essentially crowdsourced the task of content creation.

There is no simple way to quantify the extent to which nonprofessionals now contribute to the economy, but the signs of its growth are all around us—for example, there's the exponential increase in the creation of webpages. In 1997, there were 200 million. By 2005, that number had jumped to 11.5 billion, an increase attributable largely to the growth of blogs. As of January 2008, there were more than 80 million videos on YouTube, at least half of which were created by amateurs. The website Harrypotterfanfiction.com hosts an astounding 45,000 stories written by a legion of fans who have converted their passion for the venerable children's franchise into a penchant for creative fiction. The Internet itself is essentially one giant cabinet of wonders, an acme of nonprofessional achievement.

And then there's the dramatic growth in the do-it-yourself category of arts and crafts. *ReadyMade,* a "magazine for people who like to make stuff," launched in 2001 with a rate base of thirty thousand. As of January 2008, the magazine's circulation had increased to three hundred thousand.

Nowhere is the phenomenon of homemade goods as pronounced as on the Web commerce site Etsy—"Your place to buy & sell all things handmade." Interested in purchasing a whistle made out of a tin can and bottle caps? How about a "Kaleidoscope Pearberry Soapsicle"? It's far less of a niche market than it sounds: in 2007, shoppers spent $27 million at Etsy. And all this just scratches the surface. Signs of the amateur renaissance are all around us.

Take, of all things, ornithology. Before the birth of the Internet, bird-watching was the province of an enthusiastic, small cadre of devotees. But in recent years bird-watching has undergone a rapid growth in popularity. By 2006, nearly 50 million Americans were engaged in some form of "wildlife watching," according to the U.S. Fish and Wildlife Service. Declines in fishing and hunting played a role in birding's increased popularity, but much of this growth can be attributed to the concurrent growth of online communities dedicated to teaching birding basics and recording actual bird counts.

All this activity hasn't gone unnoticed by ornithologists. The Cornell Lab of Ornithology coordinates national bird counts. Eleven thousand people participated in the first bird count in 1996. In 2007, more than eighty thousand people participated. All these observations constitute an invaluable resource. "We believe it will fundamentally transform the way field ornithology is conducted," says Chris Wood, a researcher at the Cornell Lab. The enormous amounts of data being generated by amateur ornithologists are providing an unprecedented look at the distribution and migratory patterns of a multitude of species. "There's simply no other way to have this type of coverage," says Wood. "For one, there are far fewer professionals engaged in field work compared to the number of birders," and, "in many cases amateur birders are more competent at gathering, correctly identifying, and recording numbers of birds than professional ornithologists. This basic form of data collection is precisely what birders have always specialized in."

I ask for an example in which amateurs were superceding the pros. "So much about what we now know about birds comes from the birders it's hard to pick a single example," he says. But after a pause he comes up with a doozy: "There's this bird, the Cozumel thrasher, that lives on Cozumel island in Mexico. A series of hurricanes destroyed its habitat, and everyone assumed it was extinct. Then in 2004 some birders rediscovered it, and published their findings in the grey literature," non-peer-reviewed periodicals devoted to birding. "A few years later a group of scientists went down to Cozumel, saw the thrasher and came back to the U.S., and made a big announcement about how they'd rediscovered this species. The birders were like, 'That's interesting, but we did that a few years ago.'" The professionals had neglected to keep up-to-date with the amateur literature.

The point of eBird is to eliminate such duplications of effort. Launched in 2002, eBird documents bird abundance through checklists—the basic tool of the birder. The data are then fed into the Avian Knowledge Network, a master database of bird sightings used by amateurs and professionals alike. Woods shows me a chart displaying the number of observations submitted each May from 2003 through 2008. That first May, eBird collected well over 100,000 sightings—a respectable data set by any measure, but far below its potential. "We set it up as a citizen science project—'Here's how you can help us.' So we shifted the focus 180 degrees and redesigned the site to help the birders." Woods and his colleagues let people create their own home page on which they could keep their personal checklists. "There are these games birders like to play with each other, and so we built them and put them in here." In May 2008, eBird collected over 1.15 million observations, almost ten times the amount gathered in 2003.

This is crowdsourcing of a different species, so to speak. If stock photography is the first industry to be transformed by crowdsourcing, then ornithology is the first academic discipline to undergo the same process. The Internet has allowed for a felicitous marriage between amateur and professional bird researchers, so that where once professionals reigned, now a self-organizing community of amateurs shoulders a significant degree of the labor. Much of an ornithologist's job involves making routine observations. Simple data collection doesn't require a Ph.D., but before the advent of the Web it was nearly impossible to organize and coordinate with these citizen scientists, even if they wanted to lend a hand. Tapping this enthusiastic amateur research base gives the ornithologists thousands of extra sets of eyes. The data produced from this collaborative effort is then used by amateurs and professionals alike to increase their knowledge in an endless positive feedback loop.

The Reign of the Dilettante

Although the technologies behind this latest surge in amateur activity are new, the impulse itself has a venerable history. Before the age of television or spectator sports, recreation took forms scarcely recognizable to us today. So it comes as some surprise to learn that botany—the collecting, identifying, and classification of all manner of flora—ranked as one of the most popular pastimes of the nineteenth century. Calling themselves "botanizers," legions of amateurs fanned out across the abundant American forests, marshes, prairies, and deserts armed with guidebooks and specimen cases. Amateur botanists discovered a vast number of new species and were duly encouraged and mentored by the few professional botanists working at the time.

All that changed in the twilight of the century, when botany filled with ranks of professionals increasingly jealous of their amateur counterparts' contributions and dismissive of their abilities. In 1897, the professionals succeeded in having "nature study" removed from the academic curricula of American high schools, resulting in an immediate diminishing of interest in the field. Amateurs, it was felt, sullied an otherwise upstanding academic discipline. By the early years of the twentieth century, botany, along with the other sciences, had become professionalized.

More than a century of a professionalized academy has helped obscure the amateur roots of the arts and sciences, which evolved through the accomplishments of men and women who wore the mantle of amateur with great pride, and would have considered being called a professional an insult. Francis Bacon is one of the founding fathers of modern science: during the late sixteenth and early seventeenth centuries he established and popularized the inductive method of scientific inquiry. But science was really something of a sideline for Bacon, who was better known in his time as a lawyer, writer, politician, and courtier.

He was also an aristocrat, and in England as throughout Europe, the aristocracy abhorred the pursuit of any profession, the acquisition of money through labor being seen as a strictly lower-class endeavor. The pursuit of knowledge for its own sake—not particular knowledge but knowledge in the broadest sense—was commended and admired. Naturally, the only people who could afford to indulge in such time-consuming, and unpaid, intellectual toil were the wealthy. To the extent scientific collaboration, so crucial to the progress of understanding, existed at all, it was in the form of gentlemen's clubs. Academic journals were nonexistent.

Inspired by Bacon's crowning work, *Novum Organum,* in 1646, a group of philosophers, doctors, and amateur astronomers and mathematicians formed an "institution of learning" they called "the Invisible College." Colloquies were conducted via the mail, without benefit or need of the academies, which at any rate were largely devoted to preparing well-heeled young men headed for the legal courts or the parsonage. The Invisible College's purpose was to "acquire knowledge through experimental investigation," and among its members were some of the leading intellectual lights of the era, including Robert Hooke (whose fame as a scientist overshadows his contributions to architecture), Sir Christopher Wren (whose fame as an architect overshadows his contributions to science), and Robert Boyle (who is considered the founder of modern chemistry, but was also a noted theologian). These men were dilettantes, a word that carried a far more positive connotation in their day than it does in our own. This enlightened dabbling was equally dominant in the arts. To cite but one example, Jean-Jacques Rousseau is remembered for the philosophical tracts that helped inspire the French Revolution, but in his day he was as well known for his comic operas, verse, and works of fiction.

By 1660, the Invisible College had become institutionalized, and was renamed the Royal Society. For the next one hundred years Royal Society members—amateurs all, by our contemporary definition—were responsible for some of the greatest advances in human knowledge. The amateur ideal—the word's Latin root, *amare,* means "to love"—was embodied in the form of the gentleman scholar, but it was not to last. Even the first phase of the industrial revolution in the late eighteenth and early nineteenth centuries required increased specialization. A central thesis of Adam Smith's *An Inquiry into the Nature and Causes of the Wealth of Nations* focused on the principle of specialized vocations. "The division of labour, however, so far as it can be introduced, occasions, in every art, a proportionable [*sic*] increase of the productive powers of labour," he wrote. Increasing industrialization led, as Smith predicted it would, to the reduction of every man's business to "some one simple operation."

By the nineteenth century, universities were beginning to replace the aristocracy as the primary source of funding for research, and a class of professional academics emerged in the growing American and European university systems. This process of professionalization led to the spread of more rigorous methodologies, and an animus developed toward the tradition of dilettantism in the sciences as well as in the arts, which with the emergence of a commercial market were also becoming increasingly professionalized. The mathematician Charles Babbage's 1830 polemic *Reflections on the Decline of Science in England, and on Some of its Causes* accused the Royal Society of slipping into decrepitude and philistinism by catering to its richest and often most indifferent members. By contrast, Babbage pointed out, Napoleon Bonaparte had given France a flourishing system of academies that promoted merit and specialization. Divorced from their traditional patrons, these academies owed their existence strictly to government funds.

Babbage's essay had a lasting influence, beginning in 1831, when the British Association for the Advancement of Science was founded to counteract the stultifying influence of the gentlemanly culture of the Royal Society, which was administered by unpaid (and generally untrained) men whose only claim to accreditation was a purported interest in the subject. The beginning of Charles Darwin's career was typical of this new sensibility about professionalism. At a young age Darwin had already become fascinated with botany, and he carried this interest into college. His father—an eminent doctor—insisted his son pursue a career in either religion or medicine. But times had already changed by the mid–nineteenth century, and the younger Darwin was able to convince his father to let him go on his fateful journey aboard the HMS *Beagle* by pointing to the increasingly respectable community of scientific professionals.

As the nineteenth century progressed, Smith's theories concerning the division of labor manifested as the Industrial Revolution, in which workers migrated to the cities to perform ever more specialized functions, finally reaching an elegant, and stunningly efficient, apogee on the Highland Park, Michigan, assembly lines of Henry Ford's automobile plants. And by the first decades of the 1900s, a division of labor had appeared in the academy as well, culminating in the establishment of the modern research university. Now a clear distinction took hold between undergraduate education and the scholarship professors were expected to undertake in a rapidly multiplying number of disciplines.

Yet even as the arts and sciences found themselves Balkanized, undergraduate educations continued to emphasize the Renaissance ideal of an earlier, pre-industrial era. Tailored toward the education of the upper classes, universities were expected to produce "well-rounded" young men who would proceed to white-shoe law firms and corporate offices. Our universities are still essentially artifacts from the Renaissance period, representative of a time when the model citizen could wield the pen, the plow, and the protractor with equal aptitude. And that's a good thing. It makes for interesting, and interested, individuals. But such people will seek out rewarding lives full of meaningful labor. Which is where crowdsourcing comes in.

The Overeducation of the Middle Class

After World War II the demography of university students changed, even if the curricula did not. The GI Bill made college educations affordable for the middle classes for the first time. According to the College Board, "the proportion of the population 25 to 29 years of age that has completed four years of college or more has quadrupled since 1940." By 2000, a full 63 percent of high school graduates went on to college.

This, too, is a very good thing. Education is the engine that drives the information economy forward, filling an ever-increasing demand in fields ranging from financial services to marketing. But the increasing degree of specialization required at most firms is at odds with the notion of a "liberal education." Although there has been a recent trend toward more immediately applicable degrees such as engineering, business, and communications, Sheila Slaughter, a professor of higher education at the University of Georgia, observes that more than 50 percent of an undergraduate's coursework still consists of electives. So even the most focused business student might well discover a love for art history, and even the most devoted of humanities students might, as was my case, develop an affinity for meteorology. "Universities discourage specialization in the sense that they create 'play spaces,' in which students are encouraged to experiment widely and broadly," says Slaughter, noting that students may learn skills such as videography or podcasting through a class, but are likely to import it into their social lives very quickly. What begins as an elective, then, quickly becomes an extracurricular interest and—after graduation—an avocational passion, especially if it is easily stoked through online forums consisting of like-minded enthusiasts. Crowdsourcing capitalizes on the fact that our interests are more diverse than our business cards would have one believe.

Even to the extent that college students are specializing by majoring in one subject or another, fewer and fewer graduates obtain jobs that reflect their course of study. The number of art degrees granted has grown even faster than the number of general undergraduate degrees, but only a fraction of these students will make a living as a fine artist. A few will secure a precious teaching post at a university, though it will in all likelihood be an adjunct position offering scant wages and little security. A slightly larger minority will find work in applied arts such as illustration and design, and will consider themselves lucky. Nor is this scenario restricted to the arts. Few science majors will ever practice "pure science," and a chemistry graduate is as likely to become an investment banker or management consultant as he is a chemist, never mind applying the skills and knowledge he acquired in those classes *outside* his major.

The result is that a large number of people are performing their most meaningful, rewarding labor away from the workplace. Crowdsourcing has arisen organically to capitalize on the economic value the amateur class creates. And as more and more people acquire a higher education, we have inadvertently trained nonprofessionals to compete on an almost equal footing with the professionals. Is it any wonder that, given this environment, the "professional" has never been more widely distrusted, and the amateur more cheerfully embraced? People who once felt that "I could do that job as well as that guy" are now providing proof for their conviction. People like people, not experts, not eggheads, not talking heads on TV. The popularity of reality TV is certainly one manifestation of this collective mania, but the theme runs throughout every aspect of our culture. In fact, public trust in professionals has never been lower. According to a December 2006 Gallup Poll, politicians just beat car salesmen for the public's trust and respect, and journalists only beat politicians by a nose.

Such surveys mislead us into the belief that people are merely disenchanted with what we might call "the expert class." But that's only part of a deeper dynamic: the gap in knowledge that once irrevocably separated the experts from the rest of the populace has shrunk. Experts traffic in the acquisition and interpretation of exclusive information. Lawyers go to law school to understand the arcana of our legal system. Journalists cultivate sources that provide them with inside information to fuel their stories. Politicians have privileged access to classified information, or simply a window into the mechanism of government. Or at least that's how it used to work. But the architecture of the Internet conspires against closed systems. A network, by definition, is composed of a multitude of nodes, so that information multiplies rapidly and effortlessly. The architecture of a network flattens all hierarchies. The oft-repeated expression "information wants to be free"—first uttered by the writer Stewart Brand at a conference in 1984—refers not to any volition on the part of the information itself, but to the way the Web's architecture reversed the cost structure around information. On the Web, restricting information is harder—more difficult—than distributing it broadly.

Simply put, the people are empowered with enough knowledge to peek behind the Wizard's curtain; the amateurs are able to use the Web to acquire as much information as the professionals. In March 2007, the popular left-wing political blog Talking Points Memo asked its readers to comb through thousands of pages of documents released by the Department of Justice (DOJ) pertaining to the allegedly illegal firing of U.S. Attorneys under Attorney General Alberto Gonzales. Utilizing the power of many eyes in no less a potent way as had the ornithologists at Audubon or Cornell, TPM's investigative journalism arm, TPMMuckraker, was able to uncover several instances of politically motivated actions within the DOJ. This democratization of information extends far beyond politics, and for that matter beyond law, media, and medicine.

And as we saw in the case of ornithology, it's even

affecting the fields that would seem the most resistant to crowdsourcing, such as scientific research. But then, the sciences aren't immune to the same sociological and economic forces affecting any other industry. "There are plenty of people who have Ph.D.s in theoretical physics who are working on Wall Street doing stock analysis," notes Shawn Carlson, who won a MacArthur Foundation genius grant for his work in establishing the Society for Amateur Scientists. "Their first love is science, and they'll jump at the chance to come home and start practicing pure science again." Carlson himself holds a Ph.D. in nuclear physics, but he founded the SAS in 1994 in the belief that "ordinary people can participate in extraordinary science." Technology has proven to be a great equalizer, Carlson says, pointing to the fields like ornithology and astronomy that have become increasingly dependent on amateurs for gathering raw data. As the Internet disseminates knowledge, amateurs will begin to help analyze the data as well. It's hardly surprising that just as iStockphoto emerged to tap the explosive growth in skilled photographers with unrelated day jobs, a company called InnoCentive has figured out a way to tap the surplus of talented scientists whose most meaningful projects are relegated to jerry-built labs.

Benchtop Science Comes of Age

Giorgia Sgargetta isn't really an amateur scientist, though that's just the word that comes to mind when she describes her home laboratory. The petite thirty-four-year-old lives in a small town in the Abruzzo region of Italy, and after she's prepared dinner and sent her eight-year-old daughter Daiane and husband, Alessandro, off to bed,

Sgargetta dons a beat-up old lab coat, puts away her cooking utensils, and carefully takes her flasks, beakers, test tubes, and a small precision scale from the attic.

The setup wouldn't seem out of place in a high school science class, but Sgargetta is no mere dabbler. In the past few years she has spent her evenings working on research problems that have stumped some of the best corporate scientists in the world. Sgargetta is part of an extended network of scientists who work for InnoCentive, a crowdsourcing company based in Waltham, Massachusetts. InnoCentive's clients include Fortune 500 firms like Procter & Gamble (P&G), DuPont, and BASF. When the company's in-house R&D teams can't solve a problem, they hand it over to the 140,000 scientists from more than 170 countries that regularly scan InnoCentive's website looking for work. Most rewards for successful solutions pay somewhere between $10,000 and $100,000, but as Sgargetta is quick to point out, the money is not a primary motive.

"I've always loved the lab," she said, "even as a child." She excelled in her doctoral program, specializing in detergent formulations, agrochemicals, and analytical chemistry. But in Italy, as in most other countries, research positions are very difficult to obtain. Instead, Sgargetta got a job as a quality manager in a pesticides plant near her home. She's happy to work in her field, but the work is fairly rote and she misses the challenges that are part of working in a lab.

Sgargetta is hardly alone. Few scientists wind up working in pure research professions such as astronomy and physics, just as few art-school graduates wind up living off of gallery commissions. Ten years ago Sgargetta would have chalked it up to the realities of the marketplace and put her love for agrichemistry into her garden. But in an age of ultimate connectivity, she's able to put her passion to work in ways that benefit both the companies that use InnoCentive as well as her bank account.

In the four years following Sgargetta's first encounter with InnoCentive, she solved two InnoCentive challenges. In one she invented a type of dye that turned dishwater blue after the correct amount of detergent had been added. Although InnoCentive "seeker" companies are supposed to remain anonymous, Sgargetta later discovered that P&G had filed a patent referencing her and her discovery. She netted $30,000 for her kitchen-brewed coup. More recently she was awarded $15,000 for helping advance the search for a biomarker—an indicator used to measure the effects of a treatment—with which to treat ALS, or Lou Gehrig's disease. It's notable that Sgargetta had no previous experience with ALS or even with medical research.

The money has been a welcome supplement to her and her husband's normal income: "We'd really like to move someday. We have a nice view from where we live now, but the noise from the street is horrible. If I win again maybe we'll reward ourselves by buying something with a better location." But better than the money, Sgargetta said, is the feeling that she's practicing real science again. Since she began working on InnoCentive challenges she's returned to scouring technical literature, scanning the Internet for databases of chemical compounds, and filling her flasks with potentially combustible liquids.

While some members of InnoCentive's ad hoc labor force might qualify as amateurs in the strict sense that they are not professionally trained scientists, most resemble Sgargetta, passionately curious Ph.D.s who are eagerly willing to expend their free time for the sake of an intellectual challenge. The financial incentives offered by InnoCentive are hefty by crowdsourcing standards, yet a common note that solvers strike when discussing InnoCentive is that it is, first and foremost, fun. And what InnoCentive's scientists find fun is, as often as not, tackling problems outside the field in which they're trained. It's no accident that more than a few of the most successful solvers define themselves as scientific "generalists." David Tracy, a semiretired physicist from Norwalk, Connecticut, lists such disparate research interests as "algorithm development" and "optical engineering" on his bio on the InnoCentive webpage. "Nothing gets my juices flowing like a good problem in need of a novel solution," Tracy writes, adding that he's also developing a low-cost system for automating tree counts for a local nonprofit forestry organization. The intellectually inclusive spirit of Francis Bacon lives on in David Tracy.

And then some solvers really are amateurs in every sense. Not that InnoCentive discriminates. Just as solvers don't know what company has commissioned their research, neither does InnoCentive disclose the identity of the solver. "We democratize it," says Jill Panetta, InnoCentive's Chief Scientific Officer. "So the client never knows whether the solver is a Nobel laureate or a high school teacher." Only after a solution is accepted by the company is the solver's identity revealed. The companies are often surprised to learn that the solver is, in fact, to cite two actual examples, a computer programmer from Argentina or a University of Dallas undergrad.

"What we're doing is simple but profound. You have the ability as an organization to get your problem in front of an incredibly diverse array of research backgrounds," says Panetta. This pitch would seem to work well for InnoCentive, which now counts roughly thirty top-tier firms among its clients. An InnoCentive company's average earnings from a successful solution are twenty times the fee paid to a solver. Offering prize money for solving a complex problem is becoming increasingly accepted as a viable method for working out thorny scientific and technological puzzles. "I think when we launched the company six years ago we were ahead of the game. When we first approached these Fortune 500 companies they thought we were nuts, but now they get it."

In some fields, scientists won't have a choice but to utilize nonprofessionals. Dr. Ray O'Neal Jr. is a physics professor at Florida A&M University. O'Neal possesses the kind of job history—Stanford Ph.D., a post-doctoral research position with NASA—that leads to the rewarding of generous grants. But O'Neal researches cosmic rays in an era when NASA and astrophysics have fallen out of favor. "My university is chronically underfunded," he says. "I don't have ten post-docs and twenty grad students working in my lab."

Instead, O'Neal and a fellow cosmic-ray researcher, Helio Takai at Brookhaven National Laboratory, have decided to crowdsource their research project. They're creating a device that can detect cosmic rays from the sun and wirelessly transmit the data back to the lab at Brookhaven. They're recruiting citizen scientists, high school students, undergraduates, and anyone else to keep and maintain the detection stations. "Ultimately we want them all over the world. It could revolutionize our understanding of how solar rays interact with the earth's atmosphere." The Society for Amateur Scientists' Shawn Carlson says such partnerships will only increase in time. "You have all these talented people out there who are passionate about science. The professional community is going to realize what a resource this is and you'll see programs like this grow dramatically."

InnoCentive and iStockphoto provide a glimpse into

how this parallel source of labor, this shadow workforce, operates. For one, it is drawn from a global base of talent. Such networks eradicate barriers to participation, providing access to the considerable intellectual capital located in regions such as Eastern Europe, India, and China. In this sense, crowdsourcing is outsourcing on steroids. Roughly 45 percent of iStockers hail from outside North America. InnoCentive scientists have an even more cosmopolitan makeup: fewer than one third live in North America.

Two, crowdsourcing has no more regard for professional qualifications than it has for nationality. InnoCentive and iStock are meritocracies; all that matters is the final product. This is one of its greatest strengths. One revealing MIT study into InnoCentive revealed that solvers were more successful when they had *less* experience in the relevant discipline. In other words, chemists were better suited to solving life biology problems, and vice versa. This is less surprising than it seems at first blush. If a P&G chemist could have solved a stubborn predicament in his own field, it would have never wound up posted to InnoCentive's website. This is powerful mojo: The untrained are also untainted. Their greatest asset is a fresh set of eyes, which is simply a restatement of the truism that with many eyes, all flaws become evident, and easily corrected. But that concept wasn't always clear. It took a handful of renegade computer programmers to show just how powerful the law of large numbers could be.

2

FROM SO SIMPLE
A BEGINNING

Drawing the Blueprint for Crowdsourcing

In the beginning, all source code was open source code. This was due more to circumstance than design, but it would nonetheless have considerable consequences far beyond the realm of computer programming. Source code consists of the English-language commands that, once translated into zeros and ones, tell a computer what to do. Open source code is pretty much what it sounds like: open for anyone to see, copy, tweak, and use for whatever purpose they see fit. Because it was open, a spirit of collaboration and free exchange of information developed in computer programming. And because it had been open once, a small group of principled programmers determined that it should stay open. They couldn't force Microsoft or Sun Microsystems or Apple to reveal their code, but they could create a free and open alternative.

In order to do so, the founders of the open source software movement had to invent a new way to get things done. They couldn't offer anyone money, and the task before them—to write an entire operating system, requiring millions of programmer-hours—was daunting. Would highly skilled people contribute their spare time to a project that seemed doomed to fail? Actually yes, they would. Many, many people would. And because *many* people came forward, the burden did not fall heavily on the few. By the early 1990s, the crowd had produced its first substantial work: Linux, an operating system superior, in many respects, to the best products of any corporation. Open source provided a precedent— a proof of concept. If people working in their spare time—stovetop chemists, basement musicians, Sunday photographers—provide the crowdsourcing engine with fuel, it's the open source software movement that provided it with a blueprint.

No one knew any of this in 1969, of course, when Ken Thompson, a computer programmer with Bell Laboratories, suddenly found himself at loose ends. Thompson had been working on an ambitious, five-year collaboration between MIT, General Electric, and Bell. The project was supposed to create a more efficient operating system for the mainframe computers of the era, one that would be capable of performing more than a single task at a time—a limitation that had greatly slowed the processing speed of even the most advanced computers. But instead of efficiency the effort had created chaos. The manual for the operating system ran longer than three thousand pages. By that spring, Bell had lost faith and pulled out.

Facing a four-week vacation, Thompson decided to start from scratch, this time with only himself to answer to. Instead of aiming high, he would aim small. He devoted one week each to writing four components of an operating system. As Steven Weber, a political scientist and author, writes in *The Success of Open Source,* "With just one man-month and very basic hardware Thompson had to leave behind big-system mentality and do something simple." Or as one of Thompson's collaborators put it at the time, "build small neat things instead of grandiose ones."

By the end of the month, Thompson had written the elementary outlines of Unix, destined to become the most successful and long-lasting operating system ever created. But it wasn't just Unix's popularity that made Thompson's actions historic; it was his decision to make Unix out of small, discrete programs meant to do one thing but do it well. Such an architecture would eventually allow hundreds of programmers to work together in a totally decentralized fashion—in much the same way thousands of contributors work together today in a decentralized fashion to form a single reference work, Wikipedia. Breaking labor into little units, or modules, is one of the hallmarks of crowdsourcing. In this case, it facilitated the come-one, come-all approach of open source programming.

Not that there were many interested parties at the time. The field of computer science developed out of academia and quasi-academic research labs like those at Bell and MIT. Sharing computer code conformed to the general academic tradition of free exchange of information, but it was also a simple expedient: it was the only way to get anything done. One of the first commercial computers, the IBM 705, cost $1.6 million in 1953, the year it was released. (That's more than $12 million in 2008 dollars.) Beyond being expensive and requiring the larger part of a room to put it in, it required an extraordinary amount of time to write the code that told it what to do. In order to maximize their resources, the few people qualified to perform such a task pooled their time and talents.

A programmer culture emerged during these formative years, which was characterized by playful, competitive and yet highly collaborative interactions between devoted specialists. The resulting ethos prized originality and creativity and, most of all, open access to information—computer code in particular. You couldn't separate the users from the programmers, because the only people who used computers were the people who programmed them. These were the original hackers. Although the term would eventually acquire negative connotations, it originally meant someone whose mastery of computing rose to the level of art.

It wasn't until the introduction of the personal computer that a need for proprietary software developed. This created a conflict. In 1976, Bill Gates and Paul Allen—cofounders and sole employees of what was still called "Micro-Soft"—wrote "An Open Letter to Hobbyists." It did not mince words: "As the majority of hobbyists must be aware, most of you steal your software." The letter was an unequivocal condemnation of what had become a hacker habit—the free sharing of software and the source code it was based on. Gates pointed out that the royalties he and Allen had been paid for Micro-Soft's first commercial release averaged out to $2 an hour. Who would write software with such an incentive? Gates wondered. The hobbyists needed professional programmers because, after all, "What hobbyist can put 3-man years into programming, finding all bugs, documenting his product and distribute for free?" Gates could have never anticipated the answer to his question, which was that no single hobbyist could put 3-man years into such a daunting task, but thousands of hobbyists easily could.

Fighting the Good Fight

In 1983, an MIT computer scientist named Richard Stallman decided to wage a one-man war against the software industry that Gates had helped create. In doing so, he gave a name to what had previously been a vague predilection on the part of the hacker community. Stallman had arrived in Cambridge to attend Harvard University in 1970, a product of a stridently liberal upbringing in Manhattan's Upper West Side. An aggressively idiosyncratic and precocious youth, Stallman has said he didn't have friends within his peer group until he arrived at MIT's Artificial Intelligence Lab. He would spend the next thirteen years of his life there, sleeping in his office and living to write code.

In the early 1980s, Stallman watched as the hacker community that had thrived in MIT's lab fell apart. Most of his friends and colleagues left academia to create companies dedicated to developing proprietary software that would serve the booming computer market. At this point even Unix—that stalwart of hacker culture—had become proprietary. In protest, Stallman founded the GNU Project, an effort to create an operating system based on "open" or freely available source code. (GNU is a recursive acronym for "GNU-Not-Unix"—a fine example of the penchant for humorous hacker workplay.)

It was the first shot in a remarkable revolution, but few heard it at the time. Stallman severed all affiliations with MIT (although the university continued to let him use the lab and sleep in his office) and began to write an operating system based on Unix, but in a form that would allow other users to steal, copy, cut, paste, modify, and, most important, add their own contributions to the source code Stallman was writing. Attracted to the easy access of Stallman's system, other programmers began working with him on the GNU Project. "People started asking for and writing improvements," Stallman said, "and it ended up much better than I'd originally planned on its being." And because the GNU operating system was based on Unix, with its thousands of small files, it was easy for other programmers to pick and choose what individual bits they could work on, according to how much time they could devote to the project. In 1985, Stallman founded the nonprofit Free Software Foundation (FSF) "to promote computer user freedom and defend the rights of all free software users." The FSF helped Stallman support his work on GNU, but it also served to articulate his ideas: "Free software* is a matter of liberty, not price. To understand the concept, you should think of free as in free speech, not as in free beer."

By making his operating system freely accessible, Stallman was almost single-handedly keeping the hacker culture alive. By 1986, Stallman had created a C compiler, arguably the most important part of an operating system, in completely free code. In order to ensure that no enterprising programmer took the code and incorporated it into a piece of software that he or she would then put on the market, Stallman created what is a much greater contribution to the open source movement, and to culture at large: the GNU General Public License. The GNU GPL required not only that anything released under the license be made freely available, but that any software that *incorporated it* employ the same license. "The GNU GPL 'converted' software it was used with to its own license, an extraordinarily clever approach to propagating freedom," notes Glyn Moody in his history of open source movement, *Rebel Code*. This little trick has come to be known as "copyleft," as opposed to copyright.

By 1991, Stallman and a small cadre of programmers had almost completed the GNU Project. But the last

---

* In 1998, a gathering of free software's leading lights voted to adopt the term "open source software." (The terms, for our purposes, are synonymous.)

missing component, the kernel (basically the heart of an operating system) was also the hardest to write. It wasn't expected for at least another two years. Meanwhile few outside of the hacker community had even heard of GNU, much less put it to use. All this was about to change.

In August of that year, a Finnish computer science student named Linus Torvalds posted a message to an online message board: "I'm doing a (free) operating system (just a hobby, won't be big and professional like gnu). . . . I'd like to know what features most people would want." Too impatient to wait for the GNU kernel, Torvalds was writing his own—soon to be named Linux—and this open call for assistance would prove to have historic consequences. Over the next two years, thousands of coders would chip in to help improve Linux. "What had once been one hacker's 'hobby' was turning into a community," notes Moody. "The better Linux became, the more people used it; and the more people debugged it, the faster it improved: a virtuous circle that continues to drive Linux development at a vertiginous rate."

Today, Linux powers everything from supercomputers to cell phones to digital video recorders such as TiVo, to say nothing of the millions of personal computers that run Linux. And because Linux utilizes a GNU General Public license, no single company is able to use it as the basis for a commercial release. The result is a guarantee that this "virtuous circle" continues to flourish.

Linux also served to popularize open source software projects generally. There are now more than 175,000 ongoing open source projects hosted on the software development website Sourceforge.net, and open source has been widely adopted by mainstream corporations. About 70 percent of Web server software runs on the Apache

Web server, which was developed using open source methods, and more than half of all large-scale e-mail programs also use open source software. Working outside of any organizing agency, such as a company or academic institution, the open source community proved that the most intelligent networks were self-organized. Who authored Linux? The crowd.

The open source software movement has always been as much about advancing a philosophy as it has been about developing new software. Proponents of the open source model value transparency for its own sake, not simply because opening up the development process to outsiders happens to produce better code. But it is the efficacy of the open source model, not the egalitarian principles underlying it, that drove companies like IBM, and more recently even Microsoft, to begin adopting it as a way to save money and develop better products.

What makes open source so efficient? In the broadest of strokes, it's the ability for a large number of people to contribute. The open source evangelist Eric S. Raymond famously summed up this fundamental truth when he wrote, that, "Given enough eyeballs, all bugs are shallow"—which is to say that no problem is too thorny if enough people take a crack at it. Put another way, a large and diverse labor pool will consistently come up with better solutions than the most talented, specialized workforce. This is as true in fields such as corporate science, product design, and content creation as it is in software, and it is one of the central principles of crowdsourcing.

Raymond's maxim originally appeared in "The Cathedral and the Bazaar," an essay that Raymond, a software engineer by trade, presented at a conference in 1997. Written in deft, nontechnical prose, it would prove to be enormously influential in the migration of open source strategies to fields beyond software. In the essay, Raymond contrasts two methods of software development. The "cathedral" characterizes the heavily managed, hierarchical approach that had been standard operating procedure since the Industrial Revolution. Raymond contrasts this with Linux, "a world-class operating system [that] coalesces as if by magic . . . by several thousand developers scattered all over the planet, connected only by the tenuous strands of the Internet."

> Linus Torvalds's style of development—release early and often, delegate everything you can, be open to the point of promiscuity—came as a surprise. No quiet, reverent cathedral-building here—rather, the Linux community seemed to resemble a great babbling bazaar of differing agendas and approaches . . . out of which a coherent and stable system could seemingly emerge only by a succession of miracles.

In a cathedral, everything is coordinated from above. In the bazaar, everything is coordinated—if that word even applies—from below. Raymond makes a persuasive case for open source's raw, hurly-burly horsepower, which not only produced a fairly bug-free operating system, but did so at a "speed barely imaginable to the cathedral builders." When Raymond first presented his paper to the Linux Kongress of 1997, its significance was only recognized by his peers in the world of computer programming. But a much larger audience would soon take note.

Accidental Revolutionaries

We don't always know what we have wrought. While working for Western Union Telegraph Company in 1877 to improve Alexander Graham Bell's telephone, Thomas

Edison discovered a method for recording sounds as opposed to merely transmitting them over the wire. Within the month, he unveiled the Edison phonograph. The papers anointed him the "Wizard of Menlo Park," a sobriquet that has lasted to this day. Edison and his staff of assistants continued to improve his "talking machine," but he never envisioned that it might one day be used for entertainment. His goal for the phonograph was to corner the market on business dictation, and over the following three decades the Edison phonograph accomplished that task admirably. It took another man, Eldridge Reeves Johnson, to make the cognitive leap that would produce the phonograph as we know it today. Dapper, smooth-talking, and ambitious, Johnson teamed up with one of Edison's competitors and came out with a sturdier version of Edison's contraption. He adopted a nifty logo of a cock-eared dog listening to "his master's voice," christened the company Victor, and called his phonograph the Victrola. No inventor himself, Johnson single-handedly spawned the recorded-music industry. You don't have to be an inventor to innovate.

Just as Edison didn't know he'd invented the phonograph, Larry Sanger, a former philosophy professor, didn't mean to trigger the big bang of crowdsourcing. Raymond had written "The Cathedral and the Bazaar" in the context of software development, but it turned out it was relevant to a much wider world. Sanger would play a seminal role in introducing the principles of Raymond's essay to a larger public, though he didn't know that in January 2001, when he sat down to dinner with a longtime friend named Ben Kovitz. They met in San Diego at the Pacific Bar and Grill. Kovitz had recently moved from Greenwich, Connecticut, to take a job as an information engineer at a local company. He was in high spirits, unlike his companion. Sanger had left academia scarcely one year earlier, and now he was wondering whether or not he'd made the right decision. His new gig involved nothing less than the reinvention of the encyclopedia, and it wasn't going very well. In fact, Sanger feared all his efforts would be for naught.

This wasn't Sanger's first foray into the private sector. He had maintained an interest in computers since childhood, and in 1998 had started *Sanger's Review of Y2K News Reports,* a compendium of Year-2000–related news read by IT managers eager to avoid the impending disaster. The *Y2K News Reports'* mandate expired with the millennium, but it left Sanger hungry for another Internet-related venture. Then he heard that Jimmy Wales, a wealthy entrepreneur whom Sanger knew slightly from online philosophy discussion boards, was looking for Internet projects in which to invest.

Sanger approached Wales about creating a cultural news digest, but Wales had other ideas. Wales had played around with computer code in the past, and he'd recently become enamored of Stallman's Free Software movement. "The first thing Jimmy did is insist I read 'Cathedral and the Bazaar,' " Sanger recalled later. Wales had an idea for an encyclopedia that would be called Nupedia (a riff on GNU, Stallman's name for his operating system). Like *Encyclopædia Britannica* and every other iteration of the concept since Denis Diderot's seminal 1751 *Encyclopédie,* Nupedia would be put together by experts. Unlike such traditional reference works, everything on Nupedia would be available on the Internet for free and written by volunteers, just like any other open source project—or so it appeared at the time.

Sanger was enthralled—"infatuated," he remembers—by the project. But he and Wales shared some reservations.

Both were a little skeptical about the ability of amateurs to contribute meaningful knowledge to what they envisioned as an authoritative reference work. Nonetheless, Sanger came on as Nupedia editor in chief in January 2000 and immediately went about building an advisory board composed mainly of academics of his acquaintance. Over the next few months Sanger and his board created an elaborate method of screening potential authors. Once a contributor had written an entry, it would run an onerous, time-consuming seven-step review process.

At first Nupedia seemed to be progressing. Wales and Sanger were encouraged to see that by early spring a few articles had already been written, reviewed, and posted to the site. By that summer a few more articles passed through the process, and over the following months a handful more arrived. Wales and Sanger had envisioned a trickle turning into a flood. But the deluge never came, and by the time Sanger had dinner with Kovitz, Nupedia could boast of only a dozen or so articles. Intending to use Raymond's bazaar to create an encyclopedia—that most ambitious of compendiums of knowledge—Wales and Sanger had wound up with just another cathedral, and a not very impressive one at that.

"Ben listened to what I was telling him, and said he knew of a program that might open up the process," says Sanger. Not long before their fateful dinner, the renowned programmer Ward Cunningham had written a simple piece of software called WikiWikiWeb. It was meant to allow coders to more easily exchange information, but Cunningham and the small community of software developers that were the first to use it soon realized it had much broader implications. A "wiki"—named from the Hawaiian word for "quick"—allows an unlimited number of users to create and edit text on a single webpage. Even better, a wiki keeps track of every edit, which means everyone accessing the page can see what changes have been made and who made them. In early 2001, wikis were still the province of those employed in (or obsessed with) technology. But Kovitz explained to Sanger how Nupedia could use the wiki technology to speed up the laborious process of contributing, editing, and reviewing encyclopedia articles.

Sanger didn't need much convincing. "It made immediate sense to me. I think I called Jimmy [Wales] later that night and had written him a formal proposal to start using wikis before the following afternoon," remembers Sanger. Wales, too, saw the potential of wikis to help Sanger pick up the pace, although it was not speed that was foremost in his mind. Although Wales himself had made his personal fortune as a futures trader in Chicago in the 1990s, he wasn't the one funding Nupedia. This was done through one of Wales's less altruistic ventures, a Web portal called Bomis.com that featured, among other items, soft-core pornography.

If human interest in sex is constant, capital investment is considerably more fickle; Bomis was suffering alongside the rest of the technology sector. After it became clear that the hoped-for volume of contributions was not forthcoming, Sanger had proposed several ways in which Nupedia could transform its software architecture to expedite the process, but all of them involved paying the expensive hourly rates of a professional software developer. To make matters worse, *Encyclopædia Britannica* had recently changed course and posted all one hundred thousand of its entries to the Web and made it freely available, making Nupedia's entire purpose—to create a free encyclopedia—seem redundant. (Unlike *Britannica,* Nupedia used Richard Stallman's "public license," meaning users were permitted to reproduce its contents for free, not just read it.) So on January 3, 2001, when Sanger proposed wikiing up Nupedia, he found Wales receptive to any idea that involved saving Nupedia without spending more money on it.*

Even with a green light from Wales, Sanger could hardly make Nupedia a wiki by fiat. Nupedia had gathered a community of academics, philosophers, and would-be encylopedians around it. Sanger was hardly inclined to tear down a year's work and tell the Nupedians to start all over. Nine days after his fateful dinner with his friend Ben Kovitz, Sanger went live with the first Nupedia wiki. "My initial idea was that the wiki would be set up as part of Nupedia; it was a way for the public to develop a stream of content that could be fed into the Nupedia process," Sanger wrote in a short memoir about the creation of Wikipedia. Nupedia required all its authors to hold a credentialed claim on expertise in the field in which they were writing. "It turned out, however, that a clear majority of the Nupedia Advisory Board wanted to have nothing to do with a wiki." Sanger, as he happily admits to this day, was sympathetic to the view. "Their commitment was to rigor and reliability, a concern I shared with them."

A larger public didn't seem to share these reservations. According to an article in the *Atlantic Monthly*, within three weeks, contributors had created seventeen articles. That number jumped to one hundred fifty a month later, quadrupled by the end of April, and grew to thirty-seven hundred by the end of August, a far more rapid rate of growth than Nupedia had experienced. The

* For the record, Wales has claimed that he alone should be credited as founder of Wikipedia. Unfortunately, he failed to reply to several interview requests for this book.

number of contributors was growing as fast as the number of entries, as word began to spread about this new, wikified approach to aggregating knowledge. By the end of the year, Wikipedia consisted of fifteen thousand articles, and even this hardly indicated what was to come. Not only were the numbers of articles growing, but the rate of growth was rapidly increasing as well. Throughout the first years of its existence this exponential growth continued until only recently reaching a plateau. But oh, what a plateau. Wikipedia currently has 2.2 million articles—twenty-three times the number of entries in the *Britannica*—in English alone.

Sanger and Wales weren't the only ones applying Raymond's and Stallman's ideas to new fields. Around the same time Wales and Sanger were casting around for ideas to save their fledgling open source encyclopedia, Bob Kanefsky was applying open source ideas to planetary geology. A software engineer working at NASA's Ames Research Center near Sunnyvale, California, Kanefsky was trying to figure out how to apply the distributed computing model used by SETI@home to the problem of analyzing the images from Mars that were coming into Ames at the time.

In summer 2000, he called Virginia Gulick, a planetary geologist at Ames, with a question. A large part of a geoscientist's job involves identifying and measuring landforms such as craters, ridges, and valleys in satellite imagery. "It can be very labor-intensive," Gulick chuckles. All that tedium can result in a huge payoff. She and her fellow planetary geologists are scouring the universe for evidence of H_2O. "That's one reason we're going to Mars: to find evidence for water; and if there was water, there may have been life."

Kanefsky wanted to put the entire trove of Mars

images generated from the Viking missions from the 1970s online and invite amateurs to do the rote work of identifying and measuring landforms. Gulick was skeptical. "I was thinking, 'Is this really going to fly?' I really had doubts that untrained observers could tell the difference between, say, a pristine and a degraded crater." (A pristine crater has crisp edges, whereas a degraded crater is eroded due to exposure to the winds and water that have swept over Mars's surface over billions of years.) So Kanefsky and Gulick hit on a compromise. Before putting valuable work in the hands of the crowd, they would give it a test. Gulick had access to an extensive crater database of Mars imagery that had already been categorized and cataloged. A colleague of Gulick's had gone through all eighty-eight thousand images identifying, classifying, and measuring all impact craters that were visible in the Viking images. "She was very disciplined," Gulick reports. "It took her about two years."

NASA quietly posted the entire database online and asked the community of amateur astronomers who follow NASA's every move to help the pros analyze the images. They dubbed the program "Clickworkers." It was the perfect case study, because Gulick and Kanefsky had a control data set—the already completed database. Within a month several thousand contributors had successfully analyzed every image in the database. Gulick and Kanefsky were pleasantly shocked. Not only had the volunteers sped through the same job that had taken a professional planetary geologist two years to complete, but they had done it at a comparable degree of accuracy. The Clickworkers project mimics the open source model of production in several respects. First, an enormous task is distributed across a massive network. Second, there is no limit on the number of potential contributors. Finally, the work itself is broken into small, discrete tasks, so that

Clickworkers can utilize the person with five minutes to spare as well as the guy with nothing better to do on a Saturday than measure craters. This turned out to be crucial to Clickworkers's success: one study NASA put together showed that 37 percent of the project was completed by one-time contributors.

NASA restarted the Clickworkers project in 2006, but this time it was no trial run. Volunteers are now responsible for analyzing landforms found in thousands of high-resolution images returned by the HiRISE camera now circling Mars. (HiRISE stands for High Resolution Imaging Science Experiment.) "This could have a big impact on science," says Gulick. "People spend ten minutes a day doing it, but it's a huge help for us. It takes care of the rote, labor-intensive work and frees scientists up for the intellectual heavy lifting." Just as amateur birders have made invaluable contributions to ornithology through their data-collection efforts, the Clickworkers are making contributions to planetary science. Wikipedia and the Clickworkers offered dramatic proof that the open source model could be applied to fields outside software. It wouldn't be long before others would take it even further afield.

Crowdsourcing and the Problem with Patents

It's funny how fate often turns on last-minute decisions. In late October 2005, the Berkeley political scientist Steven Weber was bringing some of the smartest people he knew into a Manhattan conference room to talk about the future of business. Weber and a coauthor were writing a book about "open source methods of value creation" and wanted some heavyweights to "beat up our argument." Invitees included a former adviser to Vice President Al Gore, an editor from Harvard University Press, and various top executives at New York consulting firms. Then, just one day before the gathering, Weber's host suggested he invite Beth Noveck, a professor at the New York Law School and something of a provocateur in the legal fields. Weber vaguely remembered sharing bagels and lox with a smart, self-possessed woman at an Upper West Side deli a few years earlier, and he extended the invitation. Noveck nearly turned Weber down. She was booked, she explained, but would try to stop by for an hour or two.

On an unseasonably warm, sunny day, Weber's brain trust gathered in a windowless conference room at the offices of Monitor, a consulting company on Madison Avenue. Noveck showed up shortly after eleven a.m. Weber sat her next to David Kappos, a lawyer who managed IBM's patent portfolio. The two were soon engaged in an intense conversation. Noveck had created the Democracy Design Workshop, an online community of lawyers, scholars, and students devoted to collaborative efforts at legal reform, and was one of the legal field's chief proponents of opening closed systems to public scrutiny. Now the patent system was right in her crosshairs.

It seems unusual that IBM would want to reform a system it has used to great advantage. The technology giant was awarded 3,125 patents in 2007—the fifteenth straight year in which the firm won more patents than any other company in the United States. IBM spends roughly $6 billion per year in research, development, and engineering, and its active portfolio exceeds twenty-six thousand patents in the United States alone. But with such vast intellectual property holdings comes great expense. Since 1990 the number of patent disputes has more than doubled in the United States, with the average cost of such litigation coming in around $2 million. Welcome to David Kappos's daily headache. He didn't have twenty-six thousand patents. He had twenty-six thousand targets for rapacious, frivolous, skull-crushingly complex lawsuits.

When the group broke up for lunch, Kappos and Noveck remained in the conference room, locked in animated discussion. Noveck had recently floated a radical proposal past a select group of colleagues: Put patent applications on a wiki, and invite the public at large to help guide the patent examiner. Applications would be posted online where anyone could read, review, and comment on them. People with the relevant experience would be drawn to review patents in their fields of expertise, just as the community that tends the online encyclopedia, Wikipedia, self-organizes around areas of expertise. It would be, Noveck explained, a vast improvement over the current patent system.

The idea sounded familiar to Kappos, whose team at IBM was in fact discussing a similar approach. In recent years a consensus had emerged within the intellectual property field: the patent system was broken. Any remaining debate revolved around how to fix it. More than half of all patent applications are successful, giving rise to a rat's nest of vague, overlapping patents. "We wind up in these fights over patents where we can't tell what they mean, and the courts can't tell what they mean, and even the patentees can't tell you what they mean," Kappos says. He and his team had come up with the idea of opening patents to peer review, a system used by academic journals in which several organic chemists, say, are invited to comment on a paper written by one of their colleagues. But this didn't go nearly as far as what Noveck was suggesting.

Noveck had taken her inspiration not only from

academia, but also from the community production model employed by open source software as well as by such contemporary Internet phenomena as Amazon's user-generated product reviews, the online film database IMDb.com, and the Yahoo! Answers service, in which random people attempt—with surprisingly high rates of success—to answer your equally random questions. It's hard to imagine any of these existing if it weren't for a few steadfast iconoclasts, like Richard Stallman, propounding some very unorthodox ideas about how information should be produced and distributed. Such crowdsourcing efforts have essentially just adopted an open source approach to making products other than software. Noveck's proposal was hardly the first to attempt to harness the wisdom inherently present in large, online communities. But it was one of the most radical because it aimed to overturn one of government's most venerable functions: the awarding of legal protection for inventions and original ideas.

Kappos left the meeting intrigued, and a little scared. A few days later he called Noveck to continue the conversation and suggest they begin working together on the proposal. "I told her that we thought her plan was very powerful, but that we weren't going down the road of asking the U.S. government to cede its sovereignty over granting patents," recalls Kappos. Just the fact that the largest patent-holder in the world, IBM, and a Yale-trained law professor were discussing outsourcing patent review to the crowd was an indication of how far the model of production championed by the open source software movement had come.

Nothing could be more antithetical to the way patents are currently granted in the United States. Here's a primer: An inventor has a bright idea. She downloads a patent application from the United States Patent and Trademark Office website. She fills out the application, attaches any applicable drawings, technical descriptions, and supporting documents she deems necessary, and sends it to the patent office. Then she sits down by her phone.

She has a long wait. If the patent seeker is lucky, she might receive a judgment on her application in two and a half years—the average time between filing for a patent and a decision. The USPTO currently has a backlog of more than 1 million applications that haven't even made it to a patent examiner's desk. The examiners themselves are famously overworked and underpaid. There are currently a little fewer than 5,500 examiners employed by the patent office, and the number of patent filings has increased rapidly, reaching 467,000 in 2007. As a result the examiners are only able to allot twenty hours, on average, to reviewing even the most Byzantine applications.

When an examiner sits down with an application, he must first locate the relevant "prior art," which include previous patents and any other published material that pertains to the application in question. If our inventor has an idea for, say, a musical toothbrush (don't laugh—that's patent number 5044037), the examiner has to root through the agency's database of seven million patents for anything that might make the musical toothbrush redundant.

That may be feasible when you're talking about musical toothbrushes, but the job gets considerably more difficult when the patent involves an obscure improvement to an existing bit of programming code. Until 2005, the office did not consider training in computer science a qualification for USPTO employment. (Software engineers weren't exactly banging down the USPTO's door, either.) So the patent office has had examiners schooled in organic chemistry attempting to evaluate an application that might well puzzle Bill Gates.

Not only does the public not have a window onto the patent review process; the patent reviewers don't have access to the public. According to USPTO regulations, "a patent examiner may not consult an outside agent in the process of reviewing a patent." The fear is that such contact could compromise the agency's neutrality. Many departments within the agency even prohibit the use of the Internet as a source in patent review.

Generally speaking, the overworked and underinformed examiners have reacted in a predictable fashion, erring on the side of granting patents. This has created that Gordian knot of conflicting claims that make Kappos's job so difficult. Capitalizing on this patent promiscuity, corporations have stepped up their filings. In 2005, the *New York Times* reported that Microsoft had raised its goal of filing from two thousand patents a year to three thousand. Two of Microsoft's patent applications that year included "System and Method for Creating a Note Related to a Phone Call" and "Adding and Removing White Space from a Document."

But the effects of this patent glut are hardly comical. "There are companies out there for whom patent litigation has become a primary revenue driver," notes Kappos. Indeed, some stories have entered the realm of legend. In March 2006, the patent-holding company NTP threatened to send executives around the world scrambling for pay phones when its suit against Research in Motion (RIM), the maker of the ubiquitous BlackBerry, nearly shut down the service. RIM paid NTP a $612.5-million settlement. Clearly, something needed to be done to reform the patent process.

Soon after their first meeting, Kappos ordered his attorneys to work with Noveck on her proposal to open the patent review process to public comment. It was an unequivocal endorsement of the open source software model. Although the plan seemed oddly radical for a company such as Big Blue, in fact it conformed perfectly with the direction in which IBM had been moving since radically retooling its core business model in the 1990s. Where the company once protected its proprietary software with zeal, it now contributes thousands of programmer-hours to work on open source software projects—which bring in no revenue through licensing. It even donates some of its patents to the open source advocacy group Free Software Foundation. This is hardly philanthropy. According to the company, the income generated through providing "professional services" related to open source software has more than made up for the revenue it has lost through licensing proprietary software. The move has resulted in new innovations, new products, and a greatly enhanced reputation for IBM within the tight-knit community of software programmers.

In December 2006, Noveck and Kappos were invited to meet with some attorneys from the patent office. As it turned out, the patent office itself had been thinking about how it could tap the open source community. In 2004, President George W. Bush had appointed Jon Dudas to head the USPTO, with the mandate of patent reform. The government attorneys told Kappos and Noveck that if they could arrange a meeting, the patent office would host it. In January 2007, IBM publicly announced the creation of the "Peer-to-Patent Project" (a clever play on the term Peer-to-Peer, the popular file-sharing technology often used for illegal music downloads). The patent office, true to its word, hosted a symposium a few weeks later with some of the leading minds in intellectual property. Over the course of the year companies such as Microsoft and General Electric agreed to participate in the trial project, which launched on June 15, 2007. Though the project is still in pilot stage, Noveck has high hopes. By spring 2008, nearly thirty-three thousand people had reviewed some twenty-two patent applications and had submitted 192 instances of prior art. "The project is demonstrating that citizens have more to offer government than simply voting or answering polls. They have real expertise to contribute and are happy to do so when asked," says Noveck.

It marked a watershed moment for the open source movement. The most hidebound, secretive of government agencies had embraced the notion that, just maybe, more expertise can be found in a massive, public network than can be found among the anointed few. Twenty years earlier, the only people advocating such an approach had been a handful of obscure computer programmers, and even they never could have predicted that it would revolutionize how everything from operating systems to maps to T-shirts are created.

But making a computer program is a lot different from, say, developing an open source map or creating a video news segment. The success of open source software depended greatly on the proliferation of affordable technology and software. Open source provided a blueprint for how people might come together to work—enthusiastically, competently, and without pay—on projects outside of software. But to bridge the gap between theory and practice the crowd would need tools, and the knowledge of how to use them.

3

FASTER, CHEAPER, SMARTER, EASIER

Democratizing the Means of Production

Once upon a time there were producers and consumers. Their roles were static and well defined. But thanks to the Internet and the falling cost of the silicon chip, the line between producer and consumer has begun to blur. Amateurs provide the crowdsourcing engine with fuel, and the open source software movement provided it with a blueprint. But it's the widespread availability of the means of production that empower the crowd to take part in a process long dominated by companies. As a result, the "consumer," as traditionally conceived, is becoming an antiquated concept.

Media—publishing, filmmaking, photography, and music—comprise the vanguard in this movement. Suddenly given access to cheap equipment, user-friendly software, and cost-free distribution, an entire generation of aspiring musicians, filmmakers, writers, and other creatives is choosing to reinvent the way "product" has historically been generated, marketed, and sold. And these same dynamics are beginning to affect other fields as well, whether that involves high school students participating in astronomy projects, audiophiles building their own electronic gadgets, or craftspeople using the Internet to sell their own handmade goods. So far we've looked primarily at the companies doing the crowdsourcing. Here we'll look instead at the people who make up the crowd, and what—given the means—they're choosing to produce. People who are eschewing the established route to success. People who are creating new business models simply by virtue of following their instincts and their hearts. People like Mike Belmont.

Belmont isn't your typical public school dropout. When he was nine he would spend hours exploring the fields on the way to school from the apartment he shared with his mom in San Jose, California. He wanted to study entomology, but classes got in the way of collecting bugs. "I liked school," he says, "but I figured I could learn more on my own." Soon he'd leave for school but never arrive, spending his days in the fields instead. This hardly escaped the attention of his mother or the local truant officer. Belmont, however, was nothing if not determined. "My mom was always working, so there wasn't much she could do." For a while the truant officer would show up every morning to take Belmont to school, accompanied by the police. So he started covering his arms in Vaseline so he could wriggle away when they tried to grab him. Finally, the school gave up trying to force him to go to class and informed his mother that thenceforth he would be homeschooled—though in Belmont's case self-schooled is a more apt description. Belmont says he spent the next seven years collecting insects and reading books in the local library. When he approached the local high school at age fifteen, he tested into the eleventh grade.

Wriggling free became a pastime for Belmont, who

has since become a somewhat notorious figure in the film industry, though most people know him by his pseudonym, M dot Strange. The twenty-eight-year-old self-taught animator has created a movie, entitled *We Are the Strange,* about a doll and a small girl who search for the perfect ice cream parlor. Along the way they encounter monsters, robots, and an unusual hero named Rain. It's an original, unusual film. It looks as if it was created by someone who has spent his life immersed in video games, the Internet, and Japanese pop culture, as indeed is the case. Belmont made *We Are the Strange* without a cast, crew, or budget. But because he video-blogged the process of making the movie, he'd developed a sizable fan base before he'd even finished editing his movie. In 2006, he released a trailer for the movie on YouTube, where it quickly became a cult hit. The notoriety led to a coveted screening at the 2007 Sundance Film Festival.

Soon Belmont had obtained professional management and begun making the rounds to various indie film outfits looking to distribute the film. "It turned my stomach," he says of the experience. "They wanted everything. I couldn't have sold the movie on DVDs or over the Internet or anything." Against his manager's advice, he wriggled free of those deals as well. "The idea is that you join the system, and it'll be good for your career, even if you sign away all the rights to your work and wind up poorer," says Belmont. "Well, excuse me, but fuck the system."

Ten years ago, rejecting Hollywood would have consigned a young filmmaker to a lifetime of obscurity. The path to directing feature films started in film school, which was followed by years of working in entry-level production jobs while making low-budget short films for the festival circuit. Eventually, if the aspiring auteur possessed talent and pluck and knew the right people, he might get the financing to make a film that could, if luck happened to strike twice, get picked up by a distributor who would get the movie into a few art house theaters in New York and L.A. Only if the film held real commercial appeal would it have a chance to break out across the country. Then the director got to start the process all over again, this time with a feature to his credit. In other words, the odds were stacked against him.

But the tectonic plates beneath Hollywood are shifting. What's significant about Belmont's example isn't that he elected to reject a studio deal; plenty of artists choose to work in uncorrupted obscurity rather than compromise their vision for mainstream acceptance. What's significant is that Belmont isn't opting for obscurity at all. Intelligent, quick-witted, and charming, he knows how to work a room, online and off, and says all the right things to a journalist. His YouTube trailer has been viewed more than a million times, and his movie has been written about everywhere from *Variety* to the *New York Times*. For all his self-conscious strangeness, Belmont is also a levelheaded, no-nonsense filmmaker with every desire to reach an audience. Having rejected a theatrical distribution deal, Belmont instead released the movie through the file-sharing technology BitTorrent. He makes his money on merchandising and DVD sales.

Belmont is Hollywood's worst nightmare: cheap entertainment that commands millions of eyeballs, yet can be produced and distributed for free, leaving much of the film industry redundant. "I don't need a studio to distribute or finance my films," he says, without a trace of defiance in his voice. Unlike generations of independent filmmakers before him, Belmont doesn't hate Hollywood. He just doesn't need it.

Sometimes a Small Fraction Equals
a Large Number

In recent years a parallel universe has emerged in media and entertainment. Made up of everything from the adolescent doggerel on MySpace to reader book reviews posted to Amazon.com, this outpouring of creativity from the people formerly known as consumers goes by the somewhat dehumanizing term "user-generated content." Much of this falls along the lines of conversational ephemera—a kind of cultural dark matter that once took place inside church basements and corner bars. But a great deal of it is strange, powerful, and unique—the inspired products of people suddenly granted a forum for their creativity. No one really knows how much user-generated content is out there, but we do know that it commands an increasingly significant share of the audience's attention.

It's also clear that big corporations are becoming increasingly savvy about making money off it. User-generated content is the raw material from which companies such as Google (which owns YouTube) and News Corp (which owns MySpace) fashion their product. It's a straightforward business strategy: give people the tools to make stuff, host it on your site, and capture a slice of the growing market for online advertising. In Britain, Internet advertising is projected to exceed the broadcast ad market by 2009, and the online market in the United States isn't far behind.

For every *We Are the Strange,* there are innumerable clips of unfunny comedians or wannabe television hosts, to say nothing of grainy pet videos, awkward teen confessionals, and the inevitable kicked-in-the-groin clips. The economics of media and entertainment industries obey a power law distribution (also known as the "80/20 Rule"), in that some small fraction of hits, often less than 10 percent, carries the water for a much larger fraction of misses. The same power law distribution can be applied to the aesthetics of user-generated content. Very little of it is interesting to anyone outside the creator and his or her immediate friends and family.

But I have a corollary to this rule as it applies to user-generated content: 10 percent of a very large number is itself a large number. According to my rough estimate, as of February 2008, YouTube was hosting some 80 million videos. If even 1 percent—or 800,000 videos—can compete with some of the fare that passes for entertainment on television, it would explain the persistent and growing popularity of all the stuff on the Web that wasn't created by a major label or big movie studio. Belmont and his ilk occupy this happy fraction. Internet video isn't going to replace television or the movies, but it will continue to take an ever larger bite of advertising dollars and consumer attention. While *We Are the Strange* may not be your cup of tea—it's not mine—there's no arguing with 1 million viewers. In spring 2007, YouTube announced it would begin giving its most popular contributors—those whose videos regularly get viewed more than a million times—a cut of ad revenues, which is a strong indicator that those parallel universes are starting to collide. The future of entertainment will, at least in part, be outsourced to the crowd.

In the past ten years the cost of creating everything from movies to music to architectural designs has fallen precipitously. This is largely because the means of production have become accessible to consumers. First, the actual tools of production—professional digital video cameras, high-end sound recording equipment, and the software to make them work—have dropped in price to the point that they are affordable even to those on a modest budget. At the same time these tools have become easier to use: not so long ago film editing required manually cutting and splicing together the actual celluloid strips. Then, in the early 1990s, Avid was rolling out the first mass-market digital editing systems, but it required extensive training and was prohibitively expensive. In 1999, Apple launched Final Cut Pro, which required less money and less expertise. Apple followed this by releasing its iMovie software, which comes bundled with every Macintosh and can be mastered in less than a day (about five hours, in my case). We can see a similar series of successively cheaper and more user-friendly advances in the technology used in any number of other fields. The latest version of iPhoto—Apple's free photo-editing software—makes the connection to crowdsourcing explicit by providing a feature that allows the user to upload his or her photos to the iStockphoto website in one click.

Cheap tools would be meaningless without access to information on how to use them. Just a few years ago an aspiring director or cinematographer would have to enroll in film school or night classes to learn how to practice the craft. Now tutorials can be found for free on the Web. Current TV—a news and information cable network that airs clips submitted from viewers—offers a series of videos that teach everything from visual storytelling to film editing. And that just covers moviemaking. In 2002, MIT announced the OpenCourseWare initiative, the goal of which is to post materials from every class the university offers online—complete with textbooks, exams, and video lectures. As of late 2007, more than eighteen hundred classes were available.

Other institutions have followed suit, including the University of Michigan and the University of California at Berkeley. Meanwhile, thanks to the Internet, the cost of distribution has dropped to zero. Belmont, for instance, didn't need to send DVD trailers of *We Are the Strange* to studios and news outlets in order to generate press. He just posted it onto YouTube and let the community distribute it—via electronic word of mouth—for free.

A Template for Revolutions to Come

The 2005 Christmas season marked an important milestone, though few recognized it. For the first time a six-megapixel camera fell below $300, considered to be a magic price point—the amount a middle-class family will spend on a point-and-click camera. This might seem like a fairly mundane event, but the impact of this development touches us all. A professional photographer could now perform his or her job with a point-and-click camera. Or, more to the point, the barrier to entry for an amateur dropped below the price of a cross-continental airline ticket.

Technology moves in simple directions: cheaper, faster, smaller, and easier to use. In the early 1990s, a professional-grade digital camera cost roughly $13,000. That was almost twice as much as a new Honda Civic. What's significant about technology's inexorable progress isn't that it makes for ever cheaper, ever cooler toys around the Christmas tree, but that with every seemingly minor advance, it puts more creative power into the hands of consumers.

It's arguable that this trend started when Johannes Gutenberg invented movable type. Previously, publishing was restricted to those capable of providing room and board to a monastery full of tonsured transcribers. But Gutenberg merely shifted power from the ridiculously wealthy (the aristocracy and the church) to the merely affluent (the merchant class). It took more than five hundred years to lay the template for the upheaval we're experiencing today.

One day in the summer of 1984, Apple Computer's CEO, Steve Jobs, met with John Warnock, a cofounder of a little-known company called Adobe Software. The two had joined forces a year earlier. That year Apple had released the Macintosh, the first personal computer that displayed graphics instead of command lines of green text over a black screen. In the early 1980s, the term "personal computer" still sounded, to most people, like an oxymoron. Computers were the province of programmers, accountants, and academics. Before the Macintosh, it wasn't taken for granted, as it is today, that computers should be personal, friendly, and intuitive.

Jobs and Warnock were about to transform not just the computer industry but the world of publishing as well. Warnock and his colleagues at Adobe had written a computer language called PostScript that would allow those lush Macintosh graphics to be printed on an affordable printer using laser technology. Warnock and Jobs had asked Jonathan Seybold, a pioneer in digital printing, to come look at their invention. "I went to Cupertino [the town in California in which Apple is based] and walked into this tiny room, and there stood Jobs and Warnock with a Mac and a LaserWriter," said Seybold later. Jobs pressed a few buttons on his Macintosh, and a page slowly emerged from the printer. "I turned to Steve and said, 'You've just turned publishing on its head.' "

In January 1985, Apple launched the LaserWriter, and it wasn't long before Seybold's prediction came true. A third software company, Aldus, completed the troika by releasing a program called PageMaker that enabled graphic artists to lay out newspaper and magazine pages just as they would appear when they rolled off the press. It was a radical departure from publishing's status quo. Instead of painstakingly cutting and pasting every element of a magazine or newspaper layout onto boards, then photographing them and turning them into a printing plate, a graphic artist could now simply send the file to a machine that made the plates.

Revolutions are rarely bloodless, and the "desktop publishing revolution," as it was soon dubbed, was no exception. Between 1985 and 1990, the typesetting market cratered as publishers adopted the new technology. "At a Seybold conference shortly after the LaserWriter was announced, I was cornered by a guy who made typesetting equipment. He almost assaulted me," said Seybold. " 'You have ruined my business,' he shouted. 'You pushed PostScript and you ruined my business.' " Together Apple, Adobe, and Aldus changed the course of human creativity. "The creative professional became the driver of the printing process," notes Frank Romano, a professor of print media at the Rochester Institute of Technology.

Establishing a pattern that would be repeated time and again in the years to follow, desktop publishing put the power of production into the hands of the individual. One of those individuals happened to be me. In 1993, I was a senior at Ohio University's Scripps School of Journalism. By that time, of course, the desktop transformation was well under way. The mainstream press had already taken advantage of the cost savings associated with the streamlined workflows made possible with digital typesetting. But academia was slow to catch up.

That fall I'd arrived back at school fresh from a semester abroad studying art history in London. Coming back to Ohio University, in Athens, Ohio, I was afflicted by a cultural claustrophobia. Drunk from an intoxicating brew of new ideas and youthful grandiosity, I searched for the most intelligent, creative, and ambitious students I could find. It turned out I wasn't the only one who felt constrained by the student magazine, *Southeast Ohio*, which tended to run features with titles like "Hometown: Newark!" and "Successful Spring Turkey Hunting." I soon joined about a dozen other students in producing a magazine devoted to "alternative journalism." We covered race, sex, politics, and the kind of culture that rarely makes it to rural Ohio. The magazine was called *inside-OUT*, and for the next two caffeine-saturated years we devoted our weekends and evenings to it. We all wrote; we all edited; and we all designed. We sold the ads ourselves, making just enough to meet our printing costs with every issue. We distributed the magazine from the back of the executive editor's pickup truck, leaving stacks anywhere an Ohio college student might congregate, from Cleveland bars to Dayton cafés to the student union at Ohio State University in Columbus.

The early 1990s was an exciting time to start a new magazine. Programs like Adobe Photoshop, Illustrator, and PageMaker had liberated a new generation of writers and designers, and *insideOUT* became a laboratory for graphical and journalistic experimentation. Instead of creating a single issue as some sort of senior thesis, the new desktop publishing tools enabled us to create a magazine that looked as professional as anything else being published in Ohio at the time. During its brief lifespan, *insideOUT* twice beat the journalism school's own magazine for a Society of Professional Journalists award for best regional publication.

Not that we were exceptional magazine makers—far from it. We were typical of thousands of aspiring and amateur journalists who were freed from the constraints of daily newspapers and regional magazines. Desktop publishing may have shut the door on the typesetting industry, but it led to a renaissance in publishing. Young Turks weren't the only ones leading the way. Suddenly, everyone from church congregations to woodworking enthusiasts could create glossy, professional-looking publications. The technology dramatically altered graphic design as well, giving rise to the groundbreaking typography of magazines such as *Raygun* and *Wired*. The impact of the desktop publishing revolution has diminished over time. In an age when teenagers can broadcast their own photos, videos, and diaries to the world with a few keystrokes, putting out an "edgy" arts-and-culture magazine seems downright quaint. But the creative destruction wreaked by Jobs, Warnock, and others did more than just fill news racks with obscure magazines. It set a template for technological disruption, in which a threat to one industry leads to the creation of new industries no one could have foreseen a few years earlier. Desktop publishing was a small but irrevocable step toward placing creative power in the hands of the crowd.

Democratizing Education

More than anything, Mike Belmont, aka M dot Strange, exemplifies how the kind of knowledge and training that was once restricted to professional schools and universities is now available to anyone with an Internet connection. Belmont's path through college was no less idiosyncratic than his path through elementary school. After dropping out of school a second time, he got into a community college by simply claiming he had a high school diploma. Soon he transferred to San Jose State University to study entomology, just as he'd always intended. Then he saw David Lynch's surrealist thriller *Lost Highway,* which defied cinematic convention without straying from its own hallucinatory logic. "I was like, 'You can do *that* in a movie?' "

Belmont applied himself to his new calling with a single-minded purpose, which isn't to say he bothered to take a film class. He became particularly interested in animation and began frequenting a few of the many websites devoted to the subject. "I wasn't shy," he laughs. "I'd ask question after question and basically make a nuisance of myself." Sites such as CGSociety and C4DCafe feature message boards and tutorial videos and attract thousands of opinionated, passionate users, not all of them amateurs. "I got in a fight with one guy on CGSociety and found out he was the director of *Alien vs. Predator,*" says Belmont. But mostly Belmont's curiosity was welcomed, and rewarded. It was around this time that he started working on *We Are the Strange.*

Belmont recently started his own "film skool," posting six- to ten-minute videos to YouTube that tackle such subjects as the preproduction process and the use of subtext in movies. "I got so much from the filmmaking community, I felt I wanted to give something back," he says. Obviously, a series of short online videos can't compare with two years of film school at New York University or UCLA, but then Belmont's film skool is not for the conventional would-be filmmaker. It's for someone who—like Belmont himself—is long on talent and vision, but short on money. "There's this Buckminster Fuller quote I love," notes Belmont. " 'To build a new system you don't compete with the old one, you build a new system that makes the old one obsolete.' " Crowdsourcing requires the services of a smart, well-trained crowd, and the proliferation of valuable information over the Internet is making the crowd smarter and better-trained all the time.

Recall the connection between "amateur" and its original Latin meaning: "lover." Without an abiding love for filmmaking, Belmont would have never slaved over *We Are the Strange* for three years. Without a similar devotion other animators would have never created such online forums as CD4Cafe. The author and NYU technology professor Clay Shirky compares this kind of dedication to a Shinto shrine in Ise, Japan. The shrine has stood—in a manner of speaking—for thirteen hundred years. But the shrine is built of wood. In order to keep it from decomposing, the Imbe priests in charge of the shrine tear it down every few decades and—using wood from the same forest used to build the original—painstakingly rebuild it. "It is not a product but a process; it exists not as an edifice but as an act of love," Shirky writes in his book *Here Comes Everybody: The Power of Organizing Without Organizations.* Shirky cites the Ise shrine in the context of Wikipedia, but he could just as well be writing about CD4Cafe. "What is happening in our historical moment is that love has become a lot less squishy, and a lot less private. . . . Now we can do things for strangers who do things for us, at low enough cost to make that kind of behavior attractive. Our social tools are turning love into a renewable building material."

Filmmaking is just one area in which this kind of community-motivated labor is disseminating knowledge to anyone with some spare time, a will to learn, and an Internet connection. A similar dynamic has emerged in all forms of media creation, and is even spreading into the sciences as well. Given the long history of amateur-professional partnerships in science, it's no surprise that the Internet would trigger a resurgence in this collaboration.

Scientific discovery is fueled by the collection and aggregation of data. Just as the Internet has given ornithologists access to the eyes (and notebooks) of thousands of enthusiastic bird-watchers, the Internet has also provided forums on which professional and amateur astronomers can compare notes. The sky is large, and the number of professional observatories is small. Because of this, astronomy has always relied to some extent on the efforts of amateurs. Someone has to keep his or her eyes trained on those parts of the sky that large, institutional observatories such as that in Mauna Kea, Hawaii, can't continuously watch. Just how instrumental such amateur-professional collaborations can be became clear in the winter of 1987, when images of a supernova were captured by a former graduate student who had been helping care for an observatory in Chile in exchange for being able to use the telescope when the professional astronomers didn't need it. His findings were confirmed by observations taken by two other amateur astronomers working in New Zealand and Australia. The resulting scientific paper was coauthored by professional physicists as well as these three dedicated amateurs. In his book *Seeing in the Dark*, Timothy Ferris writes, "If one were to choose a date on which astronomy shifted from the old days of solitary professionals at their telescopes to a worldwide web linking professionals and amateurs . . . a good candidate would be the night of February 23, 1987."

In recent decades astronomers on a budget have seen their options multiply. Affordable telescopes now feature computer-guided, large-aperture lenses and "charge-coupled" devices that are capable of multiplying the amount of available light from the night sky.

Such technological advances have played an enormous role in facilitating the recent growth of amateur astronomy. But no less important has been the proliferation of websites such as Astrosurf.com, a French site that offers a complete description of the main astronomy projects amateurs can undertake as well as tutorials on how to get started. NASA quickly realized the enormous potential for amateurs to contribute to its projects. Now the agency operates a variety of efforts that strive to educate—and utilize—everyone from high school students to the armchair astronomer.

We've already seen how NASA is harnessing the crowd to help it analyze images from the asteroid belt. Another project, called INSPIRE (for Interactive NASA Space Physics Ionosphere Radio Experiments), provides schools with simple, inexpensive kits for receiving very-low-frequency radio waves in the earth's magnetosphere that are then analyzed by NASA. Similar projects exist in seismology, meteorology, and many other disciplines. "Imagine someone who was a high school athlete and always wanted to play with the pros, but didn't make the squad," says Society for Amateur Scientists founder Shawn Carlson. "Is he going to stop playing? It's the same with science. These people are dying to find a place to use their skills." Genius, to paraphrase Edison's old chestnut, is 99 percent data collection and 1 percent inspiration. And you don't have to hold a Ph.D. to count the birds in your backyard.

Democratizing the Tools

It's ten o'clock on a Sunday morning, and I'm standing against a wall in what must be the most run-down apartment in Brooklyn. Several feet away from me the actors

Bob McClure and Lindsey Broad are sitting on an abused sofa on the makeshift set of *The Burg,* an Internet sitcom about underemployed urban twentysomethings. I've decided to write about *The Burg* for *Wired,* and I have managed to convince its creators to cast me as an extra. A grungy metal gate blocks any sunlight from seeping through the cracked storefront window. The walls are bare except for a tattered Zeppelin poster. Ceiling tiles dangle from their frames. It could be a Hollywood facsimile of a Brooklyn crash pad, but *The Burg* doesn't have the money for a set designer. Besides, who needs a fake crash pad when you've got the real thing?

"Does everyone have their beers?" asks the director, Kathleen Grace. McClure and Broad hold up cans of Budweiser.

"Are Jed and I still a pseudo-couple at this point?" asks Broad, whose character had an amorous encounter with the nerd-chic nebbish played by McClure in a previous episode.

Grace ponders the question. At just twenty-seven, she is as much resourceful den mother as director. "Well," she finally answers, "you wish you were still fuck buddies."

Broad considers this. "I was talking to my drama professor," she says. "He thinks the last episode was really significant—that Jed and I crossed the Ross-and-Rachel turning point."

Grace rolls her eyes. Since its May 2006 debut, the show has attained cult status; drama professors aren't the only ones who think of it as a *Friends* for the My-Space set. "We don't want Ross and Rachel," Grace says. "We want awkward and uncomfortable."

The actors shrug. "Okay," Grace says, "let's shoot again."

Sometimes it seems as if the YouTube revolution is being waged exclusively by the video equivalent of lone gunmen, single actors performing before a bedroom web-cam. *The Burg,* on the other hand, is produced by trained producers, editors, and cinematographers using high-end digital cameras and microphones. But then, the folks behind the show aren't trying to reinvent TV; they're trying to break into it. "It's like doing an off-Broadway play," Grace says during a pause in the shooting. "The actors do it because it's creative and fun, and we give them a lot of flexibility." Not to mention exposure to agents and casting directors. Naturally, these benefits come in lieu of cash, which makes it even more like an off-Broadway play. "We pay them in Red Bull," Grace says.

Ten years ago Grace and her friends could have never afforded to create their own sitcom; that was strictly the province of professional outfits such as Carsey-Werner Productions, the company behind such Nick at Nite standards as *The Cosby Show* and *Roseanne.*

The Burg's approach does have drawbacks—chiefly, having to arrange shoots around gigs that pay in a more widely recognized currency. Jeff Skowron, one of the principal actors, was recently cast in a Broadway production, and Grace had accommodated his six-day-a-week rehearsal schedule. "What can we do?" Grace says. "We all have to pay rent."

As a collection of extras assembles downstairs, it's time to resume shooting. The script calls for a party scene featuring a Russian drug dealer and a Grim Reaper figure. Budweiser tall boys are passed around. It's Sunday afternoon, but the beer quickly disappears, necessitating an emergency "prop" run. I've spent much of the afternoon in nooks and crannies of the apartment, trying to stay out of the way. Finally, my scene comes up. It calls for me to burst into the room and shout, "This is soooo cool!" This sounds easy, but we do about ten takes. Eventually, Grace decides she's got enough footage for the scene. Most of the extras filter out, but Skowron still hasn't arrived. The actors wait, entertaining themselves with show-business horror stories while scarfing Domino's pizza. Finally, around 7:30 p.m., Skowron comes through the door, still in makeup. Matt Yeager, who will play opposite Skowron, takes his place in front of the camera. He looks down at his beer. "I've had about four of these," he says with a laugh.

The script calls for Yeager and Skowron to get into a fistfight. The two warm up by trading body blows and a few playful face slaps. The crew is cracking up, and even Grace—presumably exhausted from doling out Budweiser, hummus, and stage direction—laughs indulgently. Then it's time to roll camera. "Okay, places," she calls. "Scene twenty-six, shot K, take five. Action!" A few months later the episode is released on *The Burg*'s website. To my dismay they've cut my line, though they keep a brief shot of my face.

The Burg didn't do much for my acting career; but it's jump-started those of the regular cast and crew. McClure appeared in *The Brave One* with Jodie Foster; Broad was cast in the premiere episode of CW's hit show *Gossip Girl;* and Skowron was cast in the Freddie Prinze Jr. vehicle *New York City Serenade.* "*The Burg* became a calling card for our actors," says co-creator Thom Woodley. "They would show up at auditions and the casting director would be like, 'Oh, you were on *The Burg*—cool!' " Eventually Motorola signed on as a sponsor of *The Burg,* enabling Woodley and Grace to dole out months of back pay.

By the time the last *Burg* appeared in late spring 2007, former Disney CEO Michael Eisner had hired Woodley and Grace to produce an Internet-only series about an unknown rock band called The All-for-Nots. "Michael wanted the quality of writing to be the same," says Woodley, "but the production values will be much higher." Which is to say, *The Burg* has graduated to the big leagues.

What made *The Burg* possible was that the cost of production has fallen to levels such that young post-grads like Grace, Woodley, and company can compete for audiences with industry giants like Carsey-Werner. Before, "I don't even know what we would have shot it with," says Woodley. "A professional video camera used to cost upward of ten grand," he notes. "None of us had that kind of money." *The Burg* was mostly shot with a Canon XL1, which can be bought used for a little over $1,000. The show's director of photography supplied the camera and lighting equipment.

But the starkest illustration of the extent to which the playing field has been leveled isn't in hardware but software. "Today kids walk out of film school with a copy of Final Cut Pro," notes Woodley. "Before, to edit you had to take your film into an expensive post-production studio, and you had to know how to use Avid. Huge chunks of the filmmaking process have just been cut out, things you just don't need to do anymore."

The same forces—faster, cheaper, smaller, easier— that are rocking filmmaking are making an impact in music and product design. A FocusRite Forte recording console, used for producing and mixing music, cost $1.5 million in the mid-1980s. FocusRite now sells the equivalent package as the software program Pro Tools. Cost? $595.

Democratizing Distribution

The members of Hawthorne Heights have no business being rock stars. They play a strain of punk that has consigned innumerable bands to the obscurity of dive bars and pirate radio. For the past three decades, a devotion to this stripped-down, anti-commercial music has meant never quitting your day job. And yet here they were on a dusty summer day in Pomona, California, playing for thousands of adoring fans. The kids in the audience—a multiracial mix of teens from across the SoCal region—were in a transcendent state, crashing against one another like pinballs and screaming the lyrics to every song with red-faced intensity. They'd memorized the entire set.

In the summer of 2005, I followed Hawthorne Heights to concerts in Pomona and Cleveland. The band was a big draw for that year's Warped Tour, in which more than three hundred bands play some forty-eight concerts at venues across America. I flew coach, but the members of Hawthorne Heights toured the country in a plush tour bus. The quintet's debut album, *The Silence in Black and White,* had already sold five hundred thousand copies, a healthy performance for a down market. The group had recently appeared on *Jimmy Kimmel Live* and on MTV. These five young men from Dayton, Ohio, had achieved the rock 'n' roll dream, but like M dot Strange they had taken an unorthodox route to success. The band achieved its popularity without significant radio or TV airplay, a feat unheard of a few years earlier. They weren't signed to a major label and they didn't have an industrial-strength, multiplatform marketing campaign. Further, they didn't have fleets of trucks delivering CDs to Wal-Marts across the country. "A major label can be thought of as a bank with trucks," says longtime industry veteran Jim Griffin. "The bank lends the money to the band to make and promote the album, and the trucks carry the product to the stores."

Distribution used to be the point in the supply chain at which big companies could control the market. If smaller players couldn't get their product to retailers, they couldn't compete. The Internet turned this upside down by making distribution as easy as hitting Send on an e-mail. Hawthorne Heights didn't need the bank or the trucks. Instead it had the crowd.

Making Friends, Influencing People

For Eron Bucciarelli, the earnest, mop-headed drummer of Hawthorne Heights, a degree in communications from Ohio's University of Dayton seemed like a dead end. His heart was in punk rock. In 2001, he took a job with the local cable company and joined an unsigned pop punk quintet called A Day in the Life, after the Beatles song of the same name. The members devoted themselves to the band, gigging out at every opportunity. It was grueling: lousy venues, seedy hotels, and long road trips. "We went on tour every weekend," Bucciarelli explains. "We'd pack up the van right after work on Friday, play a show that night in Pittsburgh, play the next night in Philly, wind up in Delaware somewhere on Sunday, and then drive all night to get back to Dayton by Monday morning."

Before long, the punishing regime of day jobs and weekend tours took its toll. A brief flirtation with the indie label Drive-Thru Records fizzled. The band's lead singer, J. T. Woodruff, was disenchanted and exhausted; he had two jobs and attended night school. When the bassist quit, the other members were ready to follow his lead. But Bucciarelli wouldn't let go. He convinced his bandmates to hire another bass player, and they continued under a new name: Hawthorne Heights. "We used to tell people it was because we liked Nathaniel Hawthorne," he laughs, "but that's bullshit. We just thought it sounded cool."

The band decided to reinvent itself. "We agreed this would be our last shot," he says. "We didn't want to be in our late twenties playing some Elks hall. We'd be geezers." The first element in need of overhaul, they decided, was the music. A Day in the Life played pop punk built on catchy guitar riffs. "We dropped the classic rock influence and added breakdowns and screaming," he says. It pushed their sound closer to the post-punk genre known as screamo.

On the strength of their new sound, Hawthorne Heights soon scored a recording contract with the indie rock label Victory Records—but though the deal provided a morale boost, it didn't do much to improve the group's financial situation. "We cut a very, very different deal than we would have gotten with a major label," Bucciarelli says. In fact, the band received a paltry advance. "We got about five thousand dollars, and that immediately went to pay off our minivan."

But Bucciarelli wasn't looking for a big check. "We could have gotten a million dollars up front and all lived large for a while," he says, "but we'd have spent the rest of our careers trying to recoup." That's the way a standard-issue major label contract works: Any label's outlay associated with a band—from studio time to radio promotions—is billed against the band's advance. Instead, Hawthorne Heights kept costs low. They spent $20,000 to record their debut LP and another $5,000 on a video. And because Victory budgets a fraction of what the majors do on marketing and promotion, Hawthorne Heights needed a cheap way to build demand for their June 2004 album release.

Enter the crowd. In spring 2004, the band posted a

few songs on MySpace, which was already becoming a hub for the indie music community. They lavished attention on their budding fan base. Crowdsourcing can be a labor-intensive endeavor: on tour, each musician would spend four to five hours online every day, engaging their fans in banter and generally making themselves accessible. "The fans love it," notes Bucciarelli. "They can't believe they're getting a response. You've got a fan for life." When their album *The Silence in Black and White* came out, they already had twenty thousand "friends" on MySpace. And by frequently updating their blog and swapping in new songs on their MySpace profile, Hawthorne Heights was able to give fans a reason to return. The online buzz increased exponentially: by spring 2008, the band's MySpace fan club numbered five hundred thousand. That's a direct marketing list any major label would kill for. And every time someone opens that page, another Hawthorne Heights song blares forth. Their sophomore album, *If Only You Were Lonely,* peaked at number three on the Billboard charts.

Until recently, such a feat would have been inconceivable. Music labels exercised control over the market through two bottlenecks: radio and distribution. If the label wanted to make a hit, it paid radio stations to spin the track, and shipped the album in bulk to major retailers. Without radio support and a distribution deal, an artist couldn't begin to make headway in the marketplace. Most albums failed regardless, but at least under the old regime a few blockbusters could be counted on to finance dozens of expensive failures. This model hasn't worked too well in the digital age: music-industry revenues have declined precipitously since their peak in 1999, from roughly $15 billion to $10 billion in 2007.

By contrast, bands like Hawthorne Heights keep production and promotion costs as low as possible. They give away their best two or three songs as Internet downloads or streams, and they use social networking sites and e-mail blasts to reach an audience hungry for new music. Converts become zealots, downloading the latest releases from the band as soon as they appear on the peer-to-peer networks. The resulting loss in sales is more than made up through concert ticket sales, T-shirts, hoodies, messenger bags, posters, and bumper stickers. Electronic word of mouth becomes a marketing strategy that doubles as a distribution strategy, as more and more potential customers download the group's music and in turn—the band hopes—share it with their friends as well.

This is the music industry's first serious business model in the post-Napster era. With little fanfare, groups like Hawthorne Heights are making a full-time living selling a modest number of discs—about fifty thousand to five hundred thousand per release. As the music business is overwhelmed by crowdsourcing, the crucial functions once performed by the labels have been taken over by the fans. In a digital ecosystem, the music becomes a loss leader whose purpose is simply to create more fans, more evangelists, more ticket buyers. Most up-and-coming bands don't regard illegal peer-to-peer file sharing as piracy; they view it as a promotional and distribution channel. And while CD sales still comprise the bulk of industry revenues, digital retailers such as iTunes, Rhapsody, and eMusic are gaining in market share. The cost of making and distributing digital product is negligible.

Like Belmont, Hawthorne Heights devised their strategy in response to circumstance. There was no textbook for crowdsourcing key functions like marketing or distribution. Instead, Belmont and Hawthorne Heights acted on instinct: treating their community of fans like the invaluable resource it really is. In response, the fans did what came naturally to them, expressing their pop cultural interests by spreading the word—and the MP3 files—far and wide. This approach to distributing product has grown quickly. When I was out attending Hawthorne Heights shows, some four hundred thousand bands had profile pages on MySpace. That number has now passed 3 million. (In November 2007, guitarist Casey Calvert died from the "acute combined effects" of prescription medications and an unidentified opiate. The band, however, lives on. They released their third album in August 2008.)

Ultimately, the success of an M dot Strange or a Hawthorne Heights is inconsequential. They're merely the advance sortie of a much larger force. The hyper-competitive tech industry is eager to serve consumers increasingly interested in making things rather than simply consuming them. And it isn't just the means of producing and distributing entertainment that have become affordable—though this is how the phenomenon has first manifested—but the means of producing *anything*.

Sound dubious? Witness two fairly obscure technological developments: custom fabrication and the evolution of 3-D modeling programs. Twenty years ago just about any durable good followed a predictable path to market. First it was designed by a highly trained engineer using CAD (Computer-Aided Design) software. In the early 1980s, a Computer-Aided Design (CAD) system required its own mainframe computer and cost $150,000. Once the design was finalized, the product itself had to be manufactured—a capital-intensive process that ensured that only products intended for the mass market reached the consumer, leaving little room for grassroots innovation, which is to say, the crowd.

Enter custom fabrication—or the "fab revolution," as it's sometimes called—which uses machines that either create objects through the accretion of thousands of thin layers of metallic powders or plastics—in much the same fashion as an inkjet printer—or uses lasers to cut them from a block of some material. All that's needed to create a new model airplane or an electric guitar body or a funky Frisbee design, to use but three real-life examples, is to send a digital file to the fabrication machine. And this, as it happens, is becoming easier than ever, too. CAD programs once required users to scale a daunting learning curve, and could take years to use well. But the latest 3-D modeling software program, Google's Sketchup, can be mastered in days and is available as a free download. Custom fabrication machines aren't cheap, running around $10,000. But then, flat-screen TVs cost that much just three years ago. By 2008, a mid-range set cost less than a grand.

One day in the not distant future, says Neil Gershenfeld—head of MIT's Center for Bits and Atoms and "fab lab" evangelist—people will have personal fabricators in their home capable of creating just about anything they can dream up. When they do, it will be as easy for an amateur product designer to go up against the professionals as it was for M dot Strange to make his own movie.

4

THE RISE AND FALL OF THE FIRM

Turning Community into Commerce

If the means of production and distribution are now within the grasp of the individual, if the line between producers and consumers is blurring, where does that leave the "firm," the organizational structure that has governed how people make and deliver goods and services for over one hundred years? What constitutes an "employee" or a "manager" or "president" in a crowdsourcing environment? Of course, corporations aren't candidates for the endangered-species list quite yet. But it's useful to recall that the firm, that most conspicuous icon of the industrial era, is of fairly recent vintage and is hardly immutable.

We're not accustomed to thinking of communities in economic terms. But this wasn't always the case. Originally humans gathered into communities for reasons of survival. Larger groups made for better hunting provided greater security against rivals and made large-scale agriculture possible. The Industrial Revolution changed all that. The company organized labor into a paid workforce, and the community became the social space in which we rested from work—a respite from economic production and competition, engaging instead in religious, philanthropic, or purely social activities. Now the Internet has started to turn this paradigm on its head. The company clearly offers advantages when productivity is weighed by the pound: you'll always need a factory to produce steel. But in the realm of information production, the community is beginning to rival the corporation for primacy.

Four developments created a fertile ground in which crowdsourcing could emerge. The rise of an amateur class was accompanied by the emergence of a mode of production—open source software—that provided inspiration and practical direction. The proliferation of the Internet and cheap tools gave consumers a power once restricted to companies endowed with vast capital resources. But it was the evolution of online communities—with their ability to efficiently organize people into economically productive units—that transformed the first three phenomena into an irrevocable force.

What does the crowd (a slippery concept, especially in the context of economic production) have to do with this? First, the crowd is not composed of every living human on the planet. Because crowdsourcing is, in almost every instance, made possible by the Internet, I've come to use a synonym that reveals a bit more about the constitution of the crowd: the Billion. This is because there are a little more than one billion people online across the globe. In crowdsourcing terms, that's one billion people with the potential to contribute in some way to any given crowdsourcing project. But of course that's not how we encounter the Billion. In reality the Billion are dispersed among innumerable overlapping online communities, composed of people whose interests align, however temporarily. These communities aren't so different from those we know from the offline world. They impose a set of social norms of behavior on their constituents, and they offer rewards, in the form of enhanced reputation, for conforming to those norms or excelling at skills the community deems valuable. And in the information age, that makes for a tremendously powerful economic force. The community is the basic organizing force behind crowdsourcing.

In the past, communities formed along geographical lines. But in the decades after World War II, a number of factors conspired to break the bonds that held these communities together. Freeways, airplanes, telephones, and television all played their part in eroding geography's dominant role in organizing human affairs. Membership in social institutions such as bridge clubs and Elks lodges plummeted. People found themselves increasingly isolated—islands in a suburban sea. Robert Putnam, a Harvard political scientist, argued in his best-selling book *Bowling Alone: The Collapse and Revival of American Community* that as communities disintegrated, so did our collective stock of "social capital," the difficult-to-quantify but very real economic value derived from borrowing a cup of sugar from a neighbor or helping a friend find a job.

In this context, the spread of the personal computer seemed like one more nail in the coffin of a robust civic life. But just under the radar screen something magical was occurring. Communities were re-forming. By the late 1990s, the Internet was beginning to foster entirely new communities organized along lines of affinity. Sailing enthusiasts from Bangkok to Bangor could meet, become friends, and wind up engaging in all the gossip, chatter, and general exchange of information that formerly took place in person. More recently, new types of communities have materialized that are both local and wired at the same time.

Turning Readers into Writers

To see her at work, you wouldn't think Retina Carter represented the future of journalism. For one, Carter doesn't practice journalism full-time. Her days are spent designing new diapers for Procter & Gamble. She works for the *Cincinnati Enquirer* in her spare moments, usually at lunch and during the evenings from the home office in the modest three-bedroom colonial she shares with her husband and baby daughter. Carter writes for Cincy-Moms.com, a job she "adores," and for which she gets paid $25 a week.

The Carters had been in Cincinnati for a year when Retina's husband, Daryl, read a small advertisement printed in the back of the *Enquirer:* "Writers Needed for a Local Mom Site." It was January, the long Ohio winter had set in, and neither Retina nor Daryl had made many friends since their arrival from Georgia. "You should do this," Daryl said, showing her the advertisement. "You'd be writing"—something he knew she loved—"and you'd be getting paid for it."

Carter applied for the position, though she had no experience in online communities or professional journalism. To her surprise, she was chosen to be one of ten "moderators" on the CincyMoms site. That meant she was responsible for seeding the site with content. With the site's "soft launch" scheduled for later that month, the *Enquirer* wanted to give the staff time to work out the kinks and fill the site with articles before visitors started showing up. The CincyMoms thread followed the standard recipe for an online forum. Chatter is organized into categories, such as "Pets" or "Giving Back," and then is further divided into topics—"Puppy Classes on the East Side!"—on which users can post their thoughts and opinions. Every week Carter was supposed to create ten new topics and write twenty posts of her own, so that other moderators' topics would look lively.

Before the *Enquirer* even had a chance to publicize the site, word spread through the daycare centers and soccer fields of Cincinnati. In the first few weeks, traffic to the site doubled, then doubled again. CincyMoms doesn't look radically different from other parenting sites on the Internet. The front page consists of photographs submitted from some of the moms and, just below that, the forums. CincyMoms offered its readers something unique: local knowledge. "A lot of what women are looking for from us isn't general advice," says Carter. "They want to know the best local pizza parlor to take their kids to after a gymnastics meet, or the best pediatrician in Montgomery."

CincyMoms offers all the pleasures of the Internet— such as the ability to exchange gossip at any time of the day or night—without sacrificing the particularities of place. Unlike a bridge club or coffee klatch, however, it also provides a commodity for sale. Working for the *Enquirer*'s parent company, Gannett, Retina Carter and her friends create content for their hometown newspaper. And while Carter and nine other "discussion leaders" receive a minuscule wage for their efforts, the rest of the CincyMom community receives less tangible forms of compensation, including information, personal satisfaction, and social engagement. The *Enquirer*, in turn, receives a considerable amount of advertising revenue. It's not a bad trade-off, and for better or worse it's come to characterize a new and increasingly common relationship in the information economy.

The Internet facilitated the formation of new communities, but in the past several years companies such as Yahoo and MySpace, to name but two, have managed to convert the mundane warp and weave of community interaction into a commercial good. In a sense, of course, newspapers have always been commercializing communities. What else is the classified advertising section but a monetization of the virtual flea market? But Gannett, the publisher of *USA Today,* the *Cincinnati Enquirer,* and eighty-four other daily newspapers, is going much further, fostering communities in order to direct them to perform a specified function from which it benefits through the sale of advertising. The crowd that powers crowdsourcing isn't organized into anything we would recognize as a firm or company or even loose affiliation of freelancers. In cases running the gamut from science to journalism to product design, the crowd takes the form of a community.

Within weeks of its launch, CincyMoms was receiving fifty thousand page views a day, and advertisers were beating down the door to get onto the site. In just over three months, the site brought in $270,000 — $70,000 more than it was projected to earn in its entire first year of operation. Better yet, the moms constitute a new readership for the *Enquirer* (fewer than 20 percent of young females in the Cincinnati market previously read the paper) and, more to the point, attract the advertisers that cater to them.

CincyMoms, the *Enquirer* hopes, is a sign of a heartbeat in an otherwise chronically ill patient. In case you missed the headlines—and if you're like an increasing number of people the odds are good that you have—newspapers have entered the beginning of a painful and seemingly irre-versible decline. Fewer people read them, which means businesses pay less to advertise in them, which leads to diminished profits and falling stock prices. This causes publishers to make deep cuts in staff, which means that fewer people find anything to read in their local paper, which causes even further drops in readership.

But after more than a decade of attempting to com-pete on its own terms by, for instance, simply re-creating their primary product—the newspaper itself—online, the industry looks to be finally ready to mold itself to the new medium. In many cases, that means accepting a role of di-minished importance. Prior to the Internet, a newspaper spoke directly to its audience. That role has started to fade, but now the Internet provides the opportunity for a two-way conversation between the paper and its readers. "We really had to train our newsrooms to accept that they didn't have a monopoly on ideas and opinions," says Michael Maness, the architect of Gannett's crowdsourc-ing strategy. One sees that dialog in the comment sections that appear after the story when it's published on a paper's website. But CincyMoms, Maness notes, takes that evolution much further. The paper becomes—and here's an even larger slice of humble pie—merely the room in which the conversation takes place. Or, to use Maness's word for it, newspapers have entered the age of the "polylogue." It's better than going bankrupt. Can CincyMoms compete with a big social networking site like MySpace? Maybe. Even though a site like MySpace has the almost limitless resources of Rupert Murdoch's News Corporation behind it, MySpace still can't tell you the best pizza parlor to go to in Montgomery.

CincyMoms is just one plank of a larger plan on the part of the *Enquirer*'s owners, and the people in HQ couldn't be happier with the success of CincyMoms, which itself is based on an equally successful trial effort in Indianapolis (called, naturally, IndyMoms). Gannett hopes it's caught lightning in a bottle, and over the course of 2007 the company began throwing up "Mom sites" at thirty of its other papers.

Gannett's Mom sites represent the leading edge of a radical overhaul: the company is rethinking nearly every aspect of the way it gathers, writes, and distributes the news. The Web has become the primary vehicle for news, with frequent, round-the-clock updates. Photographers have been trained to shoot video. Reporters and editors are expected to draw from the well of ideas expressed in the reader forums. Readers themselves are being put to work as watchdogs, whistle-blowers, and researchers in large, investigative features. And everyone, it seems, is offered a chance to write a blog. All this is transforming Gannett's papers into online repositories of vital local information, overflowing with data about everything from potholes to public officials' salaries to property values. Anyone interested can dig into the treasure trove. "We must mix our content with professional journalism and amateur contributions," reads the PowerPoint presentation Gannett showed its newsrooms when launching its crowdsourcing initiative.

Welcome to the newspaper in the age of the polylogue, written for—and increasingly by—the community. There are considerable advantages to what Gannett's trying to do. For instance, if they were full-time employees, such part-time contributors as Retina Carter would need to be hired and evaluated and managed, their output directed and accounted for. But to the great satisfaction of papers like the *Enquirer,* such contributors operate autonomously. There's a trade-off for this autonomy: paid

employees can be told what to do, online communities do
what they want. But it's often a price well worth paying.

Not everyone at Gannett has been happy about the
changes. "It's adapt or die," says Tom Callinan, the *Enquirer*'s squat, gruff, no-nonsense editor. "And not everyone wants to adapt." Some of the *Enquirer*'s staff took
early-retirement buyouts or simply quit. But many—
"more than I expected," says Callinan—chose to change
with the times. Linda Parker, as it happened, was happy to
adapt. A onetime metro editor at the *Enquirer*'s crosstown
competitor, the *Cincinnati Post,* Parker is now the *Enquirer*'s "online communities editor." The words "GetPub-
lished" feature prominently on every *Enquirer* webpage.
The results land in Parker's queue, and they almost never
resemble anything commonly considered journalism.

"It used to read, 'Be a Citizen Journalist,' " Parker
says. "And no one ever clicked on it. Then we said, 'Tell
Us Your Story,' and still nothing. For some reason, 'Get-
Published' were the magic words." The *Enquirer* considers the feature to be an unequivocal success. Parker, a
cheerful woman in her mid-fifties, pores over several
dozen submissions from readers every day. These range
from a local custom car builder trumpeting his upcoming
appearance on a BET show to an emotional notice for a
play being held to raise funds for a fifth-grader's bone-
marrow transplant. Parker either rejects or approves the
submission ("I almost never reject one," she says), scans
it for "the F-word," and posts it to the sites. "A few years
ago these would have come across the transom as press
releases and been ignored."

There's a valuable lesson here: people want a voice,
but that doesn't mean they'll use the vernacular of journalism. "One of our most popular categories is called
'First-Person.' People really love to reminisce about the

1937 flood," the worst flood in Cincinnati history, says Parker. "We got great stories on that." The reader submissions do more than provide the *Enquirer* with additional content to sell ads against. "Our suburban papers"—the *Enquirer* publishes twelve of these, in addition to ten community inserts and four regional magazines—"could never fill their pages without this material." Some hyper-local stories, it turns out, have legs. One of the common criticisms levied against Gannett is that it's crowdsourcing in order to cut staff, but this misses the point entirely. Crowdsourcing actually enables the papers to expand: more webpages, more niche publications, *more ads*.

But church picnics and school closings aren't the only things readers like to cover. They're also contributing to serious journalistic investigations, breathing new life into a genre that is increasingly considered an endangered species at metropolitan newspapers. In summer 2006, the *News-Press,* a Gannett paper in Fort Myers, Florida, heard that readers from a new housing development were being charged up to $45,000 to connect to the sewer system. The standard procedure would be to assign one or more investigative reporters to the story, says Kate Marymont, *News-Press* editor. The findings would come out months later in an article that, more likely than not, would go largely unread. Instead, Marymont says, "we asked our readers to help us find out why the cost was so exorbitant."

The response overwhelmed the paper, which had to assign additional staff just to deal with the volume of tips, phone calls, and e-mails that came in. The *News-Press* posted hundreds of pages of documents to its site, and readers organized their own investigations: retired engineers analyzed blueprints, accountants examined balance sheets, and an inside whistle-blower leaked documents showing evidence of bid-rigging. The editors couldn't have been happier. Not only did the paper unearth government malfeasance (the kind of thing that makes a reporter go all warm inside), but for six weeks the story generated more traffic to the *News-Press* website than it had ever received for any event other than a hurricane. In the end, the city cut the utility fees by more than 30 percent, one official resigned, and the fees became the driving issue in a city council special election.

Gannett exported this new approach to investigative journalism to its other papers. In March 2007, in response to an article about the city's contaminated drinking water, readers of the Rochester *Democrat and Chronicle* in upstate New York unearthed locations in which toxic waste is stored. The Gannett paper *Florida Today* has set up a permanent "Watchdog" page, with a "Blow the Whistle" button that led to a series on insurance companies inflating their estimates for hurricane coverage. The "Watchlist" draws more traffic than any other page on the paper's website. The cure for what ails the newspaper may lie within the community it serves. It isn't simply that there's wisdom in the crowd, it's that the crowd—be it a crowd of amateur photographers, NASA groupies, concerned residents in Florida, or gabby moms in Cincinnati—coalesces into a community and self-organizes into a highly efficient workforce. CincyMoms demonstrates how two potent forces—geography and shared interest—can combine to create an online community. Put simply, CincyMoms is driven by a communal interest in both parenting and Cincinnati. It's of interest because it shows how the Internet is forging the kind of local communities that flourished in an era before modern communications. But physical proximity is hardly a necessary ingredient in the formation of online communities. Indeed, affinity—a shared devotion to a political ideology or a hobby or even just a TV show—has proven to be an immensely powerful factor in bringing people together.

The Company vs. The Community

By one measure at least, YouTube is a very small company. Before being acquired by Google, its sixty-seven employees fit into three floors of an unremarkable office building in San Bruno, California. That's exactly one fewer employee than works at the average American nursing home. But by another measure, YouTube is a far larger company. At the time of its acquisition by Google, YouTube was valued at $1.65 billion. That number could seem unreasonable by conventional measures, but YouTube is hardly a conventional company.

Google didn't pay for the expertise housed within that San Bruno office. It paid for the millions of users who create and submit videos to YouTube, and for the traffic they drive to the site. It paid, in short, for the community—the people who use it to engage in a conversation in a language of moving images. YouTube is far from the only company whose primary asset is its community. Facebook employs roughly seven hundred—a skeleton crew for a company that was valued, at the time of Microsoft's investment in the social networking site, in the region of $15 billion. As of early 2007, Wikipedia employed only five people. By contrast, the *Encyclopædia Britannica* was written by over four thousand paid contributors and one hundred full-time editors. In these cases, the community is taking the place of the corporation.

The conventional corporation isn't going away anytime

soon, but its hegemony is certainly under assault. Despite its unchallenged reign throughout the twentieth century, the traditional corporate structure is an artifact of the Industrial Revolution. The company's primary function, as British economist Ronald Coase observed in his 1937 essay "The Nature of the Firm," is to reduce transaction costs. Coase pointed out that contrary to the prevailing view, the market is not always efficient. Because a commodity is rarely immediately available in exactly the quantity the consumer might want, at precisely the time he or she might want it, there are additional costs that must be factored into its purchase. How long did the buyer search for it? If the purchaser is a business, did it risk revealing a business strategy, or a trade secret, in acquiring the commodity? All this and more should be factored into the transaction cost, Coase argued. A firm emerges, he wrote, when it becomes more efficient to produce a commodity in-house than to contract an outside vendor to provide it, and that firm will continue to grow until it begins to buckle under its own weight, at which point it once again becomes cheaper to outsource the work using the marketplace. This makes intuitive sense to us today, and indeed the firm continues to be the basic unit of economic production.

But times have changed since Coase wrote his article. To state the obvious, the advent of the Internet has changed the way business is conducted, with the result that the nature of the firm has changed as well. While advances in communications technology, as Coase predicted, have generally led to larger and larger companies, information technology is exercising a strong counterforce, as the MIT management professor Thomas Malone has documented. While "the main story about the organization of business in the twentieth century was centralization,"

Malone writes in *The Future of Work: How the New Order of Business Will Shape Your Organization, Your Management Style, and Your Life,* "beneath the headlines we find a more complex story." In a study conducted by Malone and his colleagues at MIT, the average size of firms in many industries was found to be shrinking—an indicator of rapidly falling transaction costs due to efficiencies created by the Internet. Tellingly, Malone points out, the largest private employer in the United States today "is not General Motors or IBM or even Wal-Mart." It's the temp agency Manpower Incorporated, which as of 2008 employed 4.4 million people.

The dramatic increase in outsourcing is one obvious indication that the firm is no longer the discrete entity of decades past. But there is, Malone argues, a deeper dynamic at play. His central argument in *The Future of Work* transcends the world of business into organizational theory. Malone has identified three stages in what he calls "an amazing pattern" in the evolution of human affairs. In stage one, people operate in small, unconnected groups. In stage two, larger groups form and decision-making is centralized. In the third stage, "the large groups remain, but decision making becomes more decentralized." In politics this has taken the form of democracy, and now the amazing pattern is taking hold in business. "We can expect to see more of this decentralization," Malone writes, "wherever (a) communication costs are falling and (b) motivation, creativity, flexibility, and the other benefits of smallness produce business gains." Malone cites such companies as Hewlett-Packard, W. L. Gore & Associates (maker of Gore-Tex fabric), and Visa International as examples of organizations that illustrate this trend toward decentralization. By this reckoning, the firm isn't so much becoming obsolete as it is evolving into just one of many deeply interconnected species in an increasingly complex ecology. Put another way, the boundaries that once separated the firm from the other creatures in that ecology—such as suppliers, contractors, customers—have become more porous.

In 2005, Eric von Hippel, the head of the Innovation and Entrepreneurship Group at MIT's Sloan School of Management, published *Democratizing Innovation,* which demonstrated how customers were taking the process of innovation into their own hands. "Users that innovate can develop exactly what they want, rather than relying on manufacturers to act as their (often very imperfect) agents," von Hippel writes. Who thought to add foot straps to windsurfing boards? Not the companies. Back in 1975, the sport's elite athletes had begun using their windsurfers to jump waves. But as windsurfer Larry Stanley recalled, "The problem was that the riders flew off in mid-air because there was no way to keep the board with you." Soon the riders were experimenting with foot straps, and not long after, the manufacturers began installing them on the factory-issued product.

Von Hippel demonstrated that in fields as wide-ranging as scientific instruments and mountain bikes and computer chips, the task of innovation was passing from the manufacturer to the user, who had both a greater need and a greater ability to improve a product's performance. Companies that embraced this change entered into a creative relationship with their customers, even going so far as to provide them with tools to help design the end products. The writer and technology professor Clay Shirky has termed this phenomenon "downsourcing," in which a manufacturer simply shifts the burden of certain functions—innovation, in this case—down the supply chain to the customer. The company then institutes the innovation and sells it back to the customer, who is, in this case, also a supplier. The customer might or might not receive direct compensation for his input. Either way, the real payoff lies in an improved product, a result from which all parties benefit.

Von Hippel offers another useful observation that we see echoed in crowdsourcing: customers don't innovate in a vacuum. "Individual users do not have to develop everything they need on their own: they can benefit from innovations developed and freely shared by others." They form, in von Hippel's terminology, "user innovation communities." They do this not so much out of a need to socialize with like minds—though that surely plays a role as well—but because the community structure offers considerable advantages to the individual innovators. "Chat rooms and e-mail lists with public postings can be provided so that contributors can exchange ideas and provide mutual assistance. Tools to help users develop, evaluate, and integrate their work can also be provided to community members—and such tools are often developed by community members themselves." Such user communities, then, are like mutual-aid societies, or cooperatives. And for such communities to operate efficiently, the individual members generally agree to abide by an accepted social norm: they "freely reveal," which is to say, relinquish any proprietary interest in, their own innovations. The community exists to improve on each other's creations.

Such communities offer the companies for which they "work" considerable advantages: they are more efficient at organizing and performing such labor than a firm would be. And not only does the firm generally not have to pay for the innovations, but the transaction costs associated with the innovations are kept to a minimum. The companies don't have to identify and hire the innovators, manage their productivity, or evaluate their output. The community does all this for them. This runs against the grain of many of our assumptions about how markets and capitalist economies function. What motivates people to act in such a seemingly selfless fashion?

It's one of the many questions the Harvard legal scholar Yochai Benkler tackles in his 2006 book *The Wealth of Networks: How Social Production Transforms Markets and Freedom.* Benkler uses case studies on Google, peer-to-peer file sharing, open source software, and Wikipedia to argue that a new model of economic production—what Benkler calls "social production"—has emerged. (Benkler defines social production as "collaborations among individuals that are organized without markets or managerial hierarchies.") Motivations fall into extrinsic and intrinsic categories. We can think of extrinsic motivations as consisting of carrots (a financial reward) and sticks (a scolding from your boss). Intrinsic motivations, on the other hand, consist of such goals as creative fulfillment, a belief in the project, the sense of community obligation, or the opportunity to enhance one's reputation in that community. According to surveys, open source software programmers are motivated more by intrinsic reasons than by extrinsic reasons. This helps explain why people might be willing to review books for Amazon, design T-shirts for Threadless, or devote countless hours to teaching newcomers on the iStockphoto site the basics of photography. More often than not, the community provides a context in which these incentives exist.

What remains to be understood, Benkler states, "is under what conditions these many and diverse social actions can turn into an important modality of economic production." In other words, what makes the online community a more efficient workforce than one managed by a firm? The short answer is that communities are better at both identifying talented people and evaluating their output. These operations increasingly lie at the heart of the information economy, the raw material of which isn't iron or steel but, in Benkler's words, "human creative labor."

That's a resource that's notoriously difficult to measure, organize, and direct. This is where the community comes in. Imagine the logjam that would have formed if Larry Sanger and Jimmy Wales had had to identify the ideal person to write each one of Wikipedia's 2.2 million entries. Or if the *Cincinnati Enquirer* had had to identify which mom should decide who the best pediatrician in Cincinnati is. Who should write about the entry on Uzbekistan? Wales doesn't know, but he doesn't have to. The person with the right combination of talent, willingness, and a few spare hours will take on the job. And, writes Benkler, "once an individual self-identifies for a task, he or she can then undertake it without permission, contract, or instruction." Transaction cost to Wikipedia? Zero.

But what if our contributor has overestimated his ability? People often do. The community's got that covered, too. At a firm, entire levels of management are devoted to quality control: evaluating the output and productivity of the company's employees. By contrast, online communities are largely self-policing. In practice, Wikipedia entries are rarely written by one person, but by a small sub-community within the larger group of contributors. This is why errors are quickly corrected. This step provides the glue that holds the community together. It's Wikipedia's dirty little secret that a manner of bureaucracy has evolved to maintain the site's editorial standards of truth and neutrality. Every Wikipedia page is monitored by a "Wikipedian," who tends that particular garden. But the organizational forms more closely mimic that of a community, again, than of a firm. Linux was put together by a freewheeling group of coders, few of whom had ever met each other in person. Linus Torvalds was able to direct their efforts, but only because his "authority is persuasive, not legal or technical, and certainly not determinative," writes Benkler. "He can do nothing except persuade others to prevent them from developing anything they want and add[ing] it to [the project]." Wikipedia works the same way.

How pervasive will social production—crowdsourcing, for all intents and purposes—be? Remember the Billion? "They may have between two and six billion spare hours among them, every day." The onus, then, isn't on the crowd; it's on companies, entrepreneurs, and anyone else with a good idea to figure out how to put that idea to work.

A Community Function

This is all less unprecedented than it seems at first blush. The origin of human communities lies in self-interest and mutual economic benefit. The first groups of humans were essentially hunting cooperatives. The cradle of mankind was a brutal and dangerous world; the power of numbers offered safety from predators and food. Eventually agriculture emerged, giving rise to cities and early civilizations in Egypt, the Fertile Crescent, and the Peruvian Andes. Crop surpluses fostered the development of trade and written languages. Soon a ruling class had formed, with priests to legitimize their rule and a bureaucracy to keep track of it all. The increasing complexity of

these early societies required the division of the workforce into vocations, from clerks to blacksmiths to stone-
masons. Once again, communities formed to serve the
mutual benefit of their members, whether that was to
further one clan's interests or to gather the city's weavers
into a guild.

Not much changed over the ensuing millennia. Communication between any two points more distant than a
day's travel by horse was difficult, so communities were
naturally organized around geographical lines. The coopers of Maastricht had little contact with the coopers of
Aachen, though the two were only twenty miles apart.
Throughout the Middle Ages and the Renaissance, the
community remained the building block for all social and
economic organization. It composed the fief, the shire,
and—in Japan—the han.

The Industrial Revolution irrevocably changed the
nature of the community. As the firm became the defining structure for economic activity, communities were el-
evated—and reduced—to serving a role outside the
measurable economy. They became the stuff of church
bake sales, bridge clubs, PTA boards, Rotary chapters,
and, yes, bowling leagues. Even in these new forms the
community still contributed to the economy, but in forms
that were difficult to identify, much less quantify. Just as
firms organized physical and human capital, the community formed the basis for social capital. In his book *Bowling Alone*, the political scientist Robert Putnam defines
social capital as "the features of social organization such
as networks, norms, and social trust that facilitate coordi-
nation and cooperation for mutual benefit." Social capital
provides the oil that keeps our economic machinery running smoothly.

Putnam distinguishes between bonding capital and

bridging capital. The former is found between family and close friends. It's integral to our emotional well-being but does little to promote economic growth. Bridging social capital, on the other hand, consists of the trust built up between acquaintances. Such social networks connect otherwise disparate groups, and according to Putnam, it's an essential component of our economy. "Bonding social capital constitutes a kind of sociological superglue, whereas bridging social capital provides a sociological WD-40," he writes.

And according to Putnam's book, this social lubricant is in increasingly scarce supply. Exhaustively researched, *Bowling Alone* demonstrates how participation in community groups reached their apex at the tail end of the long economic expansion of the 1950s and 1960s. After this high-water mark, the community, as people had come to think of it, entered a long and ostensibly irreversible decline. By the late 1990s, when Putnam's data stops (the book was published in 2000), America's civic spirit had putatively ebbed to its lowest point in the country's history. Putnam offers a raft of causes for this collective civic disengagement, including the entry of women into the workplace, the replacement of the soda counter with the mall, suburban sprawl, desegregation, white flight, and, of course, that multipurpose villain, television.

Plenty of people have beefs with Putnam's thesis. Ethnic minorities have never been big on Rotary or the Elks, Melissa Checker—an anthropologist and urbanist at City University of New York—points out. Declining membership in those organizations excludes any trends that might be occurring in minority communities. "The critique of Putnam can be summed up as this: he has a narrow definition of community. I would argue that community never entered a decline. It just took new forms."

Many of these coalesced over the Internet. And these are the communities that are causing a revolution in the way we do business. Whether one agrees or disagrees with the premise that Americans had become more isolated, more reclusive, and less likely to trust one another at the end of the millennium is, in a discussion of crowdsourcing, irrelevant. What matters is what happened next.

The Third Place

Not many people had heard of the Internet in the mid-1980s. Started as a Defense Department project in the late 1960s, for fifteen years the Internet had served mostly as a forum for computer programmers and academics. But in February 1985, an entrepreneur named Stewart Brand and the doctor and epidemiologist Larry Brilliant decided to use the technology to create a community that could overcome the limitations of geography. Their idea wasn't entirely original. In fact, J. C. R. Licklider, one of the Defense Department researchers who had developed the original computer network, predicted it would one day be used to foster communities. "Life will be happier for the online individual because the people with whom one interacts most strongly will be selected more by commonality of interests and goals than by accidents of proximity," Licklider wrote in a 1968 article.

Licklider's prediction turned out to be strikingly prescient. On April 1, 1985, Brand and Brilliant launched the WELL, an acronym standing for the Whole Earth 'Lectronic Link. A stalwart of the San Francisco counterculture, Brand had been publishing the *Whole Earth Catalog*—something of a hippie house organ—since 1968.

The WELL created a virtual "third place" (the name soci-ologist Ray Oldenburg gave to the coffee shops, bars, post offices, and other places that had once served as the heart of traditional communities) between home and workplace. Free subscriptions were provided to select members of the Whole Earth subculture. Everyone else had to pay $8 per month. Over the next ten years, the WELL would become one of the most influential commu-nities in America, even though few of its members ever met face-to-face.

The WELL's infrastructure mimicked that of an even earlier online community known as Usenet. Usenet had gotten its start when two Duke University grad students established a link with the nearby University of North Carolina. It shared with the WELL an infrastructure built around the idea of affinity. True to Licklider's prediction that online communities would be organized along lines of interest instead of geography, Usenet groups included topics such as "comp." (computers), "rec." (recreation and entertainment), and "humanities." These overarching sub-jects were then subdivided into literally hundreds of subtopics, so, for example, within "rec." you'll find "rec. sports.college.football."

The decision by a few computer scientists in these early years to create a topology based along lines of inter-est would have fateful consequences. Over the ensuing years the World Wide Web emerged to make the Internet a vastly more popular and useful medium. For the most part, the billion people with regular access to the Inter-net organize themselves along the lines of affinity. Other considerations—geography, class, education level—are rendered moot.

Groups formed along lines of affinity are uniquely adapted to the task of information production. Experts on Uzbekistan monitor the Wikipedia entry on same; a mix of novice and expert photographers gravitate to iStockphoto; and would-be video journalists gravitate to Current TV's website, among others. By organizing the Billion, the topology of the Internet has not only allowed for the rise of crowdsourcing, it has quite nearly guaranteed it.

There has been much hand-wringing over the nature of virtual communities. Critiques generally have centered on the notion that time spent online detracted from time spent engaging in the sort of informal, face-to-face socializing that forms the basic building blocks of community. What has emerged in recent years, especially in light of the explosive popularity of social networking sites such as MySpace, is that people are creating new forms of community that perform many of the same functions as those studied by Putnam.

What's clear is that online communities are leading to an increase in bridging social capital on a broad, global level. While the communities on the WELL and Usenet were small, the "third place" they managed to re-create has echoes in the massive social networking sites of our day. Facebook has 70 million members and Myspace has 110 million. Bebo—a social networking site popular in Europe—has 40 million users. And this doesn't include all the smaller online communities that are devoted to particular areas of interest, such as iStockphoto or Harry potterfanfiction.com, to name but two. The architecture of social networking sites encourages connections between, as well as among, friend groups. In this way they are almost tailored to build up stocks of bridging social capital.

We are only beginning to understand the impact the rapid growth of online communities will have on our economy and our culture. But recent studies show "a robust connection" between sites like Facebook and social capital, of the bridging variety in particular. This has a special relevance for crowdsourcing, which requires collaboration between widely dispersed individuals with only a glancing acquaintance to one another. It's a resource we've only begun to tap.

The Community at Work

Jack Hughes doesn't look like much of a revolutionary. Short, burly, and more than a little serious, Hughes wears his hair in a high and tight style a Marine might consider severe. In 1985, one year after graduating from Boston College with a degree in computer science, Hughes started a software company called Tallan. Fifteen years later he had more than six hundred people working for him, and he couldn't remember the last time he'd had a vacation. In March 2000, he called one of the companies that had been courting him and sold Tallan for $920 million.

Hughes still didn't get his vacation. One Friday in May of that year, Hughes walked out of the Tallan offices for the last time. The next Monday he walked into the office he'd leased for his next venture, which he called TopCoder. His idea was to create a website in which programmers would compete for prize money. Contests would be sponsored by big tech companies—Intel, Google, Microsoft—which would use the contests to identify young programming talent. It was a logical idea, but Hughes didn't start TopCoder just to nurture young developers. He started it because he had a bone to pick with the software industry. "It's soft," he says. "Software development has this reputation that nothing ever comes in on time, that it's always over budget and that it's always full of bugs. There's a reason for that: it's true." Hughes wanted to inject the field with some of the discipline and quality control more common in the manufacturing of traditional, tangible goods. During downtime at Tallan his programmers had competed against one another in informal contests. Hughes had noticed that the resulting code was better than what he was paying them to write. Why not make them compete against one another all the time?

TopCoder lifted the tournament structure from the NCAA and applied it directly to programming matches. Competitors were asked to create an algorithm to solve a simple problem, such as finding the quickest route through a maze or the most effective set of moves to end a chess game. Solutions had to be submitted within an hour, at which point the competitors could try to "challenge" each other by "breaking" one another's algorithms. If the entrants passed the challenge round, the TopCoder team would try to poke the solution full of holes. The winner was any programmer who managed to run this gauntlet successfully. "There are all sorts of areas of human endeavor where talent is rewarded because it's in the context of a sport. So we placed programming in that context." TopCoder even created "playing cards" for each programmer, complete with box scores. But Hughes had more in mind than just running tournaments. He'd never heard of Yochai Benkler, but he was about to put Benkler's ideas into practice.

Word slowly spread through the programming community that there was a website holding weekly competitions. The prize money wasn't spectacular, but the weekly tourneys were fun, and if you performed well, you could score a great gig with a company such as Google. For young programmers with more time than money, it was an appealing draw. Slowly and steadily TopCoder continued to grow.

But Hughes wanted TopCoder to do much more than simply administer contests. Even when TopCoder was still in a nascent stage, he knew that if he could build a big enough community he could turn their energies to producing real software for real clients. Development would still take the form of friendly competitions, except that the work completed by the winners would be compiled into part of a larger piece of software for a Fortune 1000 company. By 2003, some seven thousand programmers were regularly scanning TopCoder's weekly matches. About 20 percent of these occasionally won a contest. About 5 percent—the emerging TopCoder elite— won consistently. With his own crowdsourcing engine firing on all pistons, the time had come to put Hughes's community to work.

But before TopCoder could approach clients with its unusual model for developing software, Hughes and his staff had to engineer a method of breaking the tasks down into the smallest possible discrete parts. "We knew from the inception of the company that we'd have to break larger jobs into very short, very defined bits of work," says Hughes. So TopCoder took programs that usually might have been broken into one hundred components and figured out a way to break them down into one thousand pieces. "The idea was, the smaller the block, the more ways we can use it," says Michael Morris, TopCoder's chief of software. This proved advantageous for several reasons. One, a job has to conform to a given individual's "spare cycle," or excess capacity— those hours, essentially, between work and sleep. But the

TopCoder approach also increased speed and efficiency. "If we had five developers working on a project, they'd never have the time to modularize a task," says Morris. "They'd have to finish one thing, and then another. But we have an infinite pool of people working on a single task at the same time. The more we can break it down, the quicker the overall job gets done."

Hughes and company could have been following the crowdsourcing playbook, except of course that no such thing existed. In 2003, TopCoder was basically sui generis, employing a model that Hughes would come to call "competitive collaboration." It took a few years to fix all the bugs. "There was no crowdsourcing. No wisdom of crowds. We weren't applying theory," says Hughes. "We were a science experiment!"

By early 2006, TopCoder had built relationships with a few clients and streamlined their development process. "Our community reached a tipping point. We had about seventy thousand programmers, which we figured was a large enough user base to write industrial-scale computer code," says Hughes. "We probably had some of the best young programmers in the world competing against one another." Around this time, Sree Kotay, the Senior VP of software development at AOL, called TopCoder to ask for a meeting (Kotay has since left AOL to work at cable provider Comcast). Morris flew from Boston (TopCoder is based in Glastonbury, Connecticut) to AOL's Dulles, Virginia, headquarters to meet Kotay in person. "The irony is that he didn't even know we were building software," recalls Morris. "He just wanted to talk to us about getting involved in some contests." Instead, Morris told him AOL should be using TopCoder to develop new software for the company. He came around Kotay's desk to show him a competition that was going on live on

TopCoder's site. "That's not a contest," he told Kotay. "That's the future of software development." Soon Kotay's chief of staff and several other people were in the office watching as Morris walked them through Top-Coder's model. It was a fortuitous meeting. "Kotay was a coder back in the day. He understood how important quality code is." Not long after that first meeting, AOL commissioned TopCoder to write three programs: an en-hancement to AOL's e-mail system, a content syndication system, and an ambitious back-end system that would allow AOL's instant-messenger application to work seam-lessly with other IM clients, such as Google Talk or Yahoo Messenger.

This last job posed the greatest test of TopCoder's sys-tem. First Morris assigned an architect and a project manager to work on the program. They were the only TopCoder staffers to ever work on it. Everything else was done by the community. "They broke the IM program down into fifty-two components." Because the commu-nity had been building similar components—think of them as Lego bricks—for other projects, it turned out that twenty-two of these were already built, just ready to be plugged in.

The other thirty components had to be designed, built, reviewed, and tested. It's a rigorous process, and each step is crowdsourced. TopCoder stuck to its contest format at each step of the way. First the community com-peted to design each component. Members self-identified for each task based on their own perception of their qual-ifications. "There's a vast array of skills and specialties represented in our community," Morris says. "They gen-erally know what they're good at." Competitors submit-ted their best designs, and then TopCoder assigned a review board to evaluate each submission. "We assign the reviewers based on their qualifications. But after that it's first come, first serve." When a winning design was chosen, that, too, was posted as a competition. Then the crowd had at it once again, each attempting to code the best program according to the specifications of the chosen design. Then the review process repeated itself once more, in which the winning code was chosen. Finally there were two more contests—one for assembling all the components together and another to see who could write the best script that will run the entire program through its paces. "We let the competitors form teams. Each team will try their best to break the program." The scripts emulate a user. "It would do all the things a user might, like adding a buddy list, starting a group chat, establishing a secure link between two people." Finally TopCoder took the final program, ran it through a certification process, and handed it over to the client. The community not only performed the labor, it was responsible for quality control as well.

AOL was so happy with the final product that they've since commissioned TopCoder to work on about a dozen more programs. "They love us," says Morris. And with good reason. TopCoder's programs have an average of .98 bugs per thousand lines of code. "The industry standard is six," Morris notes with pride. "A traditional firm might have assigned six or seven developers to the project, and it would have taken well over a year to complete. It took us a little over five months."

SECTION II

Where We Are

5

THE MOST UNIVERSAL QUALITY

Why Diversity Trumps Ability

Looking for a diversion one winter evening in 1995, Caltech professor Scott E. Page built a computer model in which "artificial agents"—little computer programs that interact according to rules written into their computer code—tried to solve a difficult problem. Such computer simulations are helpful to economists because they provide a controlled environment in which to test how humans, that most unpredictable of species, interact in complex systems such as financial markets.

Page ran his simulation using two groups of agents. One was meant to represent the best and the brightest possible solvers; we'll call this the Mensa group. The other group was composed of agents with a wide variation of problem-solving ability; some of the agents were talented, but many were not. It was as if he'd stopped by the faculty lounge at a mid-tier university and culled everyone wearing brown socks. To Page's great surprise, the brown socks outperformed the Mensa agents. As a random collection of mathematicians could hardly be expected to outperform Mensa's best minds, Page decided to fiddle with his simulation, changing the rules by which the agents interacted. He got the same result. Still incredulous, he rewrote the program in a different computer language. The brown socks still won, over and over and over again. Page wanted to know why.

What began as a study break blossomed into a decade-plus research project, culminating, in 2007, with a book entitled *The Difference: How the Power of Diversity Creates Better Groups, Firms, Schools, and Societies*. Page's book applies logical rigor and mathematical precision to the burgeoning field of collective intelligence. In doing so, Page has created a theoretical framework to explain why groups often outperform experts. Why did the brown socks beat the Mensa agents so consistently? The brown socks weren't as talented as the Mensa members, but they had something better: diversity.

The results of several such experiments formed the basis for the Diversity Trumps Ability Theorem. Given certain conditions, Page writes, "a randomly selected collection of problem solvers outperforms a collection of the best individual problem solvers." At the heart of Page's theorem is the observation that people of high ability are a homogeneous group. Many of them have been trained in the same institutions, and they tend to possess similar perspectives and apply similar problem-solving techniques, or heuristics. They are indeed better than the crowd at large, but at fewer things. And many problems don't succumb to a single heuristic, or even to a set of similar ones. They require the brown socks, so to speak, to come along and try an approach that the "best minds" would never think to apply. "This theorem," Page writes, "is no mere metaphor or cute empirical anecdote that may or may not be true ten years from now. It's a logical truth."

Understanding diversity is imperative to understanding collective intelligence, and collective intelligence is an essential ingredient in one of the primary categories of crowdsourcing: the attempt to harness many people's knowledge in order to solve problems or predict future outcomes or help direct corporate strategy. Collective intelligence is the form of group cognition that we see at work in ant colonies that act like cells of a single organism. We also see it in the very human ritual of voting, in which millions of individual choices result in a single decision. Scholars from disciplines ranging from sociology to behavioral psychology to computer science have studied the phenomenon since the early years of the twentieth century, but the emergence of the Internet has given new import to collective intelligence, for the simple reason that the Internet has done more than anything else in history to facilitate it.

The types of crowdsourcing that traffic in collective intelligence take three primary forms. The first category is the prediction market, or information market, in which investors purchase "futures" pegged to some expected outcome, such as the winner of a presidential contest or of the Oscar for Best Picture. These function much like a stock market: Individuals open an account, then buy and sell shares at the going market value. If an investor buys low (a dark-horse nominee for Best Picture, perhaps), he cleans up when his prediction turns out to be correct. For instance, the best insight into the prevailing political winds in the U.S. election of 2008 isn't a poll or a pundit, but a chart on *Slate* that displays the relative price of the candidates on the futures market, Intrade. (Intrade showed Barack Obama leading Hillary Clinton just after the Super Tuesday primaries in February 2008, weeks before national polls reflected his improved fortunes.)

The second form is the problem-solving, or crowdcasting, network, in which someone with a problem broadcasts it to a large, undefined network of potential solvers. InnoCentive is an example of this, with its distributed collection of 140,000 scientists that tackle thorny R&D problems for Fortune 500 companies. The third category is the "idea jam," which is essentially just a massive, online brainstorming session that takes place over the course of weeks instead of hours. The idea jam bears a close resemblance to crowdcasting, except the call for submissions is much more open-ended. Instead of attempting to solve a particular problem, idea jams are used to generate new ideas of any stripe. People have pointed out that this is little more than an Internet-enabled suggestion box. Just so. The Internet didn't make crowdsourcing possible—it just made it vastly more effective.

As is often said of Wikipedia, collective intelligence works better in practice than it does in theory. The results it produces seem counterintuitive, running against the grain of what we thought we knew about the way the world works—basically, that Mensa should always trump brown socks. In this as in other ways, the Internet provides an opportunity to rethink our understanding of human behavior. So before we dive into crowdsourcing's practical applications of collective intelligence, we'll try to establish some theories for why it works.

Crowdsourcing is rooted in a fundamentally egalitarian principle: every individual possesses some knowledge or talent that some other individual will find valuable. In the broadest terms, crowdsourcing involves making a connection between the two. That is to say, in another counterintuitive twist, the individual—with all his or her peculiarities—is at the center of crowdsourcing. In our particulars, we are all the raw stuff of circumstance:

birthplace, family, geography, experience, and the innumerable other variables that combine in the strange alchemy that produces the unique person. When uniqueness persists in large groups we call it diversity, a term that's been saddled with some unfortunate baggage in two decades of identity politics. But as far as crowdsourcing is concerned, it's important to divorce the *concept* of diversity from the *politics* of diversity. Scholars and entrepreneurs are discovering that the sum of our differences constitutes an immensely powerful force that can be applied to solving problems or developing new products or simply making the world, online and off, a more interesting place to live. The seventeenth-century philosopher Michel de Montaigne once wrote, "There were never in the world two opinions alike, any more than two hairs or two grains. Their most universal quality is diversity." To paraphrase Montaigne, the only thing we all have in common is that we are all quite different. In the networked age, that can be a very good thing.

The Difference a Tweak Makes

Ned Gulley operates something of a petri dish for group intelligence. Gulley is a software designer at the Mathworks, the company best known for developing MATLAB, a language used by mathematicians and engineers for crunching the kinds of extravagantly complex calculations that leave most people slack-jawed. In 1999, the company decided to hold a programming contest. Previous contests had been conducted over e-mail, but judging the resulting entries was cumbersome and tedious. So Gulley suggested hosting the new competition on the website and grading it in real time.

The company's goal was to: "Provide an entertaining

diversion to the community of MATLAB users while encouraging the exchange of good programming practices." Programming contests have been a part of geek culture since the earliest days of computing, for just this reason: they make the development of skills feel like a game. Collegiate computer science departments began holding various tourneys as early as 1970, and informal matches were being held long before that. Mathworks was taking part in a venerable tradition.

At first blush, Gulley's format appeared utterly conventional. Contestants were required to solve what is commonly called a "traveling salesman problem," the classic example of which asks for the shortest possible round-trip a salesman can take through a given list of cities. Participants submitted a solution in the form of an algorithm, or computer code, that directed the salesman through a number of steps. The contest ended after ten days, at which point the most efficient algorithm would be declared the winner.

But Gulley added an extra twist: participants were allowed to steal each other's code in order to create a better solution. Every time a new solution was sent in, it was quickly scored, ranked, and posted to the website. Every other contestant could then see the programming code, in full. They could cut and paste the best bits and resubmit it with any improvements, however minor. If the tweaks, as Gulley calls them, created a more efficient algorithm, it vaulted the contestant into first place, even if he or she had only changed a few lines of code.

The result, Gulley says, closely resembles the actual process of software development. "In an office full of developers, if one person solves a problem, everyone else will gather around to see how they did it, have their 'aha' moment, then factor it into their own code," he says. "There's a pervasive myth of Thomas Edison in our culture. The smart guy who'll get us out of this fix, who'll walk into a room and come out with a brilliant solution." In reality, most breakthroughs are the product of teamwork. "I wanted to create a contest that more accurately modeled the way ideas really move through the world." To be clear, the MATLAB contest isn't so much a crowdsourcing example as it is a demonstration of the principles that make crowdsourcing so effective. In this it is closer to Page's experiments with artificial agents than it is to the TopCoder approach to software development, which of course uses the crowd to create real-world products.

Far from alienating MATLAB users, encouraging outright theft has inspired ever-greater levels of obsessive effort on their part. Nathan, a contestant from Ireland, wrote Gulley to note that he was afflicted by "physical trembling while making the final preparations to submit code." The most devoted players schedule vacations around it, or even cut classes and use sick days in the race to be at the top of the leaderboard. Gulley calls the MATLAB contest "addictive collaboration," a remarkable echo of Jack Hughes's description of TopCoder as "competitive collaboration."

"One programmer will spend all night devising a brilliant algorithm that takes the lead. "Then someone comes along, adds a little tweak, and then *they* go into first place. The first programmer is like, 'That asshole! He just cut me off by copying my code!' And so the first programmer adds another tweak in order to regain the lead." The ultimate goal, Gulley says, isn't to win. It's to come up with a brilliant tweak that will impress the other competitors. "It's like a shadow scoring system based on reputation."

But the extraordinary aspect of MATLAB isn't the fervor it inspires, but the fact that the ten-day hurly-burly— in which all intellectual property is thrown into the public square to be used and reused at will—turns out to be an insanely efficient method of problem solving. The contest has been held twice a year since its inception in 1999. On average, Gulley notes, the best algorithm at the end of the contest period exceeds the best algorithm from day one *by a magnitude of one thousand.*

This is the point at which practice would seem to leave theory in the dust, gasping for breath. How can we explain so mind-boggling an improvement? Obviously the presence of the crowd helped. Many smart programmers were able to create a better solution than any single one of them would have put forth. It's also clear that the free exchange of ideas abetted the process, as it fostered a collaborative environment in which good ideas could be tweaked into better ones. But none of this explains the exponential arc traced by each successively more efficient algorithm. What's striking is that the best programmers aren't necessarily the ones making the most valuable contributions. The novices often provided a crucial tweak that led to a breakthrough. Or as Gulley puts it: "Sometimes a script kiddie"—geek slang for an inexperienced, usually pubescent hacker—"will come along and make this tiny change, and even Edison has to rub his eyes and say, 'Whoa!' "

In other words, the brown socks beat Mensa again. This might seem counterintuitive, but in fact the power of distributed networks to solve problems was anticipated some fifty years before Page ever started pitting his computer agents against one another.

Diversity and the Market

The economist F. A. Hayek is best remembered, and not always fondly, as having composed the theories that drove the free-market policies of Margaret Thatcher and Ronald Reagan. Born in Vienna at the turn of the century, Hayek was already a highly reputed economist by the time Hitler and Stalin had come into power. At the London School of Economics and Political Science, Hayek advocated a harshly critical view of the planned economies utilized by both Nazi and Soviet states at the time. Hayek believed the marketplace was a highly efficient mechanism, the ability of which to coordinate economic activity suffered only to the extent any individual or expert attempted to meddle with it. Hayek did as much to champion Adam Smith's famous "invisible hand" as any other contemporary economist, and in 1974 he won the Nobel Prize in Economics in part for his work on this subject. With friends like Thatcher and Reagan, Hayek never wanted for enemies, but controversy has tended to overshadow the broad range of his contributions.

In a seminal 1945 paper, "The Use of Knowledge in Society," Hayek observed that society had failed to properly appreciate a category of knowledge that rested in neither the academy nor corporate boardrooms: "the knowledge of particular circumstances of time and place." Due to such "local knowledge," or what's now commonly called "private information," nearly every individual "has some advantage over all others because he possesses unique information of which beneficial use might be made." The remaining project, then, lies in obtaining all that dispersed information. Hayek writes,

> Each member of society can have only a small fraction of the knowledge possessed by all, and each is therefore ignorant of most of the facts on which the working of society rests . . . civilization rests on the fact that we all benefit from knowledge which we do *not* possess. And one of the ways in which civilization helps us to overcome that limitation on the extent of individual knowledge

is by conquering ignorance, not by the acquisition of more knowledge, but by the utilization of knowledge which is and which remains widely dispersed among individuals.

This was written before the emergence of the Internet, which has proven better at aggregating and utilizing widely dispersed information than Hayek ever could have imagined. The MATLAB contest could almost be an exercise attempting to prove Hayek's central observation: that we may well already possess the solutions to our greatest dilemmas, and that the project before us is simply to gather all that knowledge into a central storehouse. It's no coincidence that Gulley adopts the language of Hayekian economics when he speaks of the open architecture of the MATLAB contest as a way of "tickling people's private information out of each other."

Gulley has painstakingly gathered a wealth of observational data, from which he's been able to draw some conclusions about exactly why this addictive collaboration works as effectively as it does. By rendering the data visually in the form of a line graph, Gulley was able to determine that advances are made in great leaps, which are followed by longer periods of minor tweaking. "People will sniff out the slack in an algorithm, like hyenas worrying over a carcass. Then they get exhausted until someone comes along and whips the carcass into a new position, then it starts all over again."

The charts Gulley has created could just as easily be depicting the course of evolution in animal species. Genetic mutation doesn't follow a linear curve, either, but is instead characterized by, well, leaps and tweaks, an observation central to the theory of "punctuated equilibrium" developed by the evolutionary biologists Stephen Jay Gould and Niles Eldredge. Gulley is hardly unaware of the parallels and believes, on the basis of some compelling evidence, that his data on the MATLAB contest might reveal some deeper truth about how progress is rendered—in social as well as biological terms. "We're taught a version of history in which great men, Napoleon for instance, are the sole actors. But the reality is much messier and involves a complex interplay between those that make the leaps and those that make the tweaks." History requires the service of the script kiddies—the brown socks—to come along and employ their unique perspective to reorient everyone to a new viewpoint.

"We have truly brilliant people playing. One of them will make a breakthrough, and on its own it would have been the best solution in an old-school contest. Just because they're brilliant. But with the MATLAB contest, immediately people are able to come along and tweak it. No single person could do that. It's the swarm, this great big collective brain we have access to. What will really be amazing is if we can tap that brain to cure cancer."

When a Crowd Isn't a Crowd

Diversity is essential to animating the collective intelligence that emerges in models like the MATLAB contest, but the existence of diversity isn't enough. It must also be maintained. Get enough people together—be it in a bar or a chat room—and a mysterious dynamic kicks in. People either accentuate their differences and polarize into opposing camps, or they downplay their differences altogether in order to reach a consensus. Both phenomena have the same net effect: the diversity within the crowd is diminished. Humans have evolved over many millennia into highly social creatures. In many circumstances, our ability to reach an amicable agreement meant the difference between life and death: "A mammoth is charging. Shall we run or poke him with our spears?" But when collective intelligence is in play, as it is in such crowdsourcing models as information markets and problem-solving networks, consensus is counterproductive.

In 2004, James Surowiecki published *The Wisdom of Crowds.* The title of Surowiecki's book is a winking reference to Charles Mackay's 1841 classic, *Extraordinary Popular Delusions and the Madness of Crowds,* a stern indictment of the herd mentality that led to such disasters as the Dutch tulip mania of the 1630s. (Needless to say, the term "crowdsourcing" owes a debt to both authors.) While theories of group intelligence predated Surowiecki's book by decades, and in fact had recently come back into vogue in fields as disparate as sociology and business management, *The Wisdom of Crowds* captured the popular imagination in a way no other work on the subject ever had. The book contained an array of persuasive examples in which the crowd proved itself wiser than its smartest member. How did a crowd of fairgoers in rural England guess the weight of a prize-winning steer within one pound? How did a classroom of students guess the number of jelly beans in the jelly-bean jar? How did the audience for the game show *Who Wants to Be a Millionaire* consistently beat the experts? Through the wisdom of crowds. Such anecdotes have acquired an almost magical patina, entering the collective imagination and becoming fodder for cocktail conversation and water-cooler discussion. Unfortunately, they were shorn of Surowiecki's careful analysis.

In fact there's no magic to the wisdom of crowds, and the expression itself is a bit misleading. In these examples the crowd was neither wise nor even functioning as a crowd, per se. A crowd implies a group of people acting as a unit, as in "the crowd broke through the barrier and descended upon the author in a fit of hysteria." Okay, authors don't generally inspire that degree of unchecked adoration, but you get the idea. The definition of "crowd" is "a group of people united by a common characteristic." By contrast, collective intelligence is diminished by too many common characteristics. It flourishes in direct proportion to the amount of diversity contained within a group of people, and their ability to express their individual viewpoints. In order to be wise, then, the crowd can't act like a crowd at all.

There are other conditions that must be met for diversity to trump ability. First, it must be a real pickle of a problem. No one needs a diverse group of individuals to help them tie their shoes. Next, the crowd must have some qualifications to solve the problem at hand. A random collection of subway commuters could hardly be expected to outperform a group of nuclear engineers at designing a more efficient reactor; even Page's brown socks were pulled from a faculty lounge, not from the phone book. There must also be some method of aggregating and processing each individual's contribution, such as the MATLAB contest's scoring and ranking engine. But finally, participants must be drawn from a large enough pool to guarantee a diverse array of approaches, and their ability to express their individuality—their "local knowledge"—must not be impaired.

Keeping all this in mind, let's revisit some of those examples that seemed so counterintuitive at first glance. Take the case of the jelly-bean jar. Any more or less random collection of students will differ enough that they will employ a range of strategies to solving the problem.

The aggregation mechanism, in this case, is simply the teacher's ability to collect all the estimates and calculate an average. But crucially, the students are asked to write down their guesses without conferring with their neighbors, so they are able to think and act independently. (Gulley's MATLAB contestants don't confer so much as they steal from one another. Their relative isolation allows them to retain their diversity.)

Now let's look again at a game show audience's ability to accurately predict more than 90 percent of the answers. On the game show in question, *Who Wants to Be a Millionaire,* contestants are asked a series of fifteen questions of increasing difficulty. If they answer all fifteen correctly, they win $1 million. The questions are multiple-choice format, with four possible answers. When they get stuck, contestants ask for a "lifeline." This means either calling a friend—presumably chosen for their encyclopedic knowledge—for help, or polling the audience. The "experts" perform admirably, getting the correct answer 65 percent of the time. But the audience does far better, guessing the correct answer 91 percent of the time.

This seems deeply impressive. It's far better than all but the very best contestants do, and it would seem to provide ample evidence that the group is smarter than its smartest individual. But it's actually just a function of simplest arithmetic, an illustration that if even a tiny number of individuals possess the correct answer, the group itself will predict accurately. This, Page writes, is because "the mistakes cancel one another out, and correct answers, like cream, rise to the surface." This can be easily illustrated. Say the question posed to the audience, to use a real example from the show, is whether Sherpas and Gurkhas are native to (A) Nepal, (B) Morocco, (C) Ecuador, or (D) Russia. If only 4 percent of the audience

knows that the correct answer is (A) Nepal, the rest of
the audience can be expected to guess randomly among
all four answers. The result is that 24 percent of the audience will guess Morocco, 24 percent will guess Ecuador,
and 24 percent will guess Russia. But 28 percent will
guess Nepal.

Of course, there's a big difference between guessing
trivia questions and improving an algorithm by a thousand
degrees of magnitude. The latter isn't merely impressive;
it defies belief. But the same circumstances—diversity
and the proper conditions in which to express it—are at
work in both examples.

On its face, MATLAB would seem to attract mostly
Mensa-quality programmers. In other words, it's a group
that has self-selected according to its proficiency at solving such problems. A studio audience, on the other hand,
is a randomly selected group. It is certainly true that
many of the most talented MATLAB programmers participate in the contest. But the best coders have generally all
learned the same tricks and shortcuts from years of using
the MATLAB computer language. It's the inexperienced
coders—the outsiders who have to come up with their
own shortcuts—that make possible the giant cognitive
leaps that allow the winning solution to improve on the
initial solution by so many degrees of magnitude. If great
minds think alike—and in many circumstances they do—
then they really constitute only one mind. Or, as Page
puts it, "two heads aren't better than one when it's really
only one head." A diverse group of solvers results in
many different approaches to a problem. How they apply
this to real-world problems—far more involved than
guiding a salesman through a set of cities—is the subject
of our next chapter.

6

WHAT THE CROWD KNOWS

Collective Intelligence in Action

In the late fall of 2004, Karim Lakhani, a Ph.D. candidate at MIT's Sloan School of Management, was suffering from an affliction common among graduate students: research fatigue. "I hit that point where I just couldn't stand to spend any more time on my own dissertation," recalls Lakhani. He'd been analyzing how innovations emerge in open source software, but after four years of work, he was burnt out. It was time for an extended vacation. "I stopped everything and read Neal Stephenson's Baroque Cycle." Stephenson's trilogy is a work of historical fiction about the Age of Enlightenment in Europe, and it made a big impact on Lakhani. "It's all about the establishment of the Royal Society and the dawn of rational thinking about the world and the invention of calculus." By Lakhani's lights, the Baroque Cycle was a narrative history of innovation.

One passage in particular caught Lakhani's attention. One of Stephenson's books contained the true story of the longitude prize. In 1714, the British established a commission offering 20,000 pounds (roughly $12 million today) to anyone who could invent a way to determine longitude on a sailing vessel. The Royal Navy's inability to do so had resulted in the loss of untold numbers of ships and their cargoes, causing a serious drain on government finances. "The top scientific minds of that time, including Isaac Newton, had tried to develop a device, and none succeeded," notes Lakhani. The solution—a clock that operated with superb accuracy, even during the rigors of an overseas voyage—was developed by John Harrison, an uneducated cabinetmaker from Yorkshire. "I read that and thought, 'Huh. Kind of like open source. Someone poses a problem and all sorts of random, strange people show up and say I've got an answer for you, and it's never the one you'd anticipate." The longitude prize constitutes the earliest known example of crowdcasting: broadcasting a problem to the widest possible audience in the blind hope that someone, somewhere—maybe even a Yorkshire cabinetmaker—will come up with a solution.

Lakhani returned to his dissertation, but now he was determined to look at innovation with a much broader view. He'd heard of the problem-solving scientists at InnoCentive, and he wondered whether the company wasn't a modern-day version of the longitude prize. "I told them I wanted to figure out how their problems were solved. They were thrilled." Lakhani teamed up with a Ph.D. candidate at the Copenhagen Business School and two InnoCentive scientists. Over the course of the next year, they looked at 166 scientific problems that had stymied the R&D labs at 26 separate firms. In the summer of 2007, they published their findings as a Harvard Business School working paper. The results ran counter to decades of conventional wisdom in the sciences, but they probably wouldn't have surprised John Harrison. What

Lakhani and his colleagues uncovered was a real-world demonstration of Page's Diversity Trumps Ability Theorem: the people you'd least expect to solve a problem were exactly the ones most likely to crack it.

A Whole New Paradigm

The future of corporate R&D can be found above Kelly's Auto Body on Shanty Bay Road in Barrie, Ontario. This is where Ed Melcarek, one of InnoCentive's most successful solvers, keeps his "weekend crash pad," a one-bedroom apartment littered with amplifiers, a guitar, electrical transducers, two desktop computers, a trumpet, half of a pontoon boat, and enough electric gizmos to stock a RadioShack. On most Saturdays, Melcarek comes in, pours himself a Saint-Rémy, lights a Player cigarette, and attacks problems that have stumped some of the best corporate scientists at Fortune 500 companies.

The crowd possesses a wide array of talents, and some have the kind of scientific talent and expertise that used to exist only in rarefied academic environments. Forward-thinking companies are tapping this emerging well of intellectual capital and changing the face of R&D in the process. Exit the white lab coats; enter Melcarek, who, like the chemist Giorgia Sgargetta, is one of the 140,000 "solvers" who make up the network of scientists on InnoCentive. Pharmaceutical maker Eli Lilly funded InnoCentive's launch in 2001 as a way to connect with brainpower outside the company. From the outset, Inno-Centive threw open the doors to other firms eager to access the network's trove of ad hoc experts. Companies such as Boeing, DuPont, and, of course, Procter & Gamble now post their most ornery scientific problems on In-noCentive's website; anyone on InnoCentive's network can take a shot at cracking them. The companies generally pay solvers anywhere from $10,000 to $100,000 per solution. (They also pay InnoCentive a fee to participate.) Jill Panetta, InnoCentive's chief scientific officer, says more than 30 percent of the problems posted on the site have been solved, "which is 30 percent more than would have been solved using a traditional, in-house approach."

"Everyone I talk to is facing a similar issue in regard to R&D," says Larry Huston, Procter & Gamble's former vice president of innovation and knowledge. "Every year research budgets increase at a faster rate than sales. The current R&D model is broken." P&G is one of Inno-Centive's earliest and best customers, but the company works with other crowdsourcing networks as well. Your-Encore, for example, allows companies to find and hire retired scientists for one-off assignments. NineSigma is an online marketplace for innovations, matching seeker companies with solvers in a marketplace similar to Inno-Centive. "People mistake this for outsourcing, which it most definitely is not," Huston says. "Outsourcing is when I hire someone to perform a service and they do it and that's the end of the relationship. That's not much different from the way employment has worked throughout the ages. We're talking about bringing people in from outside and involving them in this broadly creative, collaborative process."

While most of InnoCentive's solvers are full-fledged scientists, many are hobbyists working from their proverbial garage, such as the University of Dallas undergrad who came up with a chemical to use in art restoration, or the North Carolina patent lawyer who devised a novel way to mix large batches of chemical compounds. Or in

Melcarek's case, a mildly eccentric electrical engineer whose lab doubles as a music studio. Yet Melcarek solved a problem that had stumped the in-house researchers at Colgate-Palmolive. The giant packaged-goods company needed a way to inject fluoride powder into a toothpaste tube without it dispersing into the surrounding air. Melcarek knew he had a solution by the time he'd finished reading the challenge: Impart an electric charge to the powder while grounding the tube. The positively charged fluoride particles would be attracted to the tube without any significant dispersion.

"It was really a very simple solution," says Melcarek. Why hadn't Colgate thought of it? "They're probably test-tube guys without any training in physics." Melcarek earned $25,000 for his efforts. Paying Colgate-Palmolive's R&D staff to produce the same solution could have cost several times that amount—if they even had solved it at all. Melcarek says he was elated to win. "These are rocket-science challenges," he says. "It really reinforced my confidence in what I can do."

Melcarek has charted an unconventional course through the sciences. He spent four years earning his master's degree at the world-class particle accelerator in Vancouver, British Columbia, but decided against pursuing a Ph.D. "I had an offer from the private sector," he says, then pauses. "I really needed the money." A succession of "unsatisfying" engineering jobs followed, none of which fully exploited Melcarek's scientific training or his need to tinker. "I'm not at my best in a nine-to-five environment," he says. Working sporadically, he has designed products such as heating vents and industrial spray-painting robots. Not every quick and curious intellect can land a plum research post at a university or privately funded lab. Some must make HVAC systems.

InnoCentive has been a ticket out of this scientific

backwater for Melcarek. For the past five years, he has logged onto the network's website a few times a week to look at new challenges. Until recently these had all been categorized as either chemistry or biology problems. Melcarek has formal training in neither discipline, but he quickly realized this didn't hinder him. "I saw that a lot of the chemistry challenges could be solved using electromechanical processes I was familiar with from particle physics," he says. Besides the fluoride-injection challenge, Melcarek also devised a successful method for purifying silicone-based solvents. That challenge paid $10,000. Melcarek has since gone on to win five additional InnoCentive challenges. "Not bad for a few weeks' work," he says with a chuckle.

Melcarek has discovered something of a winning formula: find chemistry or biology problems that he can crack using his background in physics and electrical engineering. In 2007, InnoCentive launched a category for engineering challenges, but Melcarek doesn't bother with it. All seven of the problems Melcarek has solved were in other fields.

This says a little something about Melcarek (he's a man who likes to work off hunches), but it says a lot more about InnoCentive. When Lakhani dug into InnoCentive's data, he discovered that Melcarek wasn't the exception, he was the rule: the scientists most likely to solve a problem were the ones you'd least expect to be capable of solving it.

"We actually found the odds of a solver's success increased in fields in which they had no formal expertise," Lakhani says. The farther the problem was from their specialized knowledge, the more likely it was to be solved. "Think of the problem as a flower. Except the goal is to attract not only the most insects, but the most diverse group of insects."

And Lakhani's paper contained an even more interesting gem: a full 75 percent of successful solvers *already knew the solution to the problem.* The solutions to the problems in the study—many of which, recall, had stumped the best corporate scientists in the world after years of effort—didn't require a breakthrough, or additional brainpower, or a more talented scientist's attention; they just needed a diverse enough set of minds to have a go at them. It all goes to support Hayek's proposition: progress lies not in acquiring new knowledge, but in aggregating and utilizing the knowledge we already have. When I asked Melcarek how long he spent solving InnoCentive problems, his answer was telling. "If I don't know what to do after thirty minutes of brainstorming, I give up."

Lakhani's findings may be news to people in business and science, fields in which the vogue for specialization has reigned for many decades. But they dovetail neatly with decades of research in economic sociology, echoing a principle sociologists call the strength of weak ties.

In 1970, Mark Granovetter, a Ph.D. candidate in sociology at Harvard, crossed the Charles River and asked some 282 professional, technical, and managerial workers in Newton, Massachusetts, how they'd found their jobs. Not surprisingly, many of Granovetter's respondents told him they'd used personal contacts, confirmation of the old saw: "It's not what you know, it's who you know." Granovetter, however, dug a little deeper. What kind of personal contact? Spouse? Brother? Best friend? The majority, it turned out, answered no, no, and no. Only 16.7 percent had found their job through a close acquaintance, while the rest of those who'd found their jobs through personal contacts had secured their position through someone they barely knew. The people who were most helpful were the friends of friends. The people we know well know all the same things—the same eligible singles, the same job openings, and the same available apartments—that we know. What Granovetter discovered is that it's not, in fact, who we know that gets us ahead in life, it's who we don't know well.

The strength of weak ties runs counter to a deeply entrenched bias found in corporate environments. "There's a strong tendency in human networks to homophily, which means that birds of a feather stick together," says Lakhani. "And so even when a company chooses to look to external sources for a solution to a problem, they'll rely on people and companies and labs they already know well, so they run into the same local search biases that are present in internal problem solving." In this light, it no longer seems so mysterious that the leading chemists at a company like P&G might fail to solve a problem that Ed Melcarek can knock off over a couple glasses of brandy.

The key to making it work is to broadcast the problem using a massive network like InnoCentive's. Or, to return to Lakhani's metaphor, to make your flower attractive to as many insects as possible. That's easier said than done. "Firms aren't set up to broadcast their inner problems to outsiders. Traditional corporate culture is geared to limit outsider access to insider information, not increase it." And what could be more insidery than some problem they're really stumped on? Of course, this only makes for greater opportunities for companies willing to swim against the tide.

If an uneducated cabinetmaker can solve one of the most perplexing challenges of his day, if an electrical engineer can solve some of the thorniest *chemistry* problems encountered by Fortune 500 companies, then maybe MATLAB's Ned Gulley isn't off base in suggesting that the collective brain might one day cure cancer. It's not as remote a prospect as it sounds. Taking a page from the distributed computing project SETI@home, Stanford University's chemistry department created Folding@home, which uses the excess capacity of hundreds of thousands of individual PCs to simulate protein folding—the process in which proteins combine to form biological molecules—a crucial step in understanding diseases such as cystic fibrosis, Alzheimer's disease, and cancer.

It's a short leap to go from tapping the excess capacity of thousands of computers to tapping the excess capacity of thousands of brains. It's already occurring. InnoCentive recently teamed up with the nonprofit organization Prize4Life. They are offering $1 million in prizes to InnoCentive solvers who can help advance the search for a cure for Lou Gehrig's disease. This model could easily be applied to finding the cures for other disorders. And what happens when the Billion—the approximate size of the crowd, which is to say, the number of people connected to the Internet—becomes the Three Billion? What feats of collective cognition might all these brains, working together, produce?

The potential of crowdsourcing difficult problems has even been broached in that most unlikely crucible of innovation, the federal government. In October 2007, Senator Bernie Sanders, an independent from Vermont, introduced a bill that would replace the drug monopolies given to pharmaceutical companies by the patent department with a system of cash prizes. The bill calls for the government to create an $80-billion fund, which would then be awarded for narrowly targeted medical objectives, such as developing part of a cure for malaria. At present, pharmaceutical companies have little incentive to conduct research into such lifesaving treatments. Drug firms make an easy target for their seeming callous disregard for killers like malaria, but the fact is that research and development of such drugs is incredibly expensive, and the readiest customers are also the poorest, meaning the pharmaceutical companies would have a very difficult time earning their money back on a malaria drug. Sanders's bill would address this issue by essentially guaranteeing compensation to any individual or company who successfully develops such a drug.

On the other side of the political spectrum, Newt Gingrich has proposed a similar system for alleviating government spending. As William Saleton wrote on *Slate* in October 2007, Gingrich suggests that "instead of giving $1 billion to a federal agency to deal with a problem . . . offer the money as a prize to the first company that solves it. As the conversation proceeds, Gingrich throws money at one challenge after another. Hydrogen fuel? Dangle a 10-figure prize."

But my favorite problem-solving network application has to be the Netflix Prize. In late 2006, the movie-rental company promised to give $1 million to anyone who could improve its film recommendation system by 10 percent. The contest has proven to be wildly popular with professional statisticians and all manner of amateur number-geeks. It's also great spectator sport, and a resounding affirmation of the principles displayed by Nat Gulley's MATLAB contest, but transported to a commercial setting.

Since starting up in 1997, Netflix has grown into the bane of mailmen everywhere. It currently sends 35,000 titles a day to some 7.5 million subscribers. In 2000, Netflix added a feature to its website called Cinematch, in which the site recommends movies to users based on their previous selections. Recommendation engines are a famously flawed, if ubiquitous, feature of the modern Web, and Cinematch was no exception. The system essentially attempts to predict how a user will rate a movie on a spectrum of one to five stars. Right now Cinematch has an average error rate of 0.9525, which means that it's off, on average, by one star. Given the difference in how a customer treats a three-star movie (pass) and a four-star movie (rent!), that's far from ideal. Netflix expended considerable resources in improving their system, but the company eventually decided to pay heed to Bill Joy's observation that no matter how many smart people work for you, the smartest people work somewhere else. "Those people we didn't hire we've also got working for us. It's up to them to innovate now. We're just the enablers," notes Netflix vice president for recommendation systems Jim Bennett.

After signing up, contestants receive access to an enormous database of 100 million real user ratings. By studying the connections between those ratings, participants attempt to devise an algorithm that will better predict what films individual Netflix customers will like. They submit their algorithm to Netflix, which compares it to how those users really did rate those movies. The algorithm is scored, and is placed on a leaderboard. Within two weeks of launching the experiment, Netflix had received some 169 submissions, several of which marked an improvement over Netflix's existing system. After one month, more than a thousand submissions had rolled in. The best coders quickly managed to improve on Cinematch by about 5 percent. But then progress slowed, and a year later the top contestant—a team of coders from the Information Visualization Research Group at AT&T that goes by the name "BellKor"—had still only improved on Cinematch by 8.43 percent.

The Netflix Prize resembles the MATLAB contest in its basic format. Contestants try to write an algorithm to solve a difficult problem, then they submit it and have it scored in real time. Unlike MATLAB, Netflix declined to reveal the programming code behind each submission. This is an understandable decision, given the $1 million stakes. One would expect the contestants to storm the Netflix gates in protest had the company made such a move. But as Jordan Ellenberg pointed out in a 2008 article in *Wired* about the Netflix Prize, the contestants decided to share their algorithms anyway. "The prize hunters, even the leaders, are startlingly open about the methods they're using, acting more like academics huddled over a knotty problem than entrepreneurs jostling for a $1 million payday." One contestant, "simonfunk," opted to post a complete description of his algorithm, despite the fact he was in third place, far ahead of most of his competitors. Didn't these acts of seemingly unwarranted openness compromise their ability to win the jackpot? When Ellenberg asked BellKor's leader about this, he seemed puzzled and replied, "We got a big prize by learning and interacting with other teams. This is the real prize for us."

The Netflix Prize has profited from the contributions of the most unusual of suspects, much like the script kiddies in the MATLAB contest. Gavin Potter, a forty-eight-year-old retired management consultant, decided to compete in the Netflix Prize for little more than a lark. Calling himself "just a guy in a garage," in November 2007 Potter rocketed to the top ten on the leaderboard, despite the fact that he has no math background and has little experience in the kind of sophisticated statistical algorithms used by his fellow contestants.

Instead, Potter applied what he knew about human psychology, asking fundamental questions about how users actually rate movies in the real world, such as whether recently released movies receive higher ratings. Utilizing insights gleaned from the field of behavioral economics—a new discipline that brings psychology to bear on determining why people make certain economic decisions—Potter has constructed algorithms that take account of people who, for instance, tend to rate every movie with three stars or above. This may sound elementary, but it wouldn't be obvious to a statistician working on an algorithm that treats every customer as an equally rational actor. As this book goes to press, Potter is in fifth place and less than one-half of a percentage point behind the leader.

Like the Netflix Prize, Dell's IdeaStorm attempts to capture the collective intelligence of the crowd. Unlike Netflix, however, Dell isn't trying to solve an existing problem—it's using the crowd to brainstorm new innovations. The computer maker launched the campaign in February 2007, and as this book goes to press over nine thousand ideas have been posted to the IdeaStorm website. These range from asking Dell to base its tech support call centers in the United States to a request for more USB slots on the back of its desktop computers.

Dell uses a standard social media formula to power the site. In other words, users are able to not only add new ideas but also comment on other people's ideas. In addition, they can "promote" or "demote" ideas with a thumbs-up or thumbs-down vote. Just as stories with the most "diggs" rise to the top of the social news site Digg.com, the most heavily promoted ideas get featured on the IdeaStorm home page. This last function employs another crucial element of crowdsourcing—the crowd's collective opinion—and it can be terribly effective. The day IdeaStorm launched, a user named "dhart" suggested that Dell begin offering computers with the Linux operating system preinstalled. Some 30,000 IdeaStorm users concurred, and dhart's post remained the number one idea on the site for months. As a direct result, in May 2007, Dell released three models using the Linux OS.

Dell's effort at customer collaboration is an example of a category of crowdsourcing called "idea jams." They are a close cousin to crowdcasting networks like Inno-Centive and the Netflix Prize, although idea jams aren't intended to solve a specific problem so much as create solutions to problems that don't yet exist. The term is derived from an "Innovation Jam" that IBM held in 2006. In what the company billed as the "largest brainstorming session ever," more than 150,000 people from 104 countries posted more than 46,000 ideas. Later that year the company announced it would spend $100 million to create ten new businesses based on ideas suggested during the Innovation Jam. People have pointed out that this is little more than an Internet-enabled suggestion box. Just so. The Internet didn't make crowdsourcing possible—it just made it vastly more effective.

InnoCentive, the Netflix Prize, and Dell's IdeaStorm capitalize on the power of diversity. Imagine, Page proposes, that the best solutions to any given problem were represented as a series of mountain peaks. "People with similar training are going to wind up scaling the same peak, because they conceive of the problem in a similar way. But in looking for a solution, a person with a different background"—in psychology, say—"will apply an entirely different heuristic. He will try to scale a different peak, which could well wind up being the tallest peak." This has obvious benefits to just about any company or individual facing a thorny problem. Crowdcasting's advantage is that it doesn't presume that only certain climbers are qualified to scale a given peak. In fact it doesn't presume anything at all. Instead it opens the challenge to anyone interested in taking it on. The results never fail to surprise us.

Given the proper conditions, diversity will trump ability in the case of a crowdcasting network like InnoCentive. There's a very simple reason for this: the ultimate success of one solution is not diminished by the number of unsuccessful solutions. "With the Netflix Prize, it doesn't matter how many idiots try to solve the problem. The more the merrier," says Page. As more people apply more diverse sets of problem-solving methods—no matter how harebrained—the odds that someone will crack the nut can't help but go up. And if they're wrong, you can just ignore them. But this truth only applies to crowdcasting projects like the Netflix Prize and InnoCentive. When we're using the crowd to predict the future, every response counts in the final tally. In these cases, the role of diversity is far more complex.

Investing in the Future—Prediction Markets

In 1988, the civil rights activist Jesse Jackson shocked the nation by winning the Democratic primary race in Michigan, an outcome that neither polls nor political insiders had anticipated. At the University of Iowa, a handful of political scientists and economists were intrigued by the failure of the polls to predict Jackson's victory and wondered if markets couldn't do a better job of predicting the outcome of elections. Over the course of the next several months, and well in time for the general election between George H. W. Bush and Michael Dukakis, they created the Iowa Political Stock Market. Investors could buy up to $500 in securities that paid out according to the share of the popular vote each candidate received. Shares were priced between $0.01 and $1.00, and were paid out in full. If you snatched up Bush shares when they were running at 55¢, you'd have made 45¢ for every share you purchased.

By November the results came in. The average error among all the major exit polls in the general presidential election that year was 2.5 percent. Not bad. But the Iowa Political Stock Market did much, much better, predicting the outcome to within one-tenth of a percent. "While the laws of statistics govern opinion polls," said Robert Forsythe, one of the market's creators, "the invisible hand of Adam Smith makes political markets work."

In fact the results were so impressive that the university renamed the experiment the Iowa Electronic Markets, or IEM, and began allowing trading in a range of future events, from elections in foreign countries to Google's market capitalization to the price of Microsoft stock on a certain date to upcoming decisions by the Federal Reserve. In the two decades since trading opened, the IEM has consistently outperformed the best polls.

Why would this be so? Aren't polls also tapping into the collective brain? Aren't they, too, a form of crowd-sourcing? The answer is yes, but that doesn't make them as fine-tuned a predictive model as an information market like the IEM. Polls are crude instruments. The fool-ish and the wise alike get a single, equally weighted vote. A prediction market, on the other hand, privileges the wise by offering a financial return on his wisdom. The foolish have an equal incentive to stay away, a principle Scott Page has called "Fools Rush Out."

Prediction markets offer considerable advantages

over both polls and surveys as well as prognostications issued by experts, and they are becoming increasingly attractive to everyone from the media to private companies to government. While they might differ in scope and methodology, prediction markets are no different from any futures market. Traders bet on the likelihood of outcomes involving presidential elections, say, rather than involving pork bellies. The price of a security in one of these markets, in theory, reflects the collective prediction of how likely it is to occur.

Crowdcasting networks and prediction markets both utilize collective intelligence, but in very different ways. Prediction markets are essentially just machines used to aggregate information. That doesn't mean that information markets don't exhibit their own magical qualities. The same principle we saw at work in our example from *Who Wants to Be a Millionaire* applies here. Because foolish people can be expected, on average, to vote in random patterns, even a small number of astute observers can create accurate predictions. Unlike a simple information aggregation system like *Millionaire*, however, not all "votes" are judged to be equal in a prediction market. If an investor possesses inside information, he or she is likely to invest more money than one working off a hunch. As this book goes to press, Hillary Clinton shares in the Iowa Electronic Market are going for about 13¢ (meaning each future would reap 87¢ of profit if Clinton snags the presidential nomination). If a small collection of people knew that a big scandal was about to ruin Barack Obama's shot at the Democratic nomination, they would naturally load up on Clinton futures. Prediction markets provide an incentive for people to reveal their privately held information.

Likewise, the cost of investing in such a market provides an incentive to the ignorant to keep their money in their wallets. Writing on the day before the 2004 presidential election, *Salon* staff writer Farhad Manjoo noted that while the polls put Democratic contender John Kerry ahead of President Bush by one to seven points, traders on the IEM were favoring Bush. "What accounts for the disparity between the polls and the IEM?" asks Manjoo. The answer is that no one risks money in a poll. "Betting money on an election focuses the mind. . . . I'm supporting Kerry for the White House, but I'm betting against him on the IEM." As we know now, that was a smart bet. Even while exit polls were showing a Kerry win, the IEM was predicting a Bush win. By midnight of the same day, the IEM showed Bush with 50.45 percent of the popular vote to Kerry's 49.55 percent, an uncannily accurate picture of the final outcome.

Diversity, too, exercises an influence over the results of a prediction market, but it doesn't trump ability. When it comes to prediction markets, diversity merely equals it. Scott Page again shows how this can be expressed as a mathematical theorem. Page's "Diversity Prediction Theorem" says that collective error equals the average individual error minus the diversity of the predictions. Page employs a lot of intimidating-looking formulas to prove this point, but the logic is pretty straightforward: if the variance between predictions is high—I guess forty and you guess sixty, but the answer is fifty—the diversity of predictions cancels each other out, much as it does in the *Millionaire* example. As Page writes, when it comes to prediction markets, "Being different is as important as being good."

Despite the IEM's record of accurate predictions, information markets didn't really become well known until a political firestorm broke out over the so-called terrorism futures market. In May 2001, a project manager at the Defense Advanced Research Projects Agency issued a request for proposals on using markets to predict events such as terrorist attacks, coups, and assassinations. One of the resulting $1 million grants was awarded to Robin Hanson, a pioneer in the science of prediction markets. Known as something of an unorthodox thinker, Hanson believes so profoundly in the efficacy of prediction markets that he has proposed a form of government—a "futarchy"—based on prediction markets. Working with a San Diego firm, Net Exchange, Hanson created the Policy Analysis Market, or PAM. The idea was that a select group of intelligence and policy analysis experts would try to predict the course of foreign affairs by investing up to $100 in such indexes as national stability (Will Kosovo declare independence?), economic growth (Will India's GDP grow 10 percent this year?), and military readiness (If India invaded Pakistan, could its forces successfully occupy the country?). Unfortunately for Hanson and the fortunes of the prediction market, it also included a terrorism index.

PAM fell under the purview of the Terrorism Information Awareness Office, headed by an already controversial figure, the former National Security Advisor John Poindexter, who had been convicted of perjury and other felonies during the Iran-Contra scandal. Given the charged environment following the attack on the World Trade Center on September 11, what happened next was hardly surprising. In July 2003, the news media caught wind of PAM. Betting on terrorism! In the Defense Department! Soon after the first article appeared, U.S. Senators Ron Wyden, a Democrat from Oregon, and Byron Dorgan, a Democrat from North Dakota, held a press conference deriding PAM for encouraging people to profit from terrorist attacks. Before dawn broke the following day, the Pentagon had shuttered PAM for good, extinguishing as well Hanson's dream of a futarchy.

After a week as a punch line on the late-night talk shows, PAM was effectively swept into the dustbin of history. But many economists and political scientists defended PAM's underlying premise—that markets could predict future events better than any single expert could—and, if anything, its notoriety only helped accelerate the mainstream adoption of prediction markets. The options for futures traders have expanded dramatically. The Hollywood Stock Exchange (HSX) provides a market for trades in everything from box-office grosses to Academy Awards results. The HSX boasts an impressive track record, having predicted more than 80 percent of all Oscar nominations (and that includes the more obscure categories, such as Best Sound Editing) and never missing more than one top award since its 1996 launch. There is even an academic journal—*The Journal of Prediction Markets*—devoted to the emerging discipline.

The private sector has been especially warm in its embrace of prediction markets. Companies use them internally in order to crowdsource the decision-making process in such matters as inventory, sales goals, and manufacturing capacity. In the mid-1990s, Hewlett-Packard and the Caltech economist Charles Plott devised a futures market to predict the sales of a range of HP products. Normally sales forecasts are generated by analysts on the company's sales staff, but for Plott's experiment, employees were chosen from a variety of departments. The securities represented specific intervals in sales figures. If an "investor" believed the company would sell, say, between 201 and 300 printers in a given month, she would buy shares of that security. If she was right, she would receive one dollar for every share. The market turned out to beat HP's official forecast for six of the eight products in which HP conducted the experiment. As a result, HP has since set up its own "experimental economics" group to conduct additional research into prediction markets.

The markets outperform the experts because collectively the people trading in them have access to far more data. "Quite simply, the central planners don't have all the information that the dispersed salespeople have," writes MIT Sloan School of Management professor Thomas Malone in his book *The Future of Work*. Google, Microsoft, Eli Lilly, Goldman Sachs, and Deutsche Bank have all used prediction markets to help determine corporate strategy, and Malone himself conducted a successful experiment with the computer chip maker Intel, in which an internal market was used to determine how many chips each manufacturing plant should produce in a given quarter. After some tweaks, Malone achieved a 99 percent efficiency rate, far superior to what Intel had reached by its traditional methods.

Such markets help companies adapt quickly to rapid change, notes Malone. "Because everyone has an incentive to trade as soon as possible to gain an advantage," vital information is dispersed far more quickly. "Instead of having one group of senior managers sequentially working through a single set of options," he writes, "many people can be simultaneously exploring lots of possibilities"—just as an ant colony can disperse the worker ants in many directions simultaneously to discover food. In 2006, Malone founded the MIT Center for Collective Intelligence, which is currently attempting to use prediction markets to crowdsource the viability of solutions to intransigent problems such as health care and climate change.

Nothing drives innovation like robust demand, and

companies offering ready-made software platforms for prediction markets have recently sprung up. Inkling Markets, a Chicago-based outfit that allows anyone to create his or her own prediction market, has a client list that includes Cisco, video-game maker Electronic Arts, Chrysler, tech publisher O'Reilly Media, Wells Fargo, Indiana University, Oxford University, Stanford University, and even the Los Alamos National Laboratory.

The problem is that most of these markets lack the key ingredient to a prediction market: the use of real money, which would violate prohibitions against gambling. While the IEM operates under a special exception from the Commodity Futures Trading Commission, the other prediction markets use virtual dollars. And that, economists agree, is a problem. People are animated to act by a complex welter of motivations, and financial rewards don't always figure high on that list. And it's true that participants in markets like the Hollywood Stock Exchange say they are compelled to play because of the competitive aspect. It enhances their reputation among their peers. But for a prediction market—which, unlike, say, iStockphoto or Threadless.com, doesn't tend to spawn a rabid, tightly knit community—the promise of enhanced reputation is a shaky foundation on which to build a house.

Prediction markets have also shown a tendency to suffer from the same maladies as those that affect all other stock markets: fads, information cascades, and bubbles like the one that saw tech stocks reaching dizzying, and unfounded, highs in the late 1990s. An even greater obstacle to establishing a prediction market—especially for small companies hoping to use one internally—is that the accuracy of futures trading is in direct proportion to the "thickness" of the market or the number of traders buying and selling shares at any given time. As HP and Google have discovered, it can be difficult to convince a large number of employees to participate in an internal market in exchange for meager payoffs (Google allows people to invest virtual dollars in exchange for prizes like T-shirts and gift certificates). "As a result you get thin markets, where there's not enough trading to effectively predict an outcome," says Bernardo Huberman, the director of HP's Social Computing Lab. "Secondly, a thin market can be easily manipulated by just a few trades." One salesperson might game an outcome in his favor, for instance. Without a crowd, there is no crowdsourcing.

To correct for this bias, Huberman has invented a method of counteracting the effects of a thin market, so that even a small number of traders—a corporate board, for example—could generate accurate predictions. Essentially, each participant answers a series of questions meant to evaluate their level of risk aversion. Those who throw caution to the wind are given a high rating, and those on the opposite end of the spectrum score lower. The positions they take in any prediction market are then weighted against their risk index. Huberman believes he's cracked this particular nut with his system, which HP patented, and he says other companies (he won't reveal their names) have begun licensing it. "I can imagine this being used in intelligence work," says Huberman. "A lot of people with imperfect information about, say, Azerbaijan could come together and make fairly reliable predictions about events that might occur there."

Advocates of prediction markets are also attempting to change the gambling laws to allow real money investments in nonprofit information markets, as long as they operate for small stakes. (Investment on the IEM is capped at $500 per account.) In May 2007, more than twenty eminent economists sent a letter to Congress and federal regulators urging them to create a "safe harbor" for such operations. "Using these markets as forecasting tools could substantially improve decision making in the private and public sectors [and] help manage risk more efficiently," they point out. . . .

So far we've treated crowdcasting networks and prediction markets as wholly distinct phenomena. And from the perspective of collective intelligence, they are. But theory plays a strange role when it comes to crowdsourcing—a form of economic production that forces us to apply theory to what is already occurring in practice. The Internet is catalyzing change so fast that theory is struggling to keep up. So it should come as no surprise that in the real world, some applications of collective intelligence are neither information markets nor problem-solving networks, but an intriguing hybrid of the two. Crowdsourcing doesn't offer a collection of ironclad rules. Sometimes the best strategy is intelligent improvisation.

Marketocracy: Collective Intelligence Improvised

Think of T. J. White as the argument for diversity, personified. In 1999, not many investors would have picked White as a candidate to manage their portfolios. Up to that point White had spent his life accumulating a lot of experience doing very little. He was an unremarkable student at his high school in Midland, Texas. He signed up for an unremarkable six-year stint in the U.S. Navy, followed by another six-year stint in Colorado pursuing what he calls his "second childhood," working a series of jobs meant only to "support a lifestyle" that revolved around skiing and gold prospecting. He excelled at neither.

One morning late that year White woke up, looked out at the parking lot outside his one-bedroom apartment, and had a moment of clarity. "I was a loser. I was thirty, and I had nothing. No skills, no college, no career."

A few days after New Year's Day 2000, White moved to Dallas, and the puzzle pieces started falling into place. He quickly found a job at a Home Depot not far from his house. "The manager was ex-Navy, and we hit it off," White recalls. A few weeks after that he met the woman who would become his wife, at a get-together of the Tall Texans of Dallas. "I stumbled across the website when I first moved to Dallas," explains White. "I'm six-foot-two, and Cheri's six-foot-two. We got serious pretty quickly."

And then White found what he believed to be his calling: day trading stocks over the Internet. "Everyone was talking about millionaires working at regular jobs like Home Depot. Why not me?" (Many Home Depot employees minted a fortune in company stock during the late 1990s.) White convinced Cheri to let him invest her life savings, combined it with his own, and began investing. He put $6,000 in shares of a technology company he had read about in the *Dallas Morning News,* and another $4,000 in other tech stocks. By the end of the year the bottom had fallen out of the technology sector, and White's money had evaporated.

White and his wife, Cheri, went to a local hamburger joint for a talk. He wanted her to give him the rest of her life savings—$2,000—to invest. "She looked at me across the table, took my hands in hers, and said, 'You're not good at this. You tried, and you lost.' " White emerged from the experience poorer, but the recipient of two valuable lessons. First, he'd discovered that he loved the process of investing—poring over prospectuses, studying profit-earnings ratios, and separating inflated claims from real potential for growth. More important, he realized that he should never invest in a company whose business he couldn't understand. "I don't know anything about bio-technology or computers. But I can wrap my head around someone digging a hole in the ground to look for some oil."

By the next year, White had discovered a safer outlet for his passion. An investment firm called Marketocracy allowed people to create "model portfolios" on their website. In other words, Marketocracy is like a prediction market for the stock market. After a free registration, anyone can open up to ten accounts, each of which would start with $1 million in Monopoly money. White stocked his first fund with broad investments in what he calls the "blue-collar industries." At first White continued to lose money, but soon he stopped trying to day trade and started looking for long-term values. He put an elementary formula to work, restricting his positions to companies in which growth rate exceeded their price-to-earnings ratio. This is the recipe advocated by such investors as Warren Buffett and the Fidelity fund manager and author Peter Lynch, who advocate an "invest in what you know" strategy, but White says he didn't know that at the time. "I thought I'd invented it."

White's instincts have proven remarkably effective. He has now been trading on Marketocracy for seven years, and his track record has beat even the best funds on Wall Street. If you had given White $1 million back in 2001, you would have $4,176,000 right now. Not all of White's investments have been in phony dollars. By slowly funneling his meager savings into brokerage accounts, White was able to quit his job at Home Depot soon after he and Cheri wed in 2005. "I have $166,000 invested right now, and we've paid off two cars." Cheri quit her job at a software company and now runs a doggie day care. "She hated her old job, to put it politely," says White. "That's been the best part of all this."

Discovering such unlikely investment geniuses as White is what Marketocracy does best. More than one hundred thousand people have created what the company calls "model portfolios," and roughly twenty thousand of those are considered "active traders," in that they regularly—even compulsively—monitor their portfolios. Marketocracy watches the performance of these ersatz fund managers and uses a selection of the top-performing hundred portfolios to guide the investment decisions of their Masters 100 fund, which has about $35 million in very real assets under management. That's not a lot of money for a mutual fund, but it's a considerable vote of confidence for such an unorthodox approach to investing.

On its face, Marketocracy would seem to be standard-issue collective intelligence crowdsourcing. While a large chunk of Marketocracy's so-called masters hail from stock-related industries, a surprising number are a lot like T. J. White: attorneys, chefs, geologists, and others who have a special insight into one sector of the market and a knack for sniffing out a bargain, or knowing when to take a profit on a high flier. It's what Page calls a "crowd of models"—which means Marketocracy is basing its decisions not on the crowd, but on a smaller crowd of the best performers. "It's like a crowd of experts," says Page. In this case, the experts include a mix of Mensa types with a heavy peppering of brown socks. It would seem to be a winning formula: since its inception in late 2001, the Marketocracy Masters 100 has outperformed that stock market benchmark, the Standard & Poor's 500, by an average of nearly 40 percent.

Such a track record would seem to make a clear-cut case for the virtues of a diverse crowd. But the reality behind Marketocracy's investment management approach is both more interesting and more complicated. It also reveals a lot about the tricky ways in which collective intelligence manifests, and the conditions that must be maintained to facilitate it. Over the years Marketocracy has created a fine-tuned hybrid that boasts the best qualities of both a crowdcasting network and a prediction market. It relies on a straight portfolio performance to identify the diamonds in the rough like T. J. White, but following a few disastrous quarters, the firm has also learned to exercise a great deal of discretion, sometimes following their Masters 100 elite investors and occasionally breaking from them.

Ken Kam and Mark Taguchi weren't thinking about group intelligence at all when they created the company; they were simply looking for a better system through which to scout trading talent. From 1994 to 2000, the pair helped run Firsthand Funds, which outperformed every other mutual fund in that period, averaging a 56-percent return on investors' money in its first five years. When they left to start their own fund, they were inundated with résumés. In order to identify the best trading talent, they asked applicants—and anyone else with an Internet connection—to create a mock portfolio. The hope was that some five thousand people would set up accounts with Marketocracy, and that after a year or two the pair would have enough data to hire the best traders of the bunch to help them manage their new fund.

"That goal changed pretty quickly," Taguchi laughs, exchanging looks with Kam. Some fifty thousand would-be investors signed up for mock portfolios in the first year. "We've always embraced a team idea," says Taguchi, "but that idea evolved into just using a very large team." In November 2001, Marketocracy launched the Masters 100. A lot of eyes were trained on Marketocracy. Kam and

Taguchi had been rock stars in the market's last bull cycle, and there was a lot of interest in—and skepticism about— their unusual new approach to managing a mutual fund.

At first it seemed Kam, Taguchi, and the crowd would all be vindicated. During the first year of its operation the market was in a full-scale retreat, but the Masters 100 outperformed the market from the start. By the end of the first year, Marketocracy had beat the S&P 500 by some 14 percent. By late 2002, the market hit its nadir, and stocks began climbing as the economy started heating up. At the time, Kam and Taguchi were running the fund using the simplest of formulas. The company simply allocated its assets in almost precisely the same ratios as did their Masters. "At first we equally weighted the fund's positions to reflect those of the top hundred," says Taguchi. "So if the Masters took a three-percent position in Apple, we did too."

The fund continued to outperform the market. Marketocracy's crowd-powered investment strategy worked great in the bear market of 2002 and the bull market of 2003. "In 2002 the defensive people took control," says Kam. These investors were well-suited for making decisions in a down market, but as stocks began trending northward, Kam and Taguchi wanted a different breed of trader at the helm. "In 2003 we started subbing in the more aggressive investors." It looked like a foolproof model. In 2003, the fund returned a remarkable 42.82 percent, and a flood of investment money started pouring in.

But then in 2004 the market entered a new, more complicated phase. "It was a choppy market. Up and then down, and not always the same sector." The Masters 100 started underperforming, and investors began fleeing the fund, which dropped from nearly $100 million assets under management—the key metric for an investment fund—to $50 million in just over a year.

Clearly there were bugs in Marketocracy's algorithm. For one, Kam and Taguchi realized that as the top investors got to know one another, they started conferring on their positions. (Marketocracy hosts events where members can meet and talk shop.) This had an upside—members, for instance, could learn about industries they didn't currently invest in—but it also had a big downside: deliberation is the enemy of collective intelligence because it reduces diversity. As individuals confer, they also reach consensus. One of the chief conditions that allow the crowd to make smart predictions or come up with novel approaches to a problem is autonomy: each makes his or her choice independently. "We started seeing a herd mentality emerge even among our best traders," says Kam. So Kam and his team instituted a number of changes to the site, one of which made it impossible for members to watch each other's trades. "It helped immediately."

But Marketocracy's real breakthrough was to realize that their pool of top performers—the top one hundred—was too small, and that using an algorithm to guide investments was too limited a methodology. The company wasn't benefiting from the talents and abilities of other traders who, while not performing as well as the very best, still possessed some unique expertise that might allow for a handsome profit on a trade. So Marketocracy reached out and began engaging the entire community on its decisions.

Not long after Marketocracy crashed in 2004, Kam and Taguchi put their hybrid to work. "We noticed that a certain subset of our traders was buying loads of shares in this oil-shipping firm called Knightsbridge Tankers," says Kam. No one in the Masters 100 had touched it or likely even heard of it. But a bunch of the less elite traders with accounts on Marketocracy were loading up on it. "The stock was trading at historic lows, and all these people were swimming upstream by investing in it. We wanted to know why." So they sent out some e-mails to the traders. "We received this incredibly detailed information."

It turned out that those traders were privy to information that neither the Masters nor Wall Street investors had access to. "The company had all these tankers that were about to be scrapped. How would you know that? Who would know that?" asks Kam, incredulously. "It turns out the tankers were registered in Singapore, and there were these guys who went to Singapore to look at the registrations. Incredible. The conventional wisdom is that when a tanker reaches the end of its life, it's worth zero. But the price of steel started to go through the roof in the interim, and all that was about to be returned to investors as dividends." Marketocracy made a killing.

The company effectively became a prediction market that employed important components of a crowdcasting network. "The reason diversity trumps ability in a problem-solving scenario is because you can always throw the idiots off the bus," says Page. In the case of Marketocracy, by following the Masters 100 too closely, they couldn't exercise that option. Page explains, "Picking stocks is part prediction and part problem-solving, so Marketocracy's approach makes a lot of sense."

Tapping people's collective intelligence involves trafficking in what the crowd already knows. Such crowdsourcing applications generally require small investments of time and energy on the part of individual contributors. They are also what we might think of as additive: they help people do better at their jobs, but don't threaten to replace existing employees. As we'll see, other forms of crowdsourcing promise to create much more disruption. In a few cases, that disruption is already occurring.

7

WHAT THE CROWD CREATES

*How the 1 Percent Is Changing
the Way Work Gets Done*

The activities that comprise crowdsourcing are as diverse as the crowd itself. When a patent lawyer scans InnoCentive for chemistry challenges he can tackle on his benchtop lab, that's crowdsourcing. When someone corrects a misspelling on Wikipedia, uploads a video to YouTube, or suggests an edit to an author (like this one) who has posted parts of his book online, that's all crowdsourcing, too. As far as overarching concepts go, crowdsourcing pitches a very big tent. Just as prediction markets tap the collective brain in order to elicit novel solutions, another form of crowdsourcing harnesses people's creative energies—a resource that's proving to be as endlessly inventive as it is infinitely renewable.

The product of all this creative energy falls under the loose designation of user-generated content, and it has proliferated at an explosive pace in recent years. Crowdsourcing isn't synonymous with user-generated content, but it often involves building a business around it. User-generated content bears the unfortunate stigma of being amateurish or puerile or both. There's a reason for that: much of it is.

There was a time when almost all culture would have been considered "user-generated content." Earlier I noted that many of the greatest artistic and scientific achievements were made by people we would now call amateurs. But even this observation diminishes the contributions made by the forgotten part-time poets and Sunday painters who created glorious, if ultimately ephemeral, works that were valued in their day, even if only by their close circle of acquaintances.

Before the rise of mass reproduction—the era in which photography, film, the phonograph, and the radio gave rise to the large-scale commoditization of cultural products—there was far less of a distinction between audience and creator. The centuries preceding the industrial era were characterized by a more complex and interactive relationship between creators and their audiences. New musical compositions were distributed as sheet music, which could then be interpreted according to regional preference and individual whim. In what was still a largely agrarian society, popular entertainment of the Victorian era took the form of regional theaters, church sermons, Saturday dances, and all manner of parlor games. Entertainment was a private—or at most a regional—affair composed of people entertaining one another. There were very few cultural products that we would describe as "hits" by today's standards.

This changed quickly and dramatically with the rise of modern technologies such as the phonograph, the radio, and the cinema. The mass production and distribution of culture required a more passive form of consumption. A division emerged between culture producers and culture consumers. Viewed in this historical light, the explosive growth in user-generated content is less a new phenomenon than a sign that the impulse to interact meaningfully with our media—to participate in its creation—never went away. The Internet—the very architecture of which enforces decentralization—created a natural stage for a participatory approach to media production and consumption. Indeed, the booming genre of online "fan fiction," in which readers craft new plotlines to everything from *Star Trek* to *Harry Potter,* is just a modern manifestation of the ancient oral tradition of storytelling, in which the story changes with every teller.

Long before the emergence of the World Wide Web in the early 1990s, the Internet took the form of a many-to-many communication vehicle, first through e-mail and then through Usenet groups, which were simple, all-text forerunners of the sorts of discussion forums one can find on nearly any community website or in a venue like Yahoo groups. Naturally, the first people to use the Web were those already familiar with the Internet, so early websites followed a similar model, which again prized the contributions of the individual—even if these consisted, as they do today, of mostly overheated opinions. On the Internet, the least-visited blog and the largest corporate marketing site occupy the same cultural real estate: both are just one click away.

More than just an effective cost-cutting strategy, crowdsourcing holds the potential to spawn an economy in which we aren't all forced into predetermined categories, where boys with high math scores aren't routed toward engineering schools and girls with fanciful approaches to their science projects aren't cheerfully encouraged to focus on the humanities. In the summer of 2006, I spent a few days wandering around the movable punk-rock feast known as the Warped Tour. This is no mere subculture; the Warped Tour is attended by close to a million people each year. Above and beyond being a showcase for scores of mostly unknown rock bands, the Warped Tour provides space for a bustling cultural commerce that operates out of kiosks and tents constructed around the fringes of the stages themselves. Many of the musicians here also wrote books of poetry, or ran little tattoo parlors, or operated websites. The point is that these kids didn't feel a need to describe themselves as a practitioner of one craft as opposed to another. They made stuff because it turned them on.

Crowdsourcing depends on the exceptions to this rule. Hand a camera to one hundred people and you'll get ninety-nine blurry snapshots and one indelible—or, more to the point, salable—image. The essence of crowdsourcing such creative work lies in culling the brilliant from the banal.

The mechanics of crowdsourcing content differ greatly from those that rely on collective intelligence. In a prediction market or a crowdcasting network, the task is to aggregate widely dispersed information and put it to good use. This presents its own set of challenges. The crowd must be diverse, and nominally versed in the relevant field, be it the sciences or the stock market. But the crowd needn't, generally speaking, interact with one another. In fact, as Marketocracy discovered, interaction leads to deliberation, which in turn reduces the diversity of thought through which collective intelligence thrives.

Crowdsourcing creative work, by contrast, usually involves cultivating a robust community composed of people with a deep and ongoing commitment to their craft and, most important, to one another. Because crowdsourcing eschews traditional forms of compensation—as a rule, financial rewards are nominal or nonexistent—a social environment gives creative production a context in which the labor itself has meaning. The best ideas, regardless of the medium in which they're expressed, result in enhanced status for their authors. Others naturally strive to meet or exceed the standard set by the most talented of their peers, a tendency that effectively increases the overall quality of the work produced by the community. It's also no accident that much of the interaction between community members revolves around improving their skills. People like to learn and they like to teach. The community has an unerring ability to identify its most talented members and highlight their work. Without this de facto filter, the task of sorting the good from the bad falls on the company doing the crowdsourcing. Given the voluminous submissions that characterize crowdsourcing endeavors, this is usually a burden too heavy to bear. Finally, work, even work we enjoy, is simply more fun in the company of like minds.

The incentives for companies to adopt crowdsourcing are obvious. At its best, it offers them a dedicated workforce that will perform key functions—be it investigating government malfeasance, in the case of the Fort Myers *News-Press* readers, or creating new T-shirt designs for Threadless—at little or no cost.

But crowdsourcing is no free lunch: communities can be difficult to build and even harder to maintain. The task requires managers to think in ways that run counter to decades of standard business protocol. In lieu of a regular paycheck, people will want a sense of ownership over their contributions. This often requires that the company adopt a less restrictive approach to intellectual property by either offering royalty-sharing agreements or relinquishing the rights to the work altogether. Members develop proprietary feelings over the company itself. This means opening up the decision-making process to them—a bitter pill for any firm operating in a highly competitive environment. It's the only way, however. Communities can't be directed, they can only be guided. Contributors won't brook anything less than total transparency—honesty breeds trust, but any sense that they're being used or exploited will drive them onto another site, most likely one run by a competitor.

When the company gets the recipe right, and works in harmony with its community, the result can be a highly effective (and low-cost) mode of production. iStockphoto wasn't merely able to undercut its competitors by 99 percent. It's also cultivated a large, active, and enthusiastic community of artists that is self-perpetuating and continually improving, providing iStockphoto with better and better product at no additional cost to the company. Despite the fact they are paid so little, iStockers consider themselves amply compensated, albeit through such intangible rewards as receiving mentorship and making new friends. In accomplishing this unprecedented feat, iStock didn't merely transform an industry, it invented a new one.

The Canary in the Coal Mine

There's a story people like to tell about Bruce Livingstone. In late 2005, Getty Images, the world's largest photo agency, was looking to acquire Livingstone's company, iStockphoto. Long before the contracts were drawn up, Livingstone, to show his commitment to the deal, tattooed the Getty logo across his wrist. Then he e-mailed Getty CEO Jonathan Klein photos of the tattoo with the message: "Don't make me write another word after this!"

It's just the kind of tale—emblematic of determination and fortitude and just the right amount of quirky eccentricity—that tends to burnish the reputation of its subject. In Livingstone's case, it has the added benefit of being demonstrably true.

With his penchant for muscle cars, rockabilly haircuts, and, yes, tattoos, it's tempting to call Livingstone an unlikely CEO. But I prefer to think of Livingstone as a perfectly reasonable chief for some corporation from, say, the year 2020. A company not unlike iStockphoto. Located in a single, cavernous room inside a former factory in downtown Calgary, Alberta, Canada, iStockphoto houses a tiny fraction of its actual workforce. And Livingstone, dressed in T-shirt and jeans, occupies a desk—chosen, it would seem, at random—in the middle of the floor. The corner office, it seems, loses significance in a company that thrives on decentralization.

Westeel Rosco built the factory in 1925 to manufacture nails, screws, and other bits of hardware. Unlike Westeel Rosco, iStock's products—stock photos, illustrations, and videos—aren't manufactured on site. They're created by a global, fluid workforce of fifty thousand part-time photographers and artists, fewer than 10 percent of whom make enough from iStock to live on. Yet they have a devotion to the company matched by few traditional firms. The full-time staffers who spend their days in the old Westeel Rosco plant merely play a support role for the community—and "community" is the only applicable word—that is making the product iStock brings to market every day. And that community—its members call themselves iStockers—have been very, very good to Livingstone and his investors. The company has experienced double-digit growth nearly every month of its existence, and when Getty purchased iStock in early 2006 Livingstone took home more than half of the $50 million Getty paid for the company.

The first stock photo agency was founded in 1920, and for most of the twentieth century the industry was an afterthought, trafficking in the outtakes from commercial magazine assignments. Very few photographers tried to make a living off the market in preexisting images alone. This changed after the desktop publishing revolution of the mid-1980s led to a rapid growth in the publishing industry, and to a commensurate demand for images. Suddenly photographers were making six figures a year selling photos they'd already been paid to shoot. It was like minting money. Yet stock photography remains, in comparative terms, a tiny industry. The annual global gross for the entire business is estimated to be around $2 billion, which makes it a bit bigger than the market for gift baskets, but a little smaller than the annual sales of orchids.

In just a few years the influx of talented amateurs armed with inexpensive, high-resolution digital cameras has upended the economics of the industry. In 2000, a professional-quality image was still a scarce resource. No more. This isn't to say the market for high-end photographs has disappeared. A gifted photographer will always find work. But the professional no longer has a lock on the middle and lower ends of the stock photo business. With a modicum of training, just about anyone can take a decent shot. Sophisticated cameras and photo-editing software do the rest. iStock exploits this fact. Design firms and other small companies working on a budget quickly embraced what became known as the "microstock" model. One graphic designer told me he went from paying hundreds of dollars an image to less than $10. "I pass on some of the savings to my clients and keep the rest. We're both delighted."

iStock might be great for buyers, but it's caused all sorts of headaches for professional stock photographers. Mark Harmel, a Los Angeles–based photographer specializing in healthcare imagery, has had to radically adapt to the new reality. In 2005, Harmel made roughly $60,000 from his stock image portfolio, most of it through Getty. By 2007, that income had fallen to $35,000. "If I look at the trend line, it just keeps going down. I'm really concentrating on getting assignments now," says Harmel. "I recently came back from London with seventy really wonderful shots. I'll probably use them on my website, but it's not worth my time to bother submitting them to a stock agency. They won't sell." Getty's stock price reveals that Harmel's hardly the only traditional photographer suffering. On the week in late July 2007 when I was visiting iStock in Calgary, its parent company, Getty, announced it would miss its quarterly earnings estimates. By the time I arrived home a few weeks later, the stock had slid 32 percent. In January 2008, the stock had bottomed out at $21.80, a 60-percent drop from the previous February. Shortly thereafter Getty announced its sale to the private equity firm Hellman & Friedman for $2.4 billion. In a document Getty filed with the SEC the next month, the company estimated iStock's earnings would nearly quadruple to $262 million by 2012, while its earnings from traditional stock offerings would decline from 50 percent of its overall earnings to less than 30 percent.

Despite causing such economic disruption in the industry, the crowdsourcing of stock photography also highlights the phenomenon's immense promise. Like the T-shirt company Threadless.com, iStockphoto has stumbled onto an incredibly cost-effective, profitable business model. And according to Garth Johnson, iStock's head of business development, they are only at the start of a growth cycle. Because iStock's images are so cheap,

Johnson believes the company will be able to tap an immense market in developing economies overseas. Already some 40 percent of the site's customers reside outside of North America, but in 2007 iStock launched separate websites in France, Japan, Spain, and Germany, among other countries. These sites are written in the local language and feature content from local photographers. "We haven't even begun to develop those sites," says Johnson. "This year we're going to be replicating what we did over here, growing local communities all over the world." Johnson believes the global market for stock images could be worth up to $5 billion. Microstock companies, he says, are viewed by traditional segments of the industry as barbarians at the gate. That perspective, Johnson says, is shortsighted. "They just look at the existing market and say, 'They're taking away my piece of the $2 billion pie,' instead of saying, 'I could get a smaller slice of a much, much bigger pie.'"

The upheaval roiling stock photography is only a leading indicator, like the minor volcanic eruptions that can precede a catastrophic earthquake. iStock is excelling in an industry that has entered the post-scarcity economy, in which consumable goods become so abundant that their value declines precipitously. And the dynamics that have led to the proliferation of digital images—affordable tools, a culture of amateur endeavor, communities of like-minded creators—aren't restricted to stock photography. Armed with cell-phone cameras, so-called citizen paparazzi snatch impromptu shots of stars and then sell them to new photo agencies such as Scoopt, which specialize in buying up and marketing their work. In March 2007, Getty bought Scoopt as well. "They can break the story before anybody else," said Brad Elterman, the cofounder of Buzz Foto, one of Scoopt's competitors. It's a question of probability: throngs of pedestrians along a Greenwich Village street have a much better chance of catching Gwyneth Paltrow buying coffee than does a single paparazzo.

Other commodities have begun to enter the post-scarcity phase, as the crowd acquires new skills. User-generated pornography, of all things, has caused a hemorrhage of revenues in DVD sales. The crowd is also making commercials, collaborating on TV scripts, and recording and distributing their own music. They're writing political analysis, creating their own video games, and making feature-length movies. For the time being, all this activity has taken place in something of a parallel universe, without causing any of the economic upheaval visited on the stock photo or pornography industries. But those universes are beginning to collide as more companies attempt to package all this outpouring of creativity into a marketable product. When they do, well, that's crowdsourcing, the transition from professional production to community production.

Prediction markets and problem-solving networks are additive in nature: they offer companies new ways to perform old tasks, whether that's identifying a scientific solution or more accurately forecasting the best way to allocate manufacturing resources. InnoCentive doesn't compete with P&G; it helps P&G create better products. But crowdsourcing the stuff people make—as opposed to the stuff they already know—threatens to disrupt and ultimately displace established companies. We know this because it's already occurring in stock photography, and the signs are that it could well spread into other media and entertainment fields. The question is whether the iStock secret sauce can be applied to industries like television and journalism and, possibly, even beyond to any business that traffics in bits and bytes.

The Community Is the Company

iStock has been compared to a cult, and the analogy isn't entirely unfair. It's no accident that the most successful companies in the Web's second coming—most of whom traffic in the crowd's creative output—are led by outsize personalities. "Bruce is to iStock what Tom is to My-Space," notes Garth Johnson. For those readers over the age of thirty, Tom is Tom Anderson, the president of the social networking behemoth MySpace and the first "friend" to greet any new user. Under this new archetype of a company—in which the community comes first—the cult of personality plays a crucial role in community building, and Livingstone has been as essential to the growth of the iStock community as Anderson has been to MySpace's. "Bruce has a really strong, extremely charismatic personality online," says Johnson.

Livingstone may no longer be needed, at least insofar as leading the cult is concerned. It's safe to say that iStock has left the community-building phase behind: there are now nearly fifty thousand contributors to the website. Getty's other divisions *combined* use only twenty-five hundred photographers. "We don't own anything, the community does," says iStock's Garth Johnson. "Everything we do affects these people, whether they're just earning enough to pay for their equipment, or they're making mortgage payments from their photo sales. They all want a voice, and we have to give it to them, because really, the community is the company."

The upsides to this state of affairs are obvious, but there are downsides as well: even the smallest changes can roil the fickle, passionate community of iStockers. In March 2006, iStock launched a new feature on its Web forums, a "Forumeter" that measured an iStocker's popularity through—according to the tongue-in-cheek press release announcing its release—"bafflingly complex scientific methods," including the date and number of posts to the forum. The Forumeter displayed its results through a set of red, yellow, or green bars. It did not go over well. The community questioned the principles behind measuring a community member's popularity, as well as the Forumeter's functionality. Not long after its launch, the feature had been removed. Employees may be hell on overhead, but they're paid to accept all but the most draconian policies with a polite nod. Communities, on the other hand, aren't paid to stick around, and nothing stops them from selling their photos to one of iStock's many competitors. "They don't work for us," Livingstone laughs. "We work for them."

If the iStocker feels a sense of ownership over the site, that's understandable: the iStock community predates iStock the company. Like Jake Nickell and Jacob DeHart of Threadless, Livingstone didn't set out to revolutionize an industry, he just wanted to fill a personal need and help a few friends at the same time. In 2000, Livingstone was running a small graphic design and Web-hosting firm in Calgary. Bruce is an avid photographer himself, and over the years he had developed an extensive network of photographers and designers. Early in the year he took two thousand of his images and put them online. Anyone could download his photos in exchange for giving him an e-mail address. Livingstone's friends decided they wanted to share their images with the public, too. That June the budding community instituted a credit system: a user could download one image for every image of theirs that had been downloaded by someone else.

It was a classic example of the gift economy, the non-monetary exchange that grew up alongside the World Wide Web. During iStock's early years everyone took something and gave something in turn. "The feeders and the eaters were the same people," as Livingstone puts it. Everyone profited by acquiring new images, though no one made (or spent) a dime. Soon friends of friends heard about Bruce's nifty idea and started uploading their images, too. Then around 2002 a wider public got wind of iStock, and the site began to hit critical mass. Soon Livingstone was paying $10,000 a month for the bandwidth to support it. He could have taken advertising to cover the cost of hosting, but he felt that would violate the spirit of the site. "The focus was on the community, and good design. Advertising would have cluttered the site," says Livingstone.

Instead, he started charging a quarter for each image, and he opened the system up to the public. Traffic to the site, now christened iStockphoto, started increasing exponentially. Livingstone raised the price to $1 per image. "I thought it might become a sideline business," he says. It quickly became much more than that. The quality of the images wasn't always as high (or as consistent) as a traditional stock agency's, but the differences were indiscernible to all but the most discriminating consumer, and you couldn't beat the price. By 2004, a host of other so-called microstocks had sprung up with strategies similar to iStock's. The professionals panicked. Microstock photos, they charged, were shoddy and would bring on the ruin of the industry by flooding the market with sub-par photographs. At first, the stock industry aligned itself against iStockphoto and other so-called microstock agencies such as ShutterStock and Dreamstime. But in early 2006, Getty—by far the largest agency in the business—reversed course and bought iStockphoto. "If someone's going to cannibalize your business, better it be one of your other businesses," Getty CEO Jonathan Klein told me shortly after the sale. Smaller magazines, nonprofit organizations, and all manner of websites have continued to flock to iStock's high-volume, low-cost model. As of February 2008, iStockphoto had 1 million regular customers purchasing photographs, video footage, illustrations, and animations. Though Getty won't say exactly how much revenue iStock has brought into the company, the number has more than tripled since the acquisition, making it Getty's fastest-growing business. "Bruce's brilliance," Jonathan Klein once told me, "is that he turned community into commerce."

"And I turned commerce into community," Livingstone adds when I repeat Klein's quote back to him during my visit to Calgary. And it's true. iStock offers the budding photographer all manner of free tutorials, and the forums buzz with questions about lens sizes, Polarizing filters, and F-stop settings. iStock doesn't offer a chance to get rich. It offers the chance to make friends and become a better photographer.

Livingstone and his staff spent much of the week of my visit agonizing over a press release. On my first day in the office Livingstone and about a dozen other employees were gathered inside a small conference room. Getty had been pushing iStock to raise some of its prices, and after months of resistance Livingstone had agreed to a limited increase. This fact couldn't just be declared in a boilerplate press release. Any shift in the way the product was priced, sold, and marketed had to be handled with kid-gloved delicacy. Livingstone still gets the community's approval at every step of running his company. When he says he works for the community, he laughs, but he isn't kidding.

As it happened, iStock was about to announce the

price increase on the morning I arrived at the offices. The company had begun building anticipation among the iStockers by displaying an F5 button on top of its forum pages. On a computer, the F5 button refreshes whatever webpage is displayed on the monitor. Like any good community, iStock has developed its own specific rituals and patois. "On iStock, it's code for 'Something big is coming,' " explained Livingstone. "But we're not going to tell you what!" The community had responded by "going apeshit," he noted. "We've got like seven pages on the F5 button alone."

Livingstone lapses back into a lower gear and addresses the assembled staffers, all of whom share his affection for casual office apparel and, to judge by the stickers plastered across their laptops, pop cultural ephemera. "Okay, we've got a bunch of things happening on Friday. Number one is the price change. Then we have all these cool things that are happening." The cool things iStock is announcing range from an easy way for the best-selling iStockers to sell their work through Getty's website (which still sells high-end images for hundreds of dollars) to a 100 percent sales day in which contributors receive all the money from a sale, as opposed to the standard 20 to 40 percent contributors usually receive.

I'm mystified as to why Livingstone and his staff are pouring so much energy into massaging what seems like an uncontroversial move. The price of iStock's low-range images is only going up one dime. "The fear is that the volume of sales will decline," explains Livingstone. "Somebody's always going to say the sky is falling. They're afraid that our clients will all go running to the competition." This isn't a totally unfounded fear. While iStock indisputably—and single-handedly—created the microstock photo industry, the category has become very crowded. And then there are the clients, all 1 million of them. "They'll say 'You're ruining my business because it costs me an extra three dollars to buy twenty-five images.' Well, I'm sorry, but if that's the case maybe your business isn't very good." Some debate ensues about how to introduce the price change. Livingstone discloses the exact amount of the increase, to general groans and laughter around the table. "You know, we could sit there and try to explain that illustrations haven't had a price increase in two years, and video has never had one, but we're going to do it like tearing off a Band-Aid: 'Things are changing. Here's the bad stuff.' "

In the end, Livingstone approves two separate releases. The differences between the two seem minimal, but are in fact highly revealing of how iStock handles community relations. The first release goes out to the media, and it buries the price increase at the bottom of the page. The newsletter that is sent out to the community makes the increase the lead item, with a prominent link to a forum thread that will let them immediately vent their feelings. "If we put it anywhere else they'd be like, 'Why'd you try to bury this? What are you hiding?' " Roberta McDonald, the de facto community liaison, tells me. "They're pretty clever that way." (The press, evidently, is not considered very clever in that way.) "The iStockers pick up on the price change and fill the forums with posts about it," adds Livingstone. "We just figure we'll make it easy for them to do that." This strategy has the intended effect. At 4:38 p.m. the release goes live on the site. I lean over McDonald's computer to see how the community will react. At 4:46 there are already sixteen posts about the increase. Most, to the crew's great relief, are positive.

A Jedi Mind Trick

The night before iStock made its big announcement, Livingstone hosted a dinner for various visiting dignitaries at a chichi restaurant in downtown Calgary. Over elk steak and red wine, Garth Johnson discussed the wages of iStock's success. Part of Johnson's job involves playing chaperone at the iStockphoto festivals known as—in typical iStockphoto irreverence—iStockalypses. "The iStockalypses are crazy, dude. You wouldn't believe the level of fanaticism. People come up and they're like, 'You're from iStockphoto! Oh my God! I looooove you guys!' and hug us. And the girls . . ." Johnson trailed off, taking a sip of his wine. "If I weren't married . . ."

The iStockalypses are one more way in which the company bends over backward to make shooting for iStock feel more like a big, fun game than like work. Nowhere is the iStock spirit on such lavish display as at an iStockalypse; for a company and community that revolves around a website, these offline events have become tremendously important.

The format is straightforward: the company books hotel rooms, models, and locations for shoots at a predesignated city (recent iStockalypses have been held in Prague; Austin, Texas; and Barcelona) and sells tickets to some fifty to sixty iStockers, who come to socialize, enjoy the sights, and build up their portfolios. In the beginning iStockalypses served a simple need: people who knew each other from the online forums wanted to meet in person. But they have come to illustrate one of the central dynamics of the iStock community: the best photographers want to teach and the newbies want to learn.

"There's this guy, he calls himself Subman," Livingstone said, turning toward Johnson and me. "He comes to every iStockalypse, and he's super-accomplished. He shoots for *Dwell*"—a high-end design magazine with lavish visuals—"and other big-name magazines. He comes to these events to set up and art-direct different shoots and he's just an incredible guy. And the thing is, he's the rule, not the exception. Our elite photographers want to share what they know"—a lot of which they in turn learned from other iStockers.

The iStockalypses were so popular that a few years ago the iStockers began hosting them on their own. "There was one in London a few years ago that really set the bar. It was totally run by the iStockers," Johnson told me. These events are known as "Minilypses," in contrast to those initiated by the company, because they are "totally user-generated," Johnson explained. "At first Minilypses were, like, twenty people. This one had close to fifty, people flying in from America, Sweden, Russia, Africa. Someone had a connection with the Dalí Museum, so we used that as a location. I could have never swung that, but it's incredible how individual iStockers have these connections."

But it's not just the events that cement the community together, it's the spirit behind them. There's an overwhelming impression that working for iStock is its own reward. The iStockers maintain a certain esprit de corps that runs through every forum post, blog comment, and photo critique. And there's no question that it has been an unqualified good to tens of thousands of would-be photographers. Five years ago an aspiring photographer would have regarded his passion as a terribly expensive hobby. In the wake of iStock and its competitors, it now represents an opportunity to join a robust community of other enthusiasts and, on occasion, to earn a substantial supplemental revenue. Plus, even a supplemental income in a country like the United States can comprise an affluent income in some of the markets iStock is beginning to move into, such as India.

iStockphoto has perfected the Jedi Mind Trick that's at the heart of crowdsourcing. It's an incredibly cost-effective strategy, and a lot of companies are going to make boatloads of money by implementing crowdsourcing models. iStock's profit margin is at *55 percent.* And yet this has been accomplished by creating a context—a community—in which money is a secondary concern. Ask someone in the office, and they'll tell you: *It's not about the money.* Ask an iStocker and they'll tell you the same thing. In fact—would-be crowdsources take note—if it is about the money, it won't work. It will fizzle, not sizzle, as one of iStock's designers put it. "What's funny is, the money people, they pretty quickly get pulled aside in the forums by the core people. Or they just don't have a voice. People will ignore them, like 'Oh, that's just so-and-so, they're just here to make money.' "

That doesn't mean the iStockers are totally unmotivated by self-interest. The more a photographer's images are downloaded, the more recognition they receive in the community, and the more credits they earn to download other people's photos to use in their own designs. And the additional income is welcome, of course. It's significant that people in online communities like iStock's react with great hostility to the idea that crowdsourcing equals cost savings. No one wants to feel exploited. In the end, what iStock provides is an invaluable if impossible-to-measure currency: meaning. The crowd will give away their time—their excess capacity—enthusiastically, but not for free. It has to be a meaningful exchange. The profits have to come second, or they won't come at all.

Democratizing Media

Ezra Cooperstein speaks eloquently on the subject of great
art emanating from unlikely sources. Like Livingstone,
Cooperstein—the head of the "viewer-created content" division at Current TV—has helped build a business through
crowdsourcing. Unlike iStockphoto, however, Current attempted to jump-start its community into being, with
decidedly mixed results. If iStock offers the chance to observe crowdsourcing in the wild—the community grew up
organically over a period of years—Current offers an opportunity to see how crowdsourcing fares when it's bred
in captivity.

The network launched in August 2005 with the high-
minded mission of opening up television programming
to the masses. By that measure, at least, Current has succeeded. An unorthodox "news and information network"
founded by former vice president Al Gore and a group
of investors, Current is delivered to 51 million homes
in the United States and Britain, and a full third of its
schedule consists of what it calls VC^2, or viewer-created
content. Unlike other networks that have featured Web
content on air, there are no piano-playing cats or toddler
high jinks on Current; in fact, most of its programming
compares favorably to the professionally produced fare
on other cable channels.

Current went on the air on August 1, 2005, carried in
a limited number of markets with a potential audience
of 17 million homes. The network ran spots urging viewers to send in their video clips, and Cooperstein and a
few other staffers called around to film festivals and film
schools looking for likely candidates. Within six months
they were filling one third of their schedule with videos
filed by Cooperstein's VC^2 contributors. "I think people

underestimated the amount of creativity and ability and enthusiasm that was out there waiting to be tapped," says Cooperstein.

That's not to say he was surprised, though; this was his tribe. Appointed head of the viewer-created content division when he was only twenty-five, Cooperstein is smack dab in the center of Current's target demographic of eighteen- to thirty-four-year-olds. "This creative class was just coming of age. All these young people who've grown up using Final Cut Pro and Photoshop from the time they're twelve, and they're shooting movies in their backyard and learning how to share them over the Internet. It's very powerful when someone suddenly opens up a closed system like TV to that," says Cooperstein.

Powerful for those with the interest and skills, perhaps. Cooperstein and his staff had succeeded in finding young filmmaking talent and broadcasting their videos to a national audience. It was an admirable feat, but it bore little resemblance to Current's original vision of democratizing the media. Current's website employed an "if we build it they will come" strategy. The website was well designed, sophisticated, and packed with tutorials featuring celebrity filmmakers such as Robert Redford and Sean Penn. The viewers were supposed to go to the site to upload videos, critique their friends' works, and help choose the videos that would air on Current. It didn't work out quite that way.

In the end, few came; and when they did, there was no one around to greet them. One year after launching, the destination for online video was YouTube, not Current. Around the time I showed up at Current's offices in the summer of 2007, the site was still a virtual ghost town. iStockphoto receives 37.4 posts on its forums *every minute.* Some of the forum topics I visited at CurrentTV.com hadn't been posted to in days. And when I checked the online traffic measurement site Alexa.com, Current wasn't even receiving enough traffic to register among the top hundred thousand sites in the world.

To be fair, Current was facing some daunting challenges. Making a film—even the video shorts broadcast by the network—requires the crowd to jump certain logistical hurdles that a photographer need never worry about. Like finding a crew. And staying within budget. And coping with a complex post-production process. That doesn't even broach the question of training and ability, which, as any brief tour of YouTube will amply demonstrate, varies enormously.

The fact that Current has struggled to create participatory television doesn't make its experience any less illuminating. For anyone hoping to apply crowdsourcing to their business, Current's initial missteps provide a cautionary tale. Likewise, the network's recent success— after relaunching its website in late 2007, Current has finally managed to engage a broad audience in the creation of its programming—provides a blueprint for making crowdsourcing work under difficult circumstances. Stock photography is tiny, easily dwarfed by the $65 billion global market for television. But if crowdsourcing can migrate into fields such as TV—and if Current is an indicator, it can—it has serious ramifications for the entire entertainment industry.

Current takes up several floors of a converted industrial building in the chic SoMa (South of Market) neighborhood of San Francisco. AT&T Park—home of the San Francisco Giants—looms overhead from across the street. A postmodern confection of glass and brick, Current's headquarters would be a fitting location for an art museum. Instead, behind the great walls of glass sit rows of late-model Macs and, on full view to passing pedestrians, the high-tech control room. It's the perfect facade for a company dedicated to opening up television to the masses.

On the day I visit the Current offices, Cooperstein and one of his employees are facing a dilemma: too many snow leopards. "Which piece are we looking at? Russian snow leopards?" asks Fhay Arceo, a slender young woman wearing fashionably chunky glasses.

"No," answers Cooperstein. "There are two pieces. 'Snow Leopard' and 'In Search of the Snow Leopard.' " Arceo and Cooperstein are huddled around his desk screening viewer submissions to see which "pods"—the two- to seven-minute bite-size chunks that comprise Current's programming—to show on the channel's U.K. affiliate. "The one we're about to watch is about a dad and his kids searching for the snow leopard. It's about the dad. No snow leopard," he says.

Cooperstein starts the video and he and Arceo lean toward his computer monitor to hear the audio. The piece opens with a wide shot of the Himalayas from a helicopter, as the narrator describes his father's quest to see the famously rare and elusive cat. Having made several previous trips, the family knows this one will be his last opportunity. After four days of freezing temperatures and elevation sickness, the family spots a snow leopard minutes before they begin their final descent off the mountain. The piece is long by Current's standards—nearly eight minutes. If the pod were less raw, any less obviously a product of a nonprofessional, such a climax would feel scripted. But what with the shaky camera work and earnest documentary narration, it's genuinely moving.

One can imagine how a network executive might greet "In Search of Snow Leopard," if it even made it past the mailroom. In case you hadn't noticed, neither short films nor snow leopards are in great demand at most networks. Current's content, by contrast, is determined to a large extent by a combination of viewer demand and the whims of young, hip creatives like Cooperstein and Arceo. To say that Current isn't a slave to its Nielsen ratings would be an understatement; the network isn't even rated by Nielsen.

"We're programming from our gut because we don't have that information," admits Cooperstein, as he and Arceo decide to green-light the snow leopard. "We have a vast network of friends, and a vast network of creators, and they'll call us or e-mail us and say, 'hey, that pilot was really cool,' or 'that one really wasn't.' " Current is crowdsourcing its content creation; it's crowdsourcing its programming decisions; and, to a large, if informal, degree, it's even crowdsourcing its ratings. There's a lesson in here: If you're going to invite the crowd to the party, you might as well ask them to help with the planning and cleanup. The crowd likes to be involved.

Current was started with high ambitions but modest expectations. "We are launching an exciting television network for young men and women who want to know more about their world and who enjoy real-life stories created with, by, and for their own generation," Gore proclaimed on May 4, 2004. Despite the lofty rhetoric, the executives privately anticipated that only 10 percent of its schedule would be user-generated. Cooperstein, one of the company's first employees, recalls, "This was before YouTube, and there wasn't a lot of faith that you could fill a TV network with product created by viewers."

Though Cooperstein and his staff had exceeded that original goal, the trepidation turned out to be prescient for other reasons. "We had to invent a community from scratch, and have the unusual requirement of having it be big on day one," says Robin Sloan, Current's Web strategist. "We couldn't just plant it and let it grow." Sloan notes that when the online classified site Craigslist opens a site in a new city, they do nothing to promote it. Because it's not in any rush, Craigslist can let people gravitate to the site and let it reach critical mass through organic word of mouth. Current didn't have that luxury. Instead it recruited its "viewer creators." The result, Sloan says, is that while people did start to use the website, it wasn't to interact with one another. "We established vertical relationships with each individual producer," he says. "What we should have done was create a horizontal relationship with the community. We wanted our best producers to become mentors, but they just wanted to do their own thing."

Regardless, the VC² department had hit on a productive, and by all accounts highly economical, formula. Viewers submit potential pods to the Current website. Every week other viewers vote on the pods. The two with the highest votes are subsequently aired on the network. The winners are paid between $200 and $1,000, a fraction of the roughly $60,000-per-minute cost of a scripted comedy, even after Current's production costs are factored in. The rest of the VC² programming is generally commissioned by Cooperstein and his staff, but for similar rates of pay.

"We think of ourselves as the HBO of UGC," says Cooperstein, employing the acronym for user-generated content. "We're not looking for the cat video or the fictional spoof of a dorm room." And despite the low rates of participation, Cooperstein has succeeded in producing some of the most original, if occasionally eccentric, TV on cable. Often the pods are so good that they become—in what must seem like a cruel irony to Current's online-ad sales staff—viral hits on YouTube.

A Small Crowd

Every day at 9 a.m. Cooperstein's VC^2 staff gathers inside a small, glass-enclosed conference room for a pitch meeting. Because Cooperstein's department cannot subsist on viewer-submitted videos alone, he relies heavily on regular contributors, who send his creative staff ideas for new pods that are then vetted by the staff. Attending one of these is a bit like listening to a wiretap embedded into the collective unconscious of today's youth demographic. Some of the ideas pitched on the day I sat in included a segment on competitive eating in Philadelphia ("the most unfit city in America," one staffer notes); a piece on a girls-only pillow-fighting league; and another about a regional air guitarist's quest for the national championship.

At one point I suggest a pod on a subculture I had previously considered the height of obscurity: skateboard ministries, which involves young pastors who try to convert the young through traveling shows of born-again professional skateboarders. "Done," replies one staffer, as others try to restrain themselves from rolling their eyes. This suggests the difficulty Current has remaining, well, current. Pitches follow for pods about comedy schools, nontraditional parents, and Nepal's first independent radio station. Without much apparently being decided, the meeting breaks up.

After the meeting I sit down with Cooperstein at his desk, which occupies a spot along a wall, indistinguishable from the other fifteen desks in the VC^2 area. A question nags at me. In the pitch meeting the staffers referred to their VC^2 producers by their first names, indicating that a lot of Cooperstein's pods are created by regular contributors. At least half of the VC^2 producers, Cooperstein says, are involved professionally in film and video industry. Can we really call this user-generated content? These aren't strictly amateurs, though they aren't strictly professionals, either. "It's actually a network of freelancers," Cooperstein admits. "We need a safety net of what we're doing that allows us to know we have a reliable network of people we can reach out to at any time in any city."

Cooperstein does note that he discovered a great number of these filmmakers after they' submitted their videos to the site. This raises an interesting question—and not just for Current. Does the crowdsourcing of creative work—complex creative work like television in particular—really represent the democratization of media? Or is it instead just a new approach to an old problem: identifying and nurturing young talent? To look at Current and several other examples from film and TV, the latter would seem to be the case. Everyone from Frito-Lay to MTV to Current has crowdsourced advertisements, segments, and music videos. The best entries reliably tend to come from young filmmakers with more talent than professional recognition. YouTube itself is nothing so much as a talent-finding system. None of this would diminish crowdsourcing's importance. A fair system in which filmmakers are recognized strictly on their merits would be a vast improvement over the current system, which requires mostly luck, proximity, and the right connections. But neither does it constitute television by the people, for the people.

Just before I leave the Current offices for the last time, Cooperstein asks me to follow him into an adjoining room. Inside, several staffers in beards and untucked shirttails sit editing footage on their computer monitors. "We're trying to figure out how to lower the

bar for people to participate in our programming. This,"
he says, pointing to one of the monitors, "is one of the
new formats we're working on." The video on the
screen features a kid who looks to be just out of his
teens standing in an unfurnished room talking about
the new album by the indie rock singer Conor Oberst.
"I actually was a fan of the first couple albums," the kid
tells the camera. "With *Cassadaga* I think he's run out of
magic." The segment has no flashy graphics, no spectacular camera work, and no snow leopards, but it's fun
and mildly engaging. If I cared about Conor Oberst as
much as the average twenty-four-year-old does, it might
even be provocative. "It's a CD review, on TV. The idea
is that anyone could webcam in his or her review of an
album and then we just put in a template to enhance
the production value a bit."

Cooperstein walks over to another monitor. "I'll
show you another one," he says. For the next minute a
montage of still images moves across the screen. Each
photo shows a dangerously pale hipster voguing for the
camera on some European street. The text beneath the
photos reads "STREET STYLES: OSLO." The idea, Cooperstein says, is to create a one-minute snapshot of what
fashion looks like in cities around the world. "There are
all these street fashion photographers out there. They'd
never make a video for us, but they'll upload their
photos."

Up to this point, Cooperstein says, Current has relied
on what have become known as "super contributors," a
small fraction—generally around 1 percent—of an online
community that is responsible for the lion's share of activity. One study conducted by the Palo Alto Research
Center determined that 1 percent of all Wikipedia contributors are responsible for writing roughly half of the

1 billion words contained in the English edition of the on-line reference work.

The goal with these two pilot projects, Cooperstein says, is to get a much larger fraction of people involved. "These new formats do two things. One, it's interesting content, but two, it includes a new set of creators who would never be able to play with video to take part in tel-evision." Doing this will ultimately create a ripple effect, he says. "To have that viral trend become a phenomenon, it will take the presence of a huge viewer-created content movement, and a whole new level of Web presence." The beauty of iStock's large active-user base is that it be-comes self-perpetuating and evangelizing, continually drawing in more contributors. Clearly, going back to video producers with whom you are on a first-name basis won't accomplish this.

Though I didn't know it at the time, the pilot projects were part of a larger initiative. A few months after my trip to Current, the network launched a completely over-hauled website. The old site—CurrentTV.com, which re-volved around the uploading of videos and voting on them—had been tucked away into one corner of the new site, Current.com. It represented a new approach for the network: instead of asking people to contribute videos, Current now asked them to contribute anything, anything at all—photos, comments, links, or just a tip about a devel-oping trend. The new site self-consciously emulated a so-cial networking site, allowing users to create networks of friends, à la Facebook, and a profile page. The new strat-egy incorporated all of Current's hard-won lessons, and it worked. According to Alexa.com, within a few weeks, traf-fic to the site had already grown considerably, and as this book goes to press, it continues its upward movement. At the very least, Current.com is now on the map.

The album review format Cooperstein had shown me over the summer has now been expanded into an entire genre of Current programming called "Viewpoint." Visitors to the site can record a short video of themselves, via webcam, commenting on any topic they wish. Current designed the feature so that submitting a video comment took no more effort than submitting a comment to a blog post or newspaper article would. These are then edited down and turned into video op-eds that run between longer pods on the channel. The new site capitalizes on the fact that, according to Current's internal research, 70 percent of its viewers are using their computers while they watch the network, so viewers can land their headshot and names on live TV by commenting on the pod or suggesting a link.

The problem with Current's original strategy was that it had overestimated the crowd's ability to create original videos that met their strict "HBO of UGC" standard. At the same time, it had underestimated the amount of interest people had in contributing in some other way. "The idea of rebooting the news, and being able to participate in the process, was extremely exciting to people," recalls Robin Sloan, the Web strategist who played an integral role in Current.com's relaunch. "And they would show up, but they wouldn't be video producers, so there was nothing for them to do. They would post something on the forum and then disappear. It was a huge, huge wasted opportunity. We squandered all that enthusiasm."

Sloan feels that Current is well on the way to recapturing some of that initial enthusiasm, and the numbers would seem to bear him out. "The lesson here," he says, "is that it's not so much about giving the crowd easier tasks, as it is about building a strategy around the fact that different people are good at different things, have different amounts of time to commit, or simply have different interests."

Dodging Katyushas

In the summer of 2006, Current aired "Dodging Katyushas," by a young contributor named Jaron Gilinsky. The piece shows Gilinsky and his cameraman traveling to the city of Haifa in northern Israel. A few days previous, eight Israelis had been killed when a Katyusha rocket fired from Lebanon had struck a train depot. As Gilinsky interviews one of the workers at the depot, another Katyusha is heard landing off-camera. Gilinsky moves into a nearby bomb shelter, at which point another rocket lands in the very spot where Gilinsky had just been standing.

"Dodging Katyushas" became a cult hit for Current, for the excellent reason that it's absolutely riveting television. What's striking about the segment is less the frisson of immediate danger, though that's certainly part of the appeal. It's the authenticity of Gilinsky's narration, and the unguarded attitude of the people he interviews. After the first rocket hits, Gilinsky, in a panic-stricken voice, asks, "What was that?" His interview subject, a retired colonel, looks at Gilinsky without changing his expression and says, "That was real. . . . Shall we go to the shelter?" as if gently recommending Gilinsky try the lamb souvlaki at the local restaurant. It is these details that lead us to feel as if we've watched a very well-produced home video of a rocket attack. It strips away the layers of mediation that network news shows use to make us feel safe. Clips like "Dodging Katyushas" have helped Current earn respect from the TV establishment. "Current is what viewer-created content should be: smart, well-produced pieces that give me a look at stories I otherwise wouldn't get to see reported on TV," wrote Caroline Palmer, the editor of *Broadcast & Cable,* shortly after the clip aired.

Clearly I'm an unabashed fan of Current, and not only because it employs crowdsourcing or because it provides indisputable evidence that some of the most entertaining television is made well outside of Hollywood. I just like watching it. It's reality TV for smart people. I like that I don't know what's going to be on next. I like that the news segments show sides of a conflict that never make it to CNN. I like it for the same reason I like the public radio show *This American Life:* it tells stories from the world as lived by its inhabitants, as opposed to stories force-fed to its inhabitants. Watching Current, you wonder why no one made television like this before, and why networks aren't producing more of it.

As it happens, there are some pretty good reasons for that. For half a century, TV programming has been organized around the basic unit of measure in broadcasting, the "daypart." The 8:00 to 8:30 p.m. prime-time slot is a valuable daypart; the 4 a.m. to 5 a.m. slot, not so much. Networks base their programming schedule on dayparts. Should NBC move *My Name Is Earl* from Thursdays at eight to put it against Fox's *American Idol* on Tuesdays? Or would that draw too many viewers away from *30 Rock,* which follows *Earl* on Thursdays?

Current, by contrast, is just one 24-7 loop of five- to seven-minute videos on as diverse an array of subjects as can be imagined. There are no "shows," no reasons to tune in at 8 p.m. instead of 4 a.m.; and one never knows what might be on Current. This encourages drive-by viewing, and it greatly discourages "appointment TV," which is every network's ultimate goal—to make you structure your week around its schedule. As such, Current's approach to programming flies in the face of all conventional wisdom. There is a famous precedent for this approach, of course: MTV. But the commercial infeasibility of a schedule-less schedule is exactly why MTV moved away from music videos and toward producing shows like *The Real World* and *Pimp My Ride*.

Can the small, independently owned Current succeed where MTV—which is owned by cable giant Viacom—failed? That depends on your definition of success. In September 2007, the network won an Emmy for "Creative Achievement in Interactive Television." (In a neat bit of gimmickry, the Emmy producers had MySpace president Tom Anderson deliver the award to Al Gore and his partner, the financier Joel Hyatt, via a Web telecast.) It's safe to say the network would trade the award for more viewers.

A Process of Elimination

If I sound sympathetic to the predicament Current faced in its first forays into crowdsourcing, it's because I spent the first half of 2007 making the same mistakes. In that time I helped organize an experimental journalism project called Assignment Zero, an attempt to use crowdsourcing to conduct an extensive, far-reaching journalistic investigation. It was a pioneering effort, and it's true what they say about pioneers: they're the ones with arrows in their backs. In the end, I came to think of Assignment Zero as a highly satisfying failure. On one hand, we failed to meet our optimistic goals; on the other hand, by charging heedlessly into uncharted territory, we learned a great deal about how the crowd can come together to create great journalism. The basic principles behind successful crowdsourced journalism aren't much different from those behind successful crowdsourced television or photography.

Assignment Zero was a joint effort between *Wired* and NewAssignment.Net, the experimental journalism initiative started by New York University journalism professor Jay Rosen. In early 2006, Rosen began conceiving of a journalism project that would involve both professional and amateur contributors. But Rosen needed funding to staff up with the professionals he would need. Later that year he flew to San Francisco to meet with Evan Hansen, the editor in chief of Wired.com. Newly acquired by Condé Nast, Wired.com was looking to experiment broadly and boldly, particularly in the realm of so-called citizen journalism. It was a fortuitous meeting, and together the two created Assignment Zero, indicating the nascent character of citizen journalism. The aim was to have a crowd of volunteers write the definitive report on how crowds of volunteers are upending established businesses, from software to encyclopedias and beyond. We would use the crowd, in other words, to cover crowdsourcing. Having coined the term, I was brought in as a consultant. We launched in March 2007 with the intention of producing eighty feature articles—enough to fill a dozen magazines—over the course of twelve weeks. The result, we wrote when launching the project, would be "the most comprehensive knowledge base to date on the scope, limits, and best practices of crowdsourcing." We would post the features on NewAssignment.Net and would run a selection of the best stories on Wired.com.

But our strategy, as with Current's at the time it launched, revealed a fundamental misunderstanding of the crowd's interests and abilities. In a word, we were naive. To our credit, we conceived of Assignment Zero during a cultural moment when belief in the crowd's abilities—especially their capacity to "reboot the news," as Current's Robin Sloan puts it—ran high. Some of the most exciting moments in journalism over the past few years had been produced not by a handful of intrepid reporters, but by a legion of amateur photographers, bloggers, and videographers. When a massive tsunami swept across the resort beaches of Thailand and Indonesia, who brought the event home for the rest of the world? Amateurs. When terrorists set off a series of bombs on buses and subways in London, who produced the most riveting images and sound bites? The passengers and their cellphone cameras. Hurricane Katrina served to reinforce the point: as the waters rose and then receded, professional journalists—to say nothing of the victims' families—relied on information and images from those whose journalistic accreditation started and ended with the accident of their geographical location. The news media's primary contribution was to provide the Web forum on which people gathered to distribute information and images about what was happening inside the city. Traditional journalism seemed a woebegone, antiquated model. Ripe for the crowd, in other words. We didn't stay naive for long.

Like Throwing a Party

One of the first hurdles we faced was technological. We needed to build a site that would allow large numbers of contributors to sign up and participate in meaningful ways. We used Drupal, an open source publishing system that's become one of the leading platforms for community-driven projects. We wrote our optimism directly into the architecture of the site by creating some sixty topic pages (i.e., "Crowdsourcing the Novel"), each containing up to ten separate assignments (i.e., "Interview an expert on this subject"). After several months of design and testing, we were finally ready to go public.

"It's like throwing a party," Assignment Zero executive editor Lauren Sandler told the *New York Times* the day we launched. "You program the iPod, mix the punch, dim the lights, and at eight o'clock people show up. And then who knows what is going to happen?"

Like Current, we had far more guests than anticipated. Also like Current, we didn't have anyone there to greet them when they showed up. Rather than recruit people beforehand to manage each topic—doling out assignments, corresponding with would-be contributors, or just providing a friendly face—we decided to hold off building this essential layer of community managers until after the party had already started. It was a fateful mistake. The flood of guests made Assignment Zero's design flaws quickly apparent. Potential contributors—which numbered roughly five hundred after the first week—were routed to a single Assignment Zero staffer, a former washingtonpost.com editor, Steve Fox, who couldn't begin to correspond with them all.

The net effect was to put the organizational onus on the volunteers themselves. Baffled by the overarching concept of crowdsourcing, confused by the design of the website, and unable to connect directly to a manager or organizer, most of the initial volunteers simply drifted away. Over the course of the next two weeks, around thirty volunteer editors were assigned to manage various topics. But this presented a new set of hurdles. Each editor needed to be trained to use Drupal. Even once they were up to speed, there was a lack of understanding of the nature of open source projects. "What we really needed were people who understood online organizing," says David Cohn, an Assignment Zero editor. "But many of the editors just didn't have much experience with the Internet."

Crowdsourcing was both the subject of our investigation and the methodology of how we pursued it. That proved to be another mistake. The topic was simply too meta, too nebulous, *too new,* to gain the kind of immediate traction we needed given our twelve-week deadline. Plus, our directions on what we wanted were vague. The crowd might be enthusiastic, but they're not mind readers. Our contributors didn't know if they were supposed to be writing AP-style reports, blog entries, op-eds, or the kind of polemical screeds so ubiquitous on the Internet.

"What we learned," says Rosen, "is that you have to be *way* clearer in what you ask contributors to do. Just because they show up once doesn't mean they'll show up over and over. You have to engage them right away." All volunteer projects—be it citizen journalism, an open source programming project, or simply an AIDS walk— must inspire passion. Conflict in the Middle East inspires passion. Helping photographers improve their craft inspires passion. Using the crowd to investigate crowdsourcing inspired only confusion.

After roughly six weeks—halfway through its run— Assignment Zero reached its nadir. Most of the original volunteers were gone, the majority of topic pages were deserted, and communications between staffers, volun-

teer editors, and the remaining contributors were un-
even, resulting in frequent misunderstandings. A drastic
change was required. Although much had already gone
awry, we still had one advantage working in our favor:
hard-earned knowledge from six weeks of trial and
error.

The first order of business was a site redesign. Although none of us was in contact with Current at the
time, we were devising a similar approach to increasing
participation: adopt the social networking features common to Facebook or MySpace. We placed the editor's picture and e-mail at the top of each topic page and—most
important—provided a forum in which contributors
could gather and discuss the project. We, too, had tried to
establish a vertical relationship with each contributor;
we, too, had failed to grasp that the crowd didn't want to
just talk to us—they wanted to talk to each other. The effect of this reorganization was felt immediately, as contributors could now collaborate openly with one another
and review one another's reporting. The *Cincinnati Enquirer* made deft use of this approach: don't try to control
the discussion, just provide the room in which it takes
place.

However, the majority of topic pages had yet to attract a base of interested volunteers. We had created our
topics in the belief that people would happily work on
any assignment we made available. But as Livingstone
and Cooperstein are well aware, you can't issue direc-
tives to a community, you can only offer suggestions. If
people follow you, great. If not, you follow the community. We learned this lesson through sheer necessity.
With less than six weeks left in Assignment Zero's run,
we had to jettison most of our topic pages, which required painfully excising those topics I considered most

important. We concentrated instead on the topics that had gained traction in the community—including those, such as crowdsourced novels, that I'd never have thought to assign. But that wasn't our last slice of humble pie: people might want to reboot the news, but that doesn't mean they want to write it. In response, we shifted priorities again and asked contributors to conduct Q&As with people involved in crowdsourcing efforts.

The changes had an immediate, and positive, impact. Asking our volunteers to "write the story on open source car design" had had all the appeal of asking them to rewrite their college term papers. Asking them to talk to someone they admire and respect met with a far warmer response. All efforts were now focused on what we called "interview week," which was intended to be a five-day flurry of activity, with contributors interviewing sources and transcribing the interviews to create fifty Q&As. Community activity increased exponentially. Contributors even unearthed additional subjects to interview, and our list of Q&A subjects soon exceeded seventy-five. Given clear direction and an appealing task to work on, Assignment Zero volunteers quickly rallied. "The crowdsourcing gears finally kicked in," says Cohn.

In the final two weeks of the project, Assignment Zero even began to resemble a professional journalism outfit. Editors and contributors discussed potential questions; the interviews were scheduled, conducted, transcribed, filed, and edited. And as they began pouring in, it became clear that many would exceed our expectations. In my rough count, at least sixty of the eighty interviews would stand up to professional scrutiny, which is to say the interviewer was well informed, asked challenging questions, and managed to elicit interesting (and occasionally fascinating) commentary from his or her subject. A mutual embrace of experimentation ran through all the interviews, a cheerful admission that the kinds of collaborative efforts enabled by the Internet are both powerful and yet still in their infancy. "We need to try different things," the prominent political blogger Susan Gardner told one of our contributors. "The process of elimination is undervalued. What's wrong with trying something, assessing, and taking it as positive information that this particular model doesn't work? That's not failure. That's important information."

What the interviews also make clear is that contributors volunteered to tackle subjects about which they were passionate and knowledgeable. In this they held a considerable advantage over professionals, who often must complete interviews with little time (or inclination) for advance research. It is a community's ability to allocate intellectual resources organically in this way that can make it a more efficient machine than a traditional, hierarchical organization. It's exactly this miracle of self-organization that makes crowdsourcing, in the best of circumstances, so efficient. In the final analysis Assignment Zero could boast of a significant accomplishment: it embodied the best of crowdsourcing while simultaneously studying it.

Eyes and Ears: Journalism in the Age of the Network

Not long after Assignment Zero concluded, NYU's Jay Rosen published a set of "coordinates" for crowdsourced journalism. Number one, Rosen writes, "get the division of labor right." Simply put, most participants will have a very limited amount of time to contribute. Sometimes it's ten minutes per week, sometimes it's ten hours, but tasks have to be constructed to accommodate a range of commitment levels. This is as true in other spheres of crowdsourcing as it is in journalism, and it explains why Current has rejiggered their formula to air photos and short webcam footage as well as their bread-and-butter "pods," which can take weeks to shoot and edit.

Number two is to understand participants' motivations before asking them to contribute. "The difference between an amateur journalism production and a command-and-control system like a newsroom is profound and decisive," Rosen writes. Which is why, he rightly believes, an amateur production will never replace a system of paid correspondents. But it could very well supplement one.

Assignment Zero, Rosen has said, was just the dry run. Rosen has continued to use the NewAssignment.Net platform to launch crowdsourced journalism projects. One, called Beat Blogging, helps professional journalists utilize social networking software to assemble a specialized crowd that can help improve the reporter's understanding of the complex subjects he or she is forced to tackle.

Around the time Assignment Zero ended, I helped launch a crowdsourcing initiative at the *Brian Lehrer Show,* a news-driven talk show broadcast on WNYC, National Public Radio's affiliate in New York City. Unlike Assignment Zero, Lehrer's team started small. On the morning the broadcast aired, we asked listeners to count the number of trucks or SUVs on the street outside their homes. The show received more than four hundred fifty responses from all five boroughs, allowing listeners and contributors alike to draw some interesting conclusions. This conformed to Rosen's observation that one must accommodate for people with lots of enthusiasm but little time. The SUV project only asked listeners for a few minutes of their day, and it involved a concise, easily communicated assignment. The results were unremarkable—about half of the vehicles on New York City streets were trucks or SUVs, which is about the national average—but listeners loved it. Next, the show asked people to choose a local grocery store or deli and record the price of a six-pack of Budweiser, a quart of milk, and a head of lettuce. This time the conclusions were more revealing. The radio show displayed the results on a map on its homepage showing that geography had little to do with price. Delis in the ghetto, the show discovered, often gouged their customers as cravenly as did shops in the ritziest Park Avenue neighborhoods.

This is precisely the kind of journalism at which the crowd will always prove superior to professionals, for the simple reason that the crowd outnumbers them. Journalism is fertile ground for crowdsourcing for many of the same reasons that the sciences are: much of the basic labor involved in reporting—as in scientific research—lies in the sort of data collection that requires little training. A newspaper can scarcely afford to send twenty-five reporters across the city to determine the price deviation of a head of lettuce. It falls below and beyond the newspaper's mandate. But it's important information for a resident, and, like the SUV experiment, the price survey proved highly popular with WNYC's listeners.

It's a model that works just as effectively when the stakes are considerably higher. Early in 2007, the readers of the liberal news blog TalkingPointsMemo.com, or TPM, noticed a pattern in the firings of U.S. Attorneys in Arkansas and California. Working with the community at TPM as well as his staff of reporters, Josh Micah

Marshall, TPM's editor and publisher, was able to connect the dots and determine that the attorneys were being forced out for not conforming to the Bush Administration's agenda. Mainstream outlets soon picked up the story, drawing further attention to the scandal. The awesome potency of TPM's community became clear the night of March 19, 2007, when the Department of Justice disclosed three thousand pages of e-mails, memos, and other internal records relating to the attorney firings. The "document dump," as such disclosures are called, came too late at night for newspapers to do more than skim the contents. Marshall, however, sicced his readers on the DOJ documents. The readers divided the papers into fifty-page chunks and made remarkably quick work of it. According to an article in the *New York Sun*, "The first post about the records hit the site at 1:04 a.m. Within half an hour, there were 50 summaries posted by readers gleaning the documents. By 4:30 a.m. more than 220 postings were up detailing various aspects of the files," including uncovering references to "Karl's shop," a clear indication of the White House's political involvement in the dismissals. It was a stunning display of how the crowd's sheer numbers could supplement the limited resources of a professional news outlet. In early 2008, Marshall and TPM were awarded the prestigious George Polk Award for Legal Reporting for its "tenacious investigative reporting." This is the kind of model that holds enormous promise, and that I predict we'll see much more of in coming months and years. Such examples capitalize on the crowd's most salient characteristic: the power of large numbers.

This basic epiphany—that we are all better served when the crowd complements what journalists do, rather than trying to replicate it—animates the Vancouver,

Canada-based NowPublic.com. "We think of our members as an army of eyes and ears," says Leonard Brody, the company's CEO. "But we're not asking them to be journalists. The phrase 'citizen journalism' makes about as much sense as 'citizen dentist.' " Instead, NowPublic asks their network of 130,000 users spread across 140 countries to simply upload photos and videos and in some cases do basic reporting any time they witness a newsworthy event. The company then sells the content to news organizations such as the Associated Press (AP), which recently signed a distribution deal with NowPublic. "What we learned from the experiments with citizen journalism is that people are great at recording what they see, or taking pictures, but not so great at analysis and horrible at packaging," says Brody. "We're probably closer to iStockphoto's model."

The AP has a larger network of correspondents—three thousand reporters, photographers, and videographers—than any news organization in the world. But that's a drop in the bucket compared to the number that's signed up with NowPublic, a fact Jim Kennedy, AP's director of strategic planning, is happy to admit. "It's a big world out there. We use NowPublic to get a more comprehensive map of coverage, an additional radar system beyond our own correspondents." Kennedy notes that with the Web, the goal for a news outlet is no longer to simply get one or two good photographs. "We want as much image coverage as we can get. When we talk about crowdsourcing it's focused on finding a good nugget that would add to our report, but I think it will add up to much more than that eventually. I can imagine a whole lot of contributions—amateurs as well as professionals—that could be woven into the coverage."

Crowdsourcing is going through a period of adaptation.

In the end it would be foolhardy to fault the crowd for any of Assignment Zero's missteps. The failures were those of organization, timing, and community management, not a lack of response on the part of our volunteers. What was abundantly clear, even in our limited experiment, was that there is an immeasurable amount of enthusiasm to participate in a project that people find rewarding and meaningful.

Ironically, it's just this enthusiasm—evident in iStock, Assignment Zero, and, as this book goes to press, Current as well—that has created one of crowdsourcing's greatest conundrums: the crowd responds in such great volume—think of iStock's 2 million photographs, or the 80 million videos posted to YouTube—that the task of sorting through it all is far too time-consuming to be done by all but the largest teams of employees. Fortunately, that's where the crowd performs its niftiest trick of all: the crowd, as we'll see next, is its own best filter.

8

WHAT THE CROWD THINKS

How the 10 Percent Filters
the Wheat from the Chaff

Everything you ever wanted to know about crowdsourcing can be found on the Fox television network on Tuesday and Wednesday nights. That's when *American Idol,* the hugely popular televised singing competition, puts some of the most (and least) talented crooners, divas, and rockers in the country on a national stage and lets the viewers decide who's best. Thousands of contestants audition for the show each season and, after being winnowed down by a panel of celebrity judges, the semifinalists are voted in or out via text message and phone calls by viewers. *American Idol,* like Threadless, neatly encapsulates two of the most essential aspects of crowdsourcing. The crowd provides the creative talent as well as the acumen to rank that talent.

Idol's first episode, in the summer of 2000, suffered from poor ratings, but the series didn't languish for long. Viewership increased steadily over the summer. The season finale, in which Kelly Clarkson defeated Justin Guarini, was watched by 23 million people, an almost unheard-of audience for a summer show. *American Idol* has since become a commercial juggernaut, with versions broadcast in thirty other countries and some of the most valuable advertising real estate on television. The other networks don't even bother to contest its dominance on the nights it appears. NBC staffers call *American Idol* the "Death Star" for its ability to obliterate all possible competitors. In its sixth season finale, a total of 80 million votes were cast. That's about the same number of votes cast in the 2006 midterm elections in the United States.

American Idol heralded the dawn of a new era. Voting was no longer something you did in an elementary-school gymnasium every couple of years; it was something you did every few days over your cell phone. Voting became part of the culture of consumption. Simon Fuller wasn't the first entrepreneur to use voting to engage an audience, but he revealed consumers' considerable desire to exercise greater control over what might be loosely called "the production process." Today people have the opportunity to vote on everything from the flavor of their snack chips to—if you're reading this in the United Kingdom—the cover of this book. It's part of a subtle but significant shift in power from producers to consumers.

Obviously, putting such decisions to a vote is a form of crowdsourcing. But more than that, the crowd's ability to act as a filter has become an integral element of crowdsourcing efforts ranging from iStockphoto to YouTube to Dell's IdeaStorm. Simply put, the contributions generated by the crowd are just too numerous for anyone but the crowd itself to filter. For instance, if I search for images on iStockphoto using the key word "doctor," I receive more than ten thousand results. Obviously iStock doesn't expect its clients to wade through thousands of images. Fortunately, they've already been arranged according to "Ratings" and "Downloads." Any iStock user can rate a photograph. Over time, thousands of these ratings accumulate, creating a reliable hierarchy that allows easy access to the best images on the site. "Downloads" simply measures the commercial popularity of individual photographs, like any best-seller list. In combination the two metrics create an effective system of ordering the vast numbers of photographs and illustrations—2 million and counting—on iStockphoto.

iStock isn't unique in this regard, but representative. YouTube relies on a similar combination of "Views" (which measures how many people have watched a video) and ratings. Likewise, Current's community helps determine the network's programming, both through online comments and voting. Even Peer-to-Patent—the public patent review project—uses a rating system to highlight the most useful and relevant comments on a patent application. These features are far less a clever ploy to engage a user community (though they serve that function admirably) than a survival mechanism. A traditional gatekeeper—that is to say, a paid employee—could never process and rank the millions of songs, videos, poems, video games, product designs, blueprints, and scientific formulas that flood the networks. Only the collective attention of the crowd, and its enthusiastic embrace of the five-star system, has the capacity—the sheer manpower—to create an effective filter. Without it, YouTube would be an undifferentiated morass of stupid pet tricks. With it, YouTube poses the greatest threat to Hollywood since the invention of the television.

In fact, this crowd filter is such a potent force that the

collective decisions made by millions of Internet users is being used to create a comprehensive classification system governing the massive amounts of information available on the World Wide Web. This might take the form of "social media" sites such as Digg.com, where users vote on which news stories of the day deserve attention, or of the emerging "folksonomy," through which users apply "tags," or key words, to the information they run across online, thereby creating an alternative, crowdsourced taxonomy. The principle is the same: the amount of material currently available online greatly outstrips the ability of any one individual to classify and organize it. The crowd is both the source of the information as well as the force behind its organization.

Crowdsourcing is a volume business: as such it's beholden to an axiom of user-generated content called Sturgeon's Law. This holds that 90 percent of everything (and user-generated content in particular) is, in a word, crap. Theodore Sturgeon was a well-regarded science fiction author, who composed his theory after "twenty years of wearying defense of science fiction against the attacks of people who used the worst examples of the field for ammunition." Sturgeon concluded that while 90 percent of science fiction was indeed not worth the paper it was printed on, this same rule could be applied to everything else. Sturgeon died in 1985, but he clearly anticipated the rise of YouTube.

The flipside to Sturgeon's Law, of course, is that 10 percent of everything *isn't* crap, and a somewhat smaller percentage is downright good. In the case of crowdcasting, for instance, if you're broadcasting a problem, your odds of finding a solution increase alongside the size of the group to which you broadcast it. This basic math is equally true in the crowdsourcing of creativity. As the number of submissions increases, so does the proportion that is valuable (or salable, or simply usable). Of course, this raises the problem of sifting the excellent from the execrable. Do you want to sort through ten thousand images of doctors? Of course not; who would? But spread that task across the entire spectrum of people visiting iStockphoto's site—who simply have to rate the photos as they come across them—and the job becomes not just feasible, but kind of fun.

Which brings us to another emerging rule of participatory media, the 1:10:89 rule, which says that for every 100 people on a given site, 1 will actually create something, another 10 will vote on what he created, and the remaining 89 will merely consume the creation (this is sometimes referred to as the 1:9:90 rule as well, though the principle remains the same). The numbers are hardly arbitrary. Bradley Horowitz, the VP of the Advanced Development Division at Yahoo, postulated the 1:10:89 rule after observing some common themes in the ways people used Yahoo Groups, the photo-sharing site Flickr (which Yahoo acquired in March 2005), and Wikipedia. (Jimmy Wales, Wikipedia founder, has observed that half of all edits to the online encyclopedia are made by just 2.5 percent of all users.) Horowitz's epiphany "is that we don't need to convert 100 percent of the audience into 'active' participants to have a thriving product that benefits tens of millions of users." Further, Horowitz wrote, the activity of the 10 percent—who vote and rate submissions, start and contribute to online discussions, and generally help police a site, deleting offensive or superfluous content—is as valuable to any online community as the actions of the "supercontributors" that make up the 1 percent. For this crucial 10 percent, "the act of consumption was itself an act of creation."

The previous chapter was devoted to what the 1 percent does. This chapter examines the role of an equally essential class of contributor—the 10 percent. Not everyone can design a T-shirt that is at once funny, visually pleasing, and resonant with a moment in culture, and not everyone can carry a tune. But you don't have to be a talented designer or a born chanteuse to recognize these attributes, which is why the Threadless community numbers in the hundreds of thousands instead of the tens of thousands. Clearly *American Idol*'s appeal extends well beyond aspiring performers. It takes critical mass to elicit enough contributions to ensure that a certain fraction of them is worth using, but it's equally important to build up another kind of critical mass: an active community of voters who will enthusiastically dig around in the rough to unearth a few diamonds.

Would You Buy This?

There's another advantage to having an active 10 percent of your community interacting on your site. Each week Threadless receives hundreds of submissions, only a handful of which will be printed up and sold to customers. Since its founding in 2000, Threadless has succeeded wildly in one of the riskiest possible markets, dominated by the tastes of the notoriously fickle youth demographic. Threadless's products should be marked by hits and misses, following the same kind of power law distribution seen in the music industry, in which a handful of hits pays for thousands of misses. Yet Threadless has never had a flop—it has sold out of every T-shirt it has ever produced.

How? Threadless understands that it's *fun* to vote,

and in allowing its customers the opportunity to determine the company's inventory, it is essentially serving that community, which was the company's motivation when it was founded. But as MIT Sloan School of Management professor Frank T. Piller and Kobe University professor Susumu Ogawa pointed out in a paper published in 2006, Threadless is doing something much savvier than simply offering their community a voice in the production process. "In fact, it follows a strategy that turns market research into quick sales," they write. "All products sold by Threadless are inspected and approved by user consensus before any larger investment is made into a new product." Threadless allows their users to rank T-shirt designs from zero to five, but they're also able to check an "I'd buy it!" box next to the scale. Piller and Ogawa call this strategy "collective customer commitment," and it's a useful way of looking at the dual benefits of giving your customers a vote. They're happy to be involved; for your part, you know how many widgets to make. The elegance of the Threadless model, in which users both submit T-shirt designs and vote on a winner, is that the company not only gets virtual volunteers to create their shirts, it simultaneously knows how much demand exists for every shirt it produces. Small wonder every shirt sells out.

In many ways, it's a natural evolutionary step. If the customer is always right, why not give him better tools to express his preference? And now we're endowed with a technology capable of determining what the customer wants with far greater accuracy and ease. The advantage to a manufacturer or retailer or service provider is rather clear: the better you understand consumer demand, the better you can supply it. One can think of crowd voting mechanisms as market research on steroids. Why pay to convene expensive, laborious, and ultimately dubious focus groups when a much broader swath of your customers will gladly communicate their preferences with far greater accuracy online?

By this light, Simon Fuller's most brilliant maneuver when creating *American Idol* wasn't the institution of audience voting. It was requiring each contestant to sign a contract stipulating that Fuller's management company, 19 Entertainment, would represent them. The show's notoriously brutal judge, Simon Cowell, works at the music label Sony BMG, which exercises a similar claim to sign every contestant to a recording contract. Each season's winner receives a million-dollar contract as a jackpot reward, but the real winners are Sony BMG and 19 Entertainment. The first single released by an *American Idol* contestant, "A Moment Like This," by Kelly Clarkson, had the biggest jump in *Billboard* history when it shot from number fifty-two to number one on the American pop charts in a single week, breaking a record set by the Beatles.

Subsequent winners have proven to be just as successful, and Cowell estimates that Sony BMG has sold somewhere around 100 million albums from *American Idol* contestants alone. Clarkson and her fellow *Idol* alum Carrie Underwood account for 20 million albums sold. In a *60 Minutes* interview in March 2007, Cowell said that his "only interest in *Idol* was as a vehicle to launch records." It's an ingenious strategy. Not only does the show itself act as a promotional channel, with access to one of the largest consistent audiences in television history, but the voting provides Cowell, Fuller, and the other music executives at 19 Entertainment and Sony BMG with a fine-tuned gauge of consumer demand for the singers' talents. In this light, *American Idol* isn't a TV show; it's the largest focus group in history. Consumption is the logical conclusion to the crowdsourcing process, and voters are simply customers who haven't opened their wallet yet.

Such appealing—if vaguely unsettling—logic has hardly been lost on the rest of corporate America. Frito-Lay has been actively exploring various forms of crowdsourcing. It has put the crowd to work suggesting names for new flavors, as well as choosing which of these flavors should go into long-term production. In 2006, it held a competition to create new TV ads for its Doritos brand. Then it asked visitors to the site to pick their favorite among five clips chosen by Frito-Lay. The most popular video—in which a man-size mouse crashes through a wall to get to some of those cheeeeesy Doritos—ran in the 2007 Super Bowl. For the 2008 Super Bowl, the company aired a sixty-second video by twenty-two-year-old singer-songwriter Kina Grannis, who had—you guessed it—been voted to the top from a number of entries. As this book goes to press, there are no fewer than seventeen contests on YouTube to create ads for everything from Schick razors to, somewhat improbably, the TurboTax software program.

These tactics follow an increasingly familiar formula: Ask the crowd to upload a video that demonstrates its passion for the product. Offer a grand prize of several thousand dollars and, of course, fifteen minutes of fame. Then ask everyone else to vote for the winner. In its current contest, Schick demonstrates how important it thinks the voting process is to the overall promotion: "Don't want to upload a video, or are you just plain interested in watching the submissions? Then help us choose who is going to move on to the finals by rating the videos based on their level of *experimental* creativity. The top 50 percent of videos will be considered for the finals!" The sponsor usually reserves ultimate control over which spot will appear on TV.

Nor are such promotions restricted to the creation of commercials. In October 2007, Intel launched CoolSW, which stands for "cool software." The site allows people to post write-ups on new software start-ups that have caught their interest. The rest of the CoolSW community then votes on the companies, and the ones with the most votes rise to the front page. As the moment, some of the most popular programs include a Web service that allows a user to easily convert floor plans into 3-D buildings in Google Earth, and an application that converts Power-Point presentations into Web pages. Needless to say, Intel isn't only doing this to drive traffic to its site (though that's an added bonus) or endear itself to the community of tech-watchers on the Web (though that would surely be a welcome by-product). Intel is trying to discover growth opportunities for its products. "Hardware doesn't matter at this point," said Bob O'Donnell, an analyst with research firm IDC. All the newfangled mobile devices will need chips, and Intel, O'Donnell said, clearly believes the crowd can determine which of those devices are bound for glory and which will wind up in the already overflowing technological dustbin.

And of course I couldn't very well publish a book about crowdsourcing without practicing it myself. Last December, Random House UK and the London-based design firm Apt joined up to crowdsource the dust-jacket design of the British edition of *Crowdsourcing*. And in keeping with the formula, the crowd not only submitted designs but also voted on a winner. Or rather, the votes were tallied to create a short list of twenty entries from which we selected a winner. Such an experiment—

Random House UK called it, appropriately, "coversourcing"—is a rarity in the generally cautious world of book publishing. And it served its primary purpose—the creation of a witty, appealing cover design—admirably. More than three hundred designs were submitted, and twenty thousand votes cast. By opening up the design process to the crowd, we elicited a degree of visual inventiveness and originality that is rarely on display on the shelves at the local big-box bookseller. For the most part the crowd proved astute in its judgment, voting the best entries into the top twenty.

Voting in Hypertext

In the last ten years, the quantity of information available online has since expanded at an exponential rate: there are now some 15 billion webpages, to say nothing of the images, music, videos, and other forms of media that have propagated wildly across the Internet. This information buffet has grown so large, in fact, that the task of sorting and ordering its contents has come to occupy some of the finest minds in computer science. It's a task of urgent necessity for companies that depend on their ability to create order from the chaos created by almost unlimited choice.

For the most part, crowdsourcing is still an emerging phenomenon. In one crucial respect, though, crowdsourcing has already become a predominant force in our culture. The crowd's ability to act as a filter makes a business like iStockphoto, or an effort like the Frito-Lay Super Bowl promotion, possible. But the same principle applies on a much grander scale: our collective judgment is the primary force at work in giving order to the Web, the largest storehouse of information ever known. The engine that makes all this possible? Google.

Google's search engine has transferred the power of determining the significance of information—be it in a newspaper article or a blog entry—into the hands of the crowd. This marks a dramatic departure from how people were accustomed to experiencing the Web. Before Google, experts, not the crowd, decided what merited attention. Google's founders, Sergey Brin and Larry Page, weren't intending to upset the reign of the expert. In fact, when the two were just Stanford graduate students working out the algorithm that would become the linchpin of Google's search technology, they took their inspiration from the system of annotation and citation used in academic publishing.

Scholarly journals serve another function beyond disseminating advances in fields such as physical anthropology and organic chemistry. They are the means by which academics secure tenure and establish their reputations among their colleagues. In writing an article for publication, a professor carefully builds an argument through citations to the existing literature in the field, much as a lawyer might burnish a case through citing precedent in writing a legal brief. A single scholarly paper is chockfull of citations to other scholarly papers. Collectively, the academic literature forms its own web of citations.

In the 1950s, an American linguist named Eugene Garfield conceived a method to quantify the relative importance of a given paper. Citation analysis, as it's come to be known, involves counting the number of times a paper is cited by other papers. Thus, Einstein's famous 1905 article proposing his theory of relativity is the fifth-most-"important" paper published before 1930, having been cited four hundred fifty times.

Larry Page's breakthrough was to realize that the hyperlink was really just a citation and the Web itself a densely interconnected literary corpus, no different, effectively, from that produced by decades of academic publishing. Just as an academic will cite Einstein's "On the Electrodynamics of Moving Bodies," the foodie website Chowhound.com might cite Mark Bittman's *Best Recipes in the World* in an article on ceviche. Sure, the first example might involve cosmic physics and the other a preparation for raw fish, but according to textual dynamics, the links between the two are identical.

This observation—that a link is essentially just a citation writ in hypertext—seems commonplace in retrospect, but it was a remarkable observation at the time. In 1995, the Web was barely a year old, and "search engines" were in their infancy. At the time, Yahoo—then, as now, one of the Web's most popular destinations—was just a directory of websites created by Yahoo's founders, Jerry Yang and David Filo. The Internet's contents were ranked by Filo, Yang, and their employees, not through the independent actions of the collective users of the Web. (Yahoo added a separate search function in late 1995.) Other search engines, such as AltaVista, worked by sending out "spiders" that would crawl the Internet and send back lists of webpages that would then be organized into a central index, but there was no effective way of ranking results by relevance. Someone searching for "toxic waste" would be as likely to discover a page devoted to the obscure Irish punk band by that name as an Environmental Protection Agency listing of toxic sites in the United States. The technology did little to tame the essential anarchy of the Internet.

Google formally incorporated on September 7, 1998. It employed the founders' algorithm (called PageRank, a witty play on Larry Page's last name) that essentially did for the Web what Garfield did for academic publishing. PageRank determined the relevance and importance of a website by counting the number of other sites linking to it, as well as the number of sites linking to *those* sites. Say, for the sake of argument, that both the EPA page on toxic waste sites and the Toxic Waste fan page are linked to ten times. But the EPA page has been linked to by various university websites, several newspapers, and a senator's home page, all of which are in turn linked to by hundreds of smaller sites. The total number of links in this extended network determines a site's "Googlejuice," or where it appears on the rankings. In this case, the EPA would far outstrip the band fan page, which is linked to by equally obscure websites. PageRank includes other variables as well—more than two hundred, according to John Battelle in *The Search: How Google and Its Rivals Rewrote the Rules of Business and Transformed Our Culture*—but this measurement of links remains the primary ingredient. Google's search function was so effective at determining relevance, the sine qua non of a good search engine, that the site quickly became the dominant player in the Web search industry.

What Google has demonstrated is that people's individual decisions, properly aggregated, are capable of organizing an otherwise unmanageably vast amount of information. The crowd's collective decision-making power is expressed in the form of links, which Page and Brin characterized as "votes" in their original academic paper. By relying on the uncoordinated actions of millions of individuals, rather than experts, to classify and order contents on the Internet, Google almost single-handedly overturned centuries of conventional wisdom.

The beauty of Google's system is that it requires no

additional effort on the part of individual users. The crowd expresses its judgment as part of its natural behavior. In the process, its collected actions become a database of knowledge in itself. Google doesn't have to assign people to read and analyze all 15 billion webpages. The crowd does that all on its own.

While PageRank may be the most ubiquitous system to use the crowd's collective judgments as an organizational apparatus, it's far from the only application of the idea. Amazon and Netflix both use data produced by the crowd to recommend books and movies to their customers. The current term for this is "collaborative filtering," but it's an age-old process. "At its core, collaborative filtering is any mechanism whereby members of a community collaborate to identify what is good and what is bad," write the authors of *Word of Mouse: The Marketing Power of Collaborative Filtering*. Or more to the point, what is relevant or irrelevant to the individual. Computers simply allow us to perform this task with a much greater quantity of information and for a great many more users.

The first automated collaborative filter was developed at Xerox PARC, the California computer lab behind such innovations as the computer mouse and the laser printer. In the early 1990s, the virtual message board Usenet was in wide use among PARC's researchers, who depended on Usenet articles to stay abreast of developments in their field. Articles were delivered via e-mail, which led to a plague that now afflicts anyone with an e-mail account: the overflowing inbox. In 1992, four scientists at PARC built a system called Tapestry that allowed readers to annotate each document with commentary or merely attach a "likeit" or "hateit" label. Consequently, recipients could filter the thousands of incoming messages and articles by asking the server to send on only those with favorable reviews.

But the Tapestry project was limited in scope, as it was restricted to PARC employees. A few years later a group of computer scientists from MIT and other universities released GroupLens, which also ranked Usenet articles. GroupLens improved on Tapestry in a number of ways. For one, anyone could use it, which meant that GroupLens had access to far more data than Tapestry. It worked by analyzing numerical ratings that readers assigned to various articles and then grouping like-minded users together, on the assumption that if they had agreed in the past they would agree in the future. In 1995, the MIT Media Lab applied the technology to music when it launched the Helpful Online Music Recommendations site. MIT soon rebranded the site Firefly and took on investors with the hope of selling its collaborative filtering technology to other companies. Eventually acquired, and then shuttered, by Microsoft, Firefly attracted a dedicated community of music lovers and inspired other music recommendation engines, such as the popular online service Last.FM.

But it was the giant online bookseller Amazon that popularized collaborative filters. Amazon's innovation was to analyze the connections between items rather than users. In other words, by carefully tracking what each customer purchases, Amazon can use the massive amount of resulting data to draw connections between, say, Arnold Rampersad's biography of Ralph Ellison and Junot Díaz's novel *The Brief Wondrous Life of Oscar Wao*. The books don't have anything in common and yet people who buy one often buy the other. Why? Amazon doesn't hazard a guess, and doesn't need to. Merely highlighting the relationship between the two, it has found, drives sales. Amazon's recommendations have proven so effective that similar systems have been adopted by a wide array of websites.

Although collaborative filters generally refer to recommender systems like the one employed by Amazon, they provide a useful context in which to examine how the crowd's general preferences are being used all around us every day. Such collective judgment mechanisms fall into two categories—active and passive. Amazon uses a passive filter, because it employs data that is merely the by-product of the purchases its customers make on the company's website. Passive filtering takes the data we generate simply by going about our modern, digital lives—adding links to our blogs, watching a video on YouTube, buying a mixing bowl at Williams-Sonoma.com—and uses it to organize information in some meaningful way.

PARC's experimental system, by contrast, was an active filter, because the technology relied on the conscious acts of users applying a ranking to the material at hand. Netflix uses an active filter, though the company is after the same goal as Amazon—sell (or rent, in Netflix's case) more product by recommending options that are tailored to the particular tastes of each individual user. But whereas Amazon bases its collaborative filter on the buying patterns of its customers, Netflix relies on its members to rate the movies they watch in order to power its "Cinematch" recommendation system. Likewise, the eBay rating system relies on buyers to rank sellers based on their dependability and trustworthiness.

Recently, crowd filters have spread far beyond search technologies and e-commerce. Just as librarians once created indexes to organize the contents of their libraries by subject matter, Web users are increasingly indexing both the content they create and consume with "tags."

For instance, I assign tags to every blog post I write. For a post about Frito-Lay's use of crowdsourcing to create a Super Bowl commercial, I used the tags "Doritos" and "advertising." Anyone searching the Web for "crowd-sourcing" and "Doritos" will find my post at the top of the heap. Such labels—whether it's a library card cata-log from the 1950s or the tags used to describe a blog post—are called "metadata."

Tagging started with blogs, but they were quickly ap-plied to the many other forms of social media that were emerging at the turn of this century. The Web bookmark utility Del.icio.us and the photo-sharing site Flickr rely on tags to allow individual users to categorize their book-marks and photos. But in aggregate, all this metadata com-prises a user-generated classification system. If I search Del.icio.us for webpages related to "fly-fishing" (everyone needs an escape from technology), I get 2,509 sites that different individuals tagged as pertaining to fly-fishing, in-cluding everything from a guide on various fishing knots to a site that specializes in underwater photos of trout.

This ground-up taxonomy is called a "folksonomy," and it's of great interest to library scientists. "Profession-ally created metadata is costly in terms of time and effort to produce. This makes it very difficult to scale and keep up with the vast amounts of new content being produced, especially in new mediums like the Web," notes one early paper on folksonomies. While folksonomies pose consider-able drawbacks—they are, the author notes, "fundamen-tally chaotic"—they're also incredibly responsive to a user's needs and, best of all, infinitely scalable. The advan-tage folksonomies offer is no different than that of many other crowdsourcing applications: it makes an overwhelm-ing task manageable.

The adoption of such crowd filters has far outpaced

the growth of other forms of crowdsourcing. Even the news we get has been shaped by the aggregated judgments of millions of readers. Most news outlets—from NPR to the *New York Times*—run a sidebar on their websites ranking stories according to their popularity with readers. "It can be gamed," notes David Carr, media columnist at the *Times*. "An animal, preferably a dolphin or some relationship drama, can reliably move the needle. The editors pay attention, and reporters know when they've rung the bell."

This all amounts to a sea change in how we experience the world around us. If ever there was a realm in which the expert once reigned uncontested, it was in the selection and organization of the world's knowledge. Yet in a few short years, this function has been largely democratized. And as with all forms of democracy, the positive effects never come without some disturbing consequences.

The Great Digg Riot of 2007

The *New York Times* boasts the most popular website of any newspaper in the world, with 12 million people visiting NYTimes.com every month. And yet just over half that number get their news from a site that doesn't employ a single reporter: Digg.com. Founded in 2004, Digg is one of several "social news" sites that are playing an increasingly prominent role in the complex information ecology of the Web. Like Del.icio.us and Flickr, Digg does one single thing very well. Users submit a news article or blog post or any other link. Other users then vote on, or "digg," the submission. Those with the most votes appear on Digg's home page. The result is a hodgepodge of the day's best op-ed columns, clips from *The Daily Show*, and—reflecting the demographics of Digg's core readership—news from the world of video games.

It's not Digg's popularity, per se, that makes it significant, but the fact that the links that make it to Digg's front page tend to enjoy a second life in further news stories and blog posts. Digg has an amplification effect, in other words, as do its competitors, Reddit and StumbleUpon. This multiplier effect can make or break a company or individual—a power that was once restricted to the mainstream media.

A few years back, I started receiving press releases for a social networking site called Famster. It was intended to be a MySpace for families, and I wrote it off as another pallid imitation destined for obscurity. And sure enough, when it went live on August 7, 2006, Famster had an exceedingly difficult time generating interest from consumers. Then, on August 13, Henry Wang, a seventeen-year-old from Aurora, Illinois, posted a link to Famster on Digg. "I can't believe that this site isn't widely known, even with all its features: share photos, stream videos, create a blog, upload files . . . and for free? Ridiculous." More than 1,700 people "dugg" Wang's post. Famster received roughly 50,000 unique visitors per day during the week Wang's post spent on the Digg front page, virtually guaranteeing Famster's survival in one of the most competitive marketplaces—social networking—on the World Wide Web.

And who holds this power? Not Kevin Rose or Jay Adelson, the founders of Digg. "You won't find editors at Digg—we're here to provide a place where people can collectively determine the value of content," Digg's website notes. "We're changing the way people consume information online." But change, as Rose and Adelson discovered, is a sword that cuts both ways.

An innocuous sequence of letters and numbers along the lines of "04-x3-15-00-5x-89-5c-4d-1j-55-41-69" (the actual code is widely available online) almost destroyed Digg. It was the decryption code that allowed a user to override the copy protection of HD-DVDs, and on May 1, 2007, it was published in a blog post that landed on Digg. The site's readers quickly voted the story onto the front page, and within hours the site received a cease-and-desist order from the technology consortium behind the HD-DVD technology. The site complied almost instantly: the offending article was taken down. So began the Great Digg Riot of 2007.

The Digg community interpreted Rose's decision as censorship. The code was resubmitted and taken down again. And again. And again. Soon the community banded together to vote up any submission containing the offending code. The Diggers had effectively staged a coup. Because the community determines what appears on the front page, it possesses ultimate control of what is published. Rose and his staff couldn't delete the posts fast enough, and within a few hours Digg's top five pages were overrun with articles containing the code. The Diggers wanted to know: Would Rose side with them or with the corporate interests behind HD-DVD?

For most of the day, Digg erred on the side of safety. As Jay Adelson, Digg's CEO, noted in a blog post, "Whether you agree or disagree with the policies of the intellectual property holders and consortiums, in order for Digg to survive, it must abide by the law. Digg's Terms of Use, and the terms of use of most popular sites, are required by law to include policies against the infringement of intellectual property." A reasonable enough appeal, but it wasn't heeded by the Diggers, who continued to vote up posts containing the code. Finally that evening Rose and Adelson were forced to pull the plug on their site.

And then, minutes later, Digg reappeared. A new post appeared on the front page, this one from the official Digg blog written by Rose and Adelson. Its title read: "Digg This" and then cited the code in full. Rose had made the decision to stick by his community by breaking the law himself and submitting the offensive code in his own post. "After seeing hundreds of stories and reading thousands of comments, you've made it clear. You'd rather see Digg go down fighting than bow down to a bigger company. We hear you, and effective immediately we won't delete stories or comments containing the code and will deal with whatever the consequences might be," he wrote. "If we lose, then what the hell, at least we died trying."

By standing behind his community, Rose took a principled and, depending on your views on copyright, possibly even heroic stance. But the Digg Riot also constitutes an object lesson in the new realities of crowd-powered media: When the people "collectively determine the value of content," they also possess the power to make crucial editorial decisions that have heretofore rested in the hands of a few sober-minded, highly experienced journalists. The editor of a paper is its final firewall, the person who determines whether or not he's about to publish the equivalent of the Pentagon Papers or simply open the paper to crippling litigation. As Rosen and Adelson discovered, Digg doesn't enjoy such a firewall. They didn't intend to let the crowd decide whether to publish the HD-DVD decryption code. But then, they didn't have a choice. The crowd made the decision for them.

Digg, eBay, and other sites that rely on crowd filters to create order from chaos are also susceptible to being gamed by nefarious actors. As its power and influence has increased, Digg has been plagued by those who trade diggs—their votes, essentially—for money. Getting "fronted" on Digg can lead to millions of page views, and all the advertising revenue and sales that can result from such traffic. As a result, companies have sprung up that promise to drive their clients' websites to the top of Digg in exchange for a fee. Assignment Zero contributor Derek Powazek interviewed Ragnar Danneskjold, the founder of one such firm, Subvert and Profit, who explained that his company "fills the niche market for 'darker' crowdsourced actions." With a name like Subvert and Profit, Danneskjold can afford to be brazen. In fact, Danneskjold is a pseudonym. Most crowdsourcing gigs won't buy you a Lexus, and the dark side, it turns out, isn't any different. Dannerskjold receives $2 per vote, half of which he distributes to his members.

Digg has done its best to create algorithms that catch consistently similar patterns of voting and ban certain users if it suspects they are in league with companies like Subvert and Profit, but it's a never-ending battle.

And all this ignores another, possibly more ominous danger. By democratizing the roles of gatekeeper and editor, we are trusting that the crowd can better determine the significance of a news item (or work of art, for that matter) than professionals with a lifetime of experience playing cultural arbiter. Not everyone is comfortable with that notion. "As I write, there is a brutal war going on in Lebanon between Israel and Hezbollah. But the Reddit user wouldn't know this because there is nothing about Israel, Lebanon, or Hezbollah on the site's top twenty 'hot' stories," notes the critic Andrew Keen in his 2007 book *The Cult of the Amateur.* "Instead, subscribers can read about a flat-chested English actress, the walking habits of elephants, and underground tunnels in Japan. Reddit is a mirror of our most banal interests."

Keen hates Wikipedia, despises the blogosphere, and believes YouTube is killing off the cinematic arts. In *Cult of the Amateur,* he argues that we're diving headlong into an age of mass mediocrity in which the mob replaces experts and we all become collectively dumber. I share Keen's concern, if not his general condemnation of social media. Google, YouTube, and Digg all constitute a form of mob rule, and as their importance increases, so does the mob's influence. But there's a fine line between mobocracy and democracy, and some tolerance of the former is generally required to achieve the latter. Crowdsourcing—and crowd voting mechanisms in particular—correct a long-standing inequity. The culture industry has long been controlled by a select few, and as any tour of prime-time network television reveals, they haven't had too much trouble finding the lowest common denominator all on their own. If anything, a dose of democracy could be just the tonic the culture industry needs.

And dystopian visions to the contrary, the death of the expert is hardly nigh. Right now the crowd has the elite on the run, but it's my conviction that the situation will stabilize, leading to a more complex ecosystem in which social media and traditional media coexist in harmony. The vision Keen summons of a populace sustained entirely on sites like Digg, Reddit, and YouTube is highly unlikely. In the years I've worked at *Wired,* I've watched people's information diets become far more varied and, I would argue, more healthy. For the vast majority of users, Digg and YouTube comprise interesting—if occasionally spicy—side dishes. And then, mob rule has its advantages. It allows people to cut out the middleman. Not a bad thing, even—especially—when it comes to combining the power of collective judgment with the power of the collective pocketbook.

9

WHAT THE CROWD FUNDS

Reinventing Finance, Ten Bucks at a Time

The stories below differ in one essential aspect from other applications of crowdsourcing we've explored so far. In other cases, the crowdsourcer taps people's excess capacities. What has come to be called crowdfunding, by contrast, isn't dependent on the crowd's knowledge, creative energies, or judgments. It merely taps their spare dollars, pounds, and pesos. And yet crowdfunding has more in common with the other forms of crowdsourcing than is immediately apparent. First, it radically shifts the organization of an existing field. Two, it flattens hierarchies, by directly connecting people with money to the people who need it. And crowdfunding shares crowdsourcing's generally democratic impulse.

If there is one single paragon of this new model of financing, it is Kiva.org, which bills itself as the "world's first person-to-person micro-lending Website." The description diminishes the graceful simplicity of Kiva's strategy: use the Internet to connect small businesses in the Third World with philanthropically minded lenders in the First World. In its few years of existence Kiva has already managed—thanks to glowing praise from luminaries such as Oprah Winfrey, Bill Clinton, and *New York Times* columnist Nicholas D. Kristoff—to raise $20 million in capital to help fund some 225,000 small businesses in eleven countries. Kiva now faces a problem rare among charitable nonprofits: too many donors. Its popularity with its lenders often outstrips its ability to identify recipients for the loans, frequently resulting in "check back later" signs on its webpages.

Kiva constitutes a sea change in a field—microfinance—that is already creating wholesale changes in international development. The concept of microlending originated in an experiment conducted in 1976 by a Bangladeshi economics professor named Muhammad Yunus. By giving small loans to poverty-stricken people who would otherwise never have access to credit, Yunus saw that he could jump-start local economies. Yunus's first loan was of $27 to forty-two villagers to create a crafts business. Seven years later he founded Grameen Bank based on just this principle. Dependent at first on government grants and philanthropic bequests, Grameen became self-sustaining in 1995, with an astonishing 67 percent of its savings deposits coming from the same people who utilized its low-interest loans. Yunus discovered that loans could do what traditional aid could not: create an escape route out of endemic, multigenerational destitution. According to internal surveys, a full 58 percent of Grameen's 7.4 million borrowers have escaped poverty. This idea has become one of the most influential of our time—behemoth international institutions such as Citigroup now operate for-profit microfinance divisions— and in 2006 Yunus and Grameen Bank shared the Nobel Peace Prize "for their efforts to create economic and social development from below."

Kiva applies the global connectivity of the Internet to make it even easier to harness spare capital and route it to those who need it most. Just as other forms of crowd-sourcing capitalize on our excess capacity to design new products, tweak a scientific formula, or rate the latest clips on a video-sharing site, crowdfunding taps the collective pocketbook, allowing people to finance projects they believe in with just a few dollars here and there.

The appeal of such an approach to allocating credit hasn't been lost on other entrepreneurs. Crowdfunding has also been called "social banking," and it is already making an impact on fields far outside micro-credit. Those who use the Internet as a medium for fraud have unsurprisingly found crowdfunding attractive, too. Kiva discovered during a routine audit that one of its field partners—in-country affiliates who decide which borrowers are credit-worthy, and disburse the loans to them—was keeping part of the money for itself. Kiva used the democratic nature of the Internet once again in creating a mechanism to guard against such malfeasance: field partners are now rated based on past performance, allowing lenders to evaluate the risk level of working with them.

The Difference a Bus Ticket Makes

Elizabeth Omalla of Uganda started her first business in 2000 with a $100 grant from a local micro-credit organization, the Village Enterprise Fund. The money allowed her to establish a stand selling vegetables and cooking oil. The VEF is just one of many micro-credit organizations working on the African continent. Sub-Saharan Africa is the poorest region in the world, and it's getting poorer. Nearly half of its 770 million residents live in extreme poverty—surviving on less than $1 a day—and that number continues to climb every year. Like other developing economies, Africa doesn't lack for entrepreneurial energy. It just lacks capital.

Omalla quickly realized that in order to succeed she would need to expand her wares to include fish, a popular staple in Uganda. After finding a supplier, Omalla was able to sell roughly six fish a day on the street in her village. Her supplier was a middleman who would bring the fish up from Lake Victoria, more than two hours away. But Omalla, with eight children to feed, was barely covering her expenses. The only way to expand her business was to establish a direct link with the fishermen on Lake Victoria. In order to pay for transportation and sufficient quantities of fish, she needed considerably more money—$500, a large loan by micro-credit standards—than she could obtain through existing sources. The Village Enterprise Fund loans max out at $100, and banks in the developing world generally require cumbersome documentation and collateral and charge interest rates of up to 30 percent. Informal lenders—we would call them loan sharks—charge up to 300 percent interest. For the time being, Omalla was stuck. She had her business, but her dreams were stalled.

At the time, Omalla had never met Matt and Jessica Flannery, for the perfectly good reason that they lived on the other side of the world, but their paths would soon cross. When Matt and Jessica got engaged in early 2003, they did thirteen weeks of premarital counseling at their local church. At one point the pair were asked to describe their career goals. "I want to live in the [San Francisco] Bay Area and be an entrepreneur," answered Matt. "I want to go to Africa and do microfinance," answered Jessica. At this point Matt was writing software for TiVo and trying to come up with a new business idea every day. "Three hundred sixty-five ideas was my goal," he later wrote. His fiancée was working at the Stanford Graduate School of Business, and she had invited Matt along to hear Yunus address a class at the school. They were both inspired by the lecture. "I thought it was a great story from an inspiring person. For Jessica, it was more of a call to action that focused her life goals." Despite their seemingly contradictory ambitions, Matt and Jessica were married that summer. Six months later Jessica was on her way to work for the Village Enterprise Fund, which had offered her a consulting position in East Africa.

While Jessica spent her days traveling through Kenya and Tanzania interviewing VEF recipients, Matt stayed in San Francisco working at TiVo. They spoke frequently over the phone and began to hatch a start-up that would combine their interests, a company that contributed to poverty alleviation, but through loans, not donations. Matt took a month-long trip to Africa and the two refined their idea.

Soon after the pair returned from Africa, Matt had a skeleton version of Kiva.org up and running. From there Jessica began researching partners within the microfinancing industry and setting up their organization as a nonprofit. There were of course lots of questions. Would the U.S. Securities and Exchange Commission get involved? Would lawyers be needed? Would existing microfinance banks feel competitive with Kiva, or work with it for the greater good?

Before they could launch Kiva to the public, Matt and Jessica needed to find the borrowers. When Jessica was in Uganda she had met a village pastor, Moses Onyango, and now the Flannerys signed on Onyango to identify likely loan candidates. The first on his list was Omalla's struggling fishmongering business. Soon Onyango had found six other local businesses, including a goat herder and a seller of secondhand clothing. Onyango played a crucial role. Without local partners, it would be impossible for Kiva to gauge the credit-worthiness of prospective borrowers. Onyango—a portly, softspoken man who commanded great respect in his community—was the perfect person for the role. Using a digital camera provided by Kiva, Onyango took pictures of the seven loan candidates and uploaded the photos along with descriptions of their businesses.

All Kiva had to do next was find lenders. Their first "crowd," as it were, was purposefully small and defined. They sent out an e-mail to their entire wedding list and waited to see how the three hundred friends and family members would react. Within a weekend, Kiva had raised enough money—$3,500—to fund all seven loans. "We were blown away," Matt recalled. "Everything worked."

In March 2005, Omalla received her $500 loan. The money allowed her to travel directly to Lake Victoria, where she was able to buy enough fish to supply not only her village, but surrounding villages as well. That December, Omalla paid off her loan in full. She also was able to save $130 and purchase two cows and five goats, no small feat; in Uganda, such four-legged capital means the difference between feast and famine. But now that Kiva was off the ground, the Flannerys faced the dual challenge of finding new funders as well as new businesses to fund. The primary obstacle, Matt had recognized early on, would be in trying to build Kiva into a large enough operation to be self-supporting and continue the kinds of efforts that had made so great a difference in Omalla's life.

Kiva formed a partnership with Village Enterprise

Fund to address the problem of identifying borrowers, but Kiva was still unknown to the crowd—the people who held all the capital. Meanwhile, Matt was spending his days at TiVo and Jessica had started business school at Stanford. It seemed as if Kiva might always remain a pet project. Then one morning Matt woke to find a thousand e-mails in his inbox. Their site had been featured on the home page of the liberal blog Daily Kos. That morning more than a million people read about Kiva, and their pet project was flooded with $10,000 in loan capital. Glowing praise in the press soon followed, providing Kiva with enough momentum to allow Matt to quit his job that December. Kiva was able to establish partnerships with microfinance institutions all over the world, and in September 2007 Bill Clinton endorsed Kiva in his book *Giving: How Each of Us Can Change the World.*

Turning Fans into Believers

Crowdfunding isn't new. It's been the backbone of the American political system since politicians started kissing babies. Political fundraising over the Internet first started gathering speed in 2000 and by the election cycle of 2008 Barack Obama had turned it into a science, raising some $272 million from more than 2 million, mostly small, donors. And that was just for the primary. The Internet so accelerates and simplifies the process of finding large pools of potential funders that crowdfunding has spread into the most unexpected nooks and crannies of our culture—such as music and movies.

This makes more sense than is at first apparent. To make a commercially viable album or movie generally requires a large, up-front investment. Both production and marketing costs can go well into the millions—or, in the case of films, tens of millions—of dollars. Artists are thus generally at the mercy of movie studios and music labels, who decide which projects to bankroll. But there's always been something a little strange about placing such power in the hands of so few people. The decision of which movies get made ultimately rests with the five major studio heads in Hollywood, who try to intuit the tastes and interests of hundreds of millions of moviegoers. The system isn't only undemocratic, it's terribly inefficient. The situation is little different at the music labels, where green-lighting power also resides in the hands of a few dozen executives. No amount of focus grouping or test marketing—which the studios and labels engage in aggressively—can change the essential difficulty of discerning what separates a hit from a dud.

Crowdfunding, on the other hand, allows artists to appeal directly to consumers. By asking people to place a small financial stake in the careers of musicians and filmmakers (I have yet to see the model used by authors or other creators, but I bet that will occur before 2008 is out), artists are able to appeal directly to the very constituency that will ultimately consume their wares. Would you watch this? Would you listen to this? If so, give me a few bucks to help me make my album/movie. Who better to decide what should be created than the same people who will ultimately consume the product?

The application of crowdfunding to the cultural sphere hasn't reached quite the kind of success achieved by Kiva, but neither does it remain in the realm of theory. The British writer and filmmaker Matt Hanson started a crowdfunded film project—appropriately called A Swarm of Angels—because he wanted to make an end run around the studio system. Hanson hopes to gather enough capital—approximately $2 million—to make a feature-length film. To do this he has put up a shingle on the Web and is soliciting £25 ($50) from anyone interested in becoming an angel. Hanson eventually hopes fifty thousand people will participate. In a nifty twist, Hanson has incorporated other elements of crowdsourcing into the production of the movie. The first thousand investors have contributed ideas to the scriptwriting process and will ultimately decide which of two separate scripts Hanson has written will go into production.

It's not as far-fetched as it sounds: In April 2007, William Brooks, a thirty-six-year-old copywriter in England, launched MyFootballClub with the aim of collecting £35 each from fifty thousand people that would then be spent in purchasing a professional football team. By November 2007, Brooks had raised more than £700,000 and completed the takeover of the Ebbsfleet United Football Club. Brooks's crowd decides, via online vote, everything from what jerseys the team wears to who should coach the team.

For his part, Hanson wants to "kick-start a creative and business model for the viable production of large-scale free cultural works." The resulting film will be distributed free over the Internet, and it will be copyrighted under a Creative Commons license, under which other people can "download it, remix and distribute it" for any nonprofit use. And the raw footage itself will be uploaded for commercial use as well. What has been interesting, Hanson notes, about charging people in order to participate in a crowdsourcing community like A Swarm of Angels is that it has ensured people's participation is meaningful. "Why pay twenty-five quid to be an asshole? In essence, you're turning cinema from what it has become, a business, back to what it was originally, an art form. Instead of having to please some producer with purse strings, you're dealing with a community. It makes the process much more open."

The impetus to discover new models to support artistic production is even more pronounced among musicians. As the sales of CDs continue to plummet, a number of possible business models have emerged, but one of the most interesting has been a crowdfunding outfit based in Holland called SellaBand. The brainchild of Pim Betist, a former account manager with Royal Dutch Shell, SellaBand allows any band to create a profile page, à la MySpace, on which they write a bio and stream music. Unlike MySpace, though, SellaBand isn't looking to collect "friends," but investors. These "believers," as they're called on SellaBand, can buy a share in the band's future proceeds at $10 a pop. If the act can raise $50,000, SellaBand hooks them up with a veteran producer and mixer and brings them all into the studio to cut a record. The "believers" each receive a complementary album when the recording is done, as well as a share of the advertising revenues from the SellaBand site.

SellaBand started in 2005 after Betist tired of his corporate work at Shell and approached Johan Vosmeijer, a veteran in the European music industry. Vosmeijer had worked as a producer at labels such as Epic and Sony. Within three months, Vosmeijer and Betist had put together the financial wherewithal to fund the company. They launched SellaBand.com in August 2006. Shortly afterward, SellaBand began attracting attention from the music industry and the press (including an article I wrote in *Wired*). After about ten weeks, the first SellaBand act hit the $50,000 mark. The second band, the Salt Lake City–based act Cubworld, achieved the same feat in January 2007. "I read about the site and how it worked and I

thought, 'This is like a bank account for my dreams,' "
said Jacob Kongaika, the creative force behind Cubworld.
Kongaika strikes an uncanny echo with A Swarm of Angels's Matt Hanson. Asked the best thing about Sella-
Band, he doesn't mention the money or the publicity, but
the fact that he's "not tied down to the industry bosses
saying I have to write seventy songs before I go into a
studio. The fans have spoken and it is being done."

After recording a six-song demo, SellaBand pressed
and shipped Cubworld's CD out to their "believers." For
the first year after the date on which SellaBand signs an
act, the company keeps 40 percent of the publishing proceeds. In many cases this will amount to 40 percent of
nothing, but if one of the SellaBand acts scores a major
hit, or even has a song licensed for a TV commercial, the
publishing income will be substantial. Unlike Kiva, Sella-
Band is out to turn a profit. All download sales, advertising, and online CD sales are split three ways between the
band, the "believers," and SellaBand.

Not only does SellaBand transfer the cost of production onto the crowd, it also creates a social media wave in
the process. Since a band's fans are also literally invested
in the band, they tend to be much more proactive than
your average fan. In marketing parlance, SellaBand believers are "evangelicals," and it's what every band (and
everyone else with a product on the market) aspires to
attract. Crowdfunding doesn't just raise money for Sella-
Band artists, it really does build a core group of "believers." To date SellaBand has helped twenty-one bands
reach the $50,000 mark.

SellaBand comes at an interesting juncture in the
recording industry, which is still reeling from the effects
of large-scale peer-to-peer file sharing, in which millions
of music consumers download their music for free over

the Internet. Musicians, managers, and label executives have tried a number of different methods to counteract this unrelenting tide, including simply letting customers pay what they want—as the band Radiohead did in the fall of 2007. But amid all this uncertainty, the crowd-funding approach that SellaBand is pioneering holds a particular appeal to both musicians and the fans that support them. After waging a bitter, six-year legal war against its best customers (between 2003 and 2008 the RIAA issued 28,000 lawsuits against alleged "music pirates"), the recording industry has generated an immense amount of hostility on the part of young fans as well as many of the musicians themselves, who never really believed the labels were acting in their best interest. As a result, there has been a lot of talk in the music industry about removing the middlemen and going direct from "band to fan." For years that was merely warm-and-fuzzy rhetoric, but SellaBand has hit on a model in which the fans play the banks once played by the labels. As Kongaika says, "The fan has spoken."

SECTION III

Where We're Going

10

TOMORROW'S CROWD

The Age of the Digital Native

There are reasons to believe that the current manifestation of crowdsourcing is just a prelude to a far more pervasive transformation. Actually, there are about 200 million reasons to believe it. That's the rough number of kids around the world that currently have Internet access. Marc Prensky, a writer and video-game developer, coined the term "digital native" to describe the cohorts that are coming of age in the Internet era. The rest of us he aptly identifies as "digital immigrants." Like most immigrants, we often struggle to understand the incomprehensible customs of the natives.

Reared on social media, always on Internet connections, cell-phone cameras, Machinima, and YouTube, digital natives live on the same planet as digital immigrants, but inhabit a very different universe. They can concentrate on multiple projects simultaneously, they collaborate seamlessly and spontaneously with people they've never met, and most important, they create media with the same avidity that previous generations consumed it. This is the crowdsourcing generation, a demographic perfectly adapted to a future in which online communities will supplant the conventional corporation.

If the revolution is to be waged by children, then it's appropriate that one of the first shots would be fired by a teenage video-game designer. In 1999, Minh Le was a Vietnamese immigrant in his last year of the computer science program at Simon Fraser University, in Vancouver, British Columbia. After classes Le would return to his apartment and play games like *Doom* (man kills zombies), *Quake* (man kills extra-dimensional monsters), and *Half-Life* (man kills extra-dimensional monsters and zombies). Le loved playing these games so much that he started making his own "mods," or modifications to these games. A mod can range from creating a customized weapon to a "total conversion"—writing an entirely new game, in which only the underlying game engine remains the same. In June of that year, Le and another young game designer, Jess Cliffe, released a total conversion of *Half-Life* that they called *Counter-Strike*. *Counter-Strike* brought *Half-Life* down to earth, so to speak. Instead of shooting mutants, gamers played on teams composed of either terrorists or agents. The former attempts to perform nefarious acts; the latter tries to stop them. Much bloodshed ensues. Mods generally attract a very limited audience, but then, most mods weren't nearly as good and well executed as *Counter-Strike*. Within weeks it had been downloaded thousands of times. When I spent a month in Uzbekistan on assignment for *Wired* in 2002, it was almost impossible to find an open terminal on which to check e-mail. The boys of Tashkent (like the boys of Bali and Boulder and Bombay) were all playing *Counter-Strike*.

Valve, the game studio behind *Half-Life* (on which *Counter-Strike* is based), reacted curiously to *Counter-Strike*'s explosive popularity. Rather than send out cease-and-desist letters to Le—who had, after all, used the company's intellectual property in order to build his game—Valve encouraged its proliferation. In fact, Valve had made *Counter-Strike* possible by releasing modding software along with its games. Mods are an integral part of gaming culture, and further, Valve understood that mods didn't hurt sales of the original game; they helped them: to play *Counter-Strike*, you need to be running *Half-Life* on your computer. Soon Valve had licensed the rights to sell the mod commercially and put Le on its payroll.

It was a prescient move, presaging the kinds of crowdsourcing strategies other companies would adopt years later. Valve was using a customer to create innovations around its product. It was arguably the smartest move Valve ever made. Working closely with Le, the company released the official version of *Counter-Strike* in November 2000. By 2003, it had become the most popular game on the Internet, with 2.5 million active players. The online gamer magazine *GameSpy* even credited *Counter-Strike* as the number one reason *Half-Life* had maintained its popularity well into the millennium. Chris Baker, a senior editor at *Wired,* says the game was so pervasive that it drove the slump in PC sales in the early years of the decade. "New games generally drive computer upgrades, but so many people were happy with *Counter-Strike* there wasn't any reason to buy a new computer," says Baker.

Counter-Strike is exceptional so far as mods go, but it's hardly sui generis. Mods have been a venerable part of gamer culture for decades. Traditionally, however, modding required extensive time and skill. What's changing is that the gaming industry is making great pains to lower the bar, making it possible for ever more kids to create their own games. *Half-Life*, for instance, is much more than a video game—it's an ever-evolving collaboration between customers and company, an example of how crowdsourcing can both create better products as well as improve a company's bottom line. *Half-Life* represents something else as well: it's the future of work.

The New Fluency

Mike Webber is hard at work, though that's not immediately apparent from looking at him. He is sitting in front of three oversize computer monitors. The British zombie comedy *Shaun of the Dead* plays on the left screen. The Greek gore-fest *300* plays on the right. But Webber leans closely toward the middle screen, which displays the dingy hallways, empty courtyards, and flat, bullet-pocked walls that characterize the *Counter-Strike* physical environment. Webber, like most of the other high schoolers sitting nearby, is making his own mod. He glances left just in time to catch a zombie impaled on a pipe. He and two other teenage boys groan in unison. "That's so the best part," he mutters, then returns to building a better battlefield.

Webber, a spiky-haired sixteen-year-old in a Metallica shirt, cargo shorts, and sandals, is attending his generation's distinct take on summer camp—cyber camp. He is one of twenty-eight teenagers who every morning trickle into a cafeteria on the Adelphi University campus on Long Island, New York. Cybercamps Academy runs some one hundred twenty such camps across America every summer. The curriculum includes everything from Flash design to robotics, but most of the kids at Adelphi are here to pursue an abiding passion—creating avatars, levels, and weapons for the immensely popular game *Half-Life*.

The kids in attendance ranged in age from ten to seventeen. Computers were neatly arranged along a series of folding tables. A riot of cables ran underfoot. The shades were closed against the bright August sun, giving the cafeteria the feel of the basement of a house inhabited exclusively by sixteen-year-old boys. Clearly, these campers were not at risk for poison ivy or sunburn. I spent the day observing the teens at play and work, and talking to them about their interests and goals.

Few of the campers said they wanted to create games for a living, despite an almost obsessive enthusiasm for the craft. Making games, to them, seemed less like the kind of thing one does for a living than a highly desirable skill, like playing the guitar or doing a kickflip on a skateboard. Put another way, making games had become a natural extension of playing games, a complementary but hardly discrete ability. Their relationship to video games was much more complicated than mine. I grew up playing them and, to my wife's chagrin, I can still fritter away entire nights immersed in *Halo* or *Medal of Honor*. But it would never occur to me that I could reach through the set and re-create the game to suit my whim. And it would never occur to the kids at Adelphi that they couldn't.

It would be easy to dismiss them as the exceptions, not the rule. Haven't geeks gone to computer camps for decades? But the kids at Adelphi aren't geeks; they're just kids. "The constituency of the campers has really shifted since I started running the camps," says Josh Block, a computer science teacher at an area high school and the director of a Cybercamp in Westchester County, New York. "It's really a cross-section of school society—geeks, jocks, and everything in between." Cybercamps started in 1997 with 122 campers. Ten years later it registered more than 10,000 youths for the week-long program, an increase in line with the company's competitors. The "tech camp" market is now worth between $400 and $500 million.

The teens at Adelphi are generally the product of affluent, highly educated communities. One would expect them to possess talents and abilities far exceeding their counterparts in less privileged settings. What's surprising, according to much of the research into teens and media behavior, is how representative they really are.

These Are Not the Smurfs You're Looking For

The video-game industry is hardly unaware of this trend. In fact, Valve provides Cybercamps with discounted versions of the software that allows gamers to create new mods. The company has wisely recognized that by encouraging this sort of creativity they can significantly extend the shelf life of their commercial releases. Long after their customers get bored with the initial product, they will continue to redesign new variations on it, keeping the veterans entertained and bringing new customers into the fold.

Valve hardly invented this strategy, though the company deserves credit for avidly adopting it. The history of modding video games stretches back nearly as far as the technology itself. The original gamers were mostly hackers and otherwise technically inclined computer enthusiasts. The first mod is generally considered to be a reinvention of a simple strategy game called *Castle Wolfenstein*, in which the player battles Nazi soldiers. In 1983, one fan created the *Castle Smurfenstein* mod (in which all the characters were replaced with Smurfs), displaying the irreverent wit and pop-culture savvy that would come to characterize mods for years to come.

As games evolved, they became increasingly labor- and processor-intensive affairs requiring thousands of man-hours to produce. But somehow the amateurs managed to keep pace. In 1990, Apogee, the game publisher for the then-popular *Duke Nukem*, discovered that players were not only creating their own levels for the game, but had even written their own level editors—separate programs that help automate basic coding tasks involved in software development. "This was a fascinating development," recalls Apogee founder Scott Miller. "We just didn't expect players to take the time and effort to create their own development tools."

It was just the beginning. Modding would fully blossom in the 1990s, primarily through the first-person-shooter genre. In 1992, Apogee published *Wolfenstein 3-D*, recasting the original Allies vs. Nazis story in the round. It was an immediate success, and just as immediately apparent—according to an excellent history of modding written for *Salon* by the technology writer Wagner James Au—was the significant role that modding would play in the game's commercial fortunes. The title's lead programmer, John Carmack, was a firm believer in open source principles, and when Carmack and his colleagues released the immensely popular game *Doom* the next year, they actively encouraged their fan base to create their own mods.

Doom and its successors, such as *Quake* and then in 1998, *Half-Life*, not only popularized first-person shooters (so-called because the gamer actually plays from the point-of-view of the avatar), but they also institutionalized the convention of modding. This represented an astute understanding of how copyright was evolving toward more permissive models, but it was also smart business. Cliff Bleszinsky, the lead designer for one of the most popular first-person shooters of this decade, *Unreal*

Tournament, estimates that about half of the 2 million plus people who bought the game have played on user-generated mods. "Many of the best game companies now count on modders to show them the way creatively and to ensure their own survival in a savagely competitive market," Au notes in *Salon.*

This all stands in marked contrast to the copyright stance taken by other sectors of the entertainment industry, such as the music and movie businesses, which avidly prosecute even the most benign reuses of copyrighted work. According to a study conducted by American University, most of the user-generated videos that the entertainment industry claims are in violation of copyright law are protected under the "fair use" interpretation of the statutes governing copyright. (Fair use allows derivative creations that use short excerpts from a copyrighted book, movie, or other copyrighted work. It is, for instance, what allows me to quote other authors in this book.)

One can see how well this scorched-earth policy has worked out for the recording industry: it suffered its catastrophic declines in the same period that gaming industry revenues increased more than 30 percent. First-person shooters have sustained a robust market by freely crowdsourcing the creative energy that goes into making new games. Recently, the gaming industry at large seems eager to embrace user-generated games. In the fall of 2008, some of the gaming industry's biggest releases will bank on the notion that what gamers most want isn't new games but the tools necessary to make their own. Sony will release a game for its PlayStation 3 console called *LittleBigPlanet,* in which users create their own objects, obstacle courses, or entire environments. Around the same time, Will Wright—the vaunted designer who created *The Sims* franchise—will release the long-awaited *Spore,* in which players guide their own creatures through every stage of evolution, from single-celled organisms to interplanetary traveler life-form. *Spore* allows gamers to upload their creations to YouTube and even to a specialized website called Sporepedia, on which player's can rate one another's creations. Each copy of the game will search Sporepedia on its own and populate the tens of thousands of planets in each player's galaxy with the highest-rated content. The *Spore* universe itself will be a creation of the crowd.

The tradition of collaboration between producers and consumers of games is so strong that it threatens to mislead us into thinking that this dynamic is somehow endemic to games, rather than just one manifestation of a larger phenomenon. If this book could be reduced to a single theme, it would be that the erosion of the boundary between producer and consumer has begun to exercise a considerable effect on our economy and our culture. The crowd has begun to take on the burden of product creation, with great glee and enthusiasm, as the evolution of video gaming makes clear. And kids are getting their hands dirty in far more than just video games, as we're about to see.

Kids Today

In 2005, the Pew Internet & American Life Project released the findings of a large-scale survey called "Teen Content Creators and Consumers." The Pew survey revealed that well over half of all teens with Internet access weren't just surfing the Web, but were actively creating content for the Web. The portrait that emerged from the study was of a parallel information ecosystem that operated independently of professional content producers such as NBC or, say, *Wired* magazine. These kids were creating and consuming their own multimedia narratives, composed of text, photographs, and videos. The study was enormously influential and was quoted extensively in the following months.

Then in late December 2007, Pew released a sequel to the original report, "Teens and Social Media." The findings of the study, which had been conducted over the course of 2006, were even more startling. They not only reinforced Pew's original conclusions, but they demonstrated that as a trend, teen content creation is rapidly becoming even more prevalent than first indicated. "The tools needed to produce and distribute digital media are readily available and utilized in some way by most teen Internet users," the Pew authors wrote. According to Pew, about 93 percent of all American twelve- to seventeen-year-olds are regular Internet users. That means more than 23 million teenage Americans are online. Of those, some 64 percent—nearly 15 million teens—are creating content for the Internet.

Pew asked its respondents whether they engaged in several activities the researchers considered to be "hallmarks of online content creation." One, do you work on a webpage? Two, do you contribute to someone else's webpage? Three, do you share original artwork, photos, stories, or videos? And finally, do you remix content you find online? Well over half of all teens answered yes to one of those questions. But what was more significant was that 40 percent, more than 9 million teens in the United States alone, are engaged in at least three of those activities. More teens are spending more time creating more online content in a greater variety of ways than ever before, a trend that seems to be on the rise.

This has clear implications for our economy: online communities such as iStockphoto, InnoCentive, and Threadless are already making significant contributions to the overall economy, and teens make up only a small percentage of their users. When this demographic reaches adulthood, they will bring behaviors and attitudes honed through thousands of hours in front of a computer, constructing their own experience and working collaboratively in various online communities.

A profound shift is afoot, which was nowhere more evident than at the Adelphi Cybercamp. Most of the campers seemed to be working on four or five projects at once—some of which had little to do with the curriculum. One mop-headed thirteen-year-old was making an animated video in Flash, the multimedia authoring tool that powers much of the content on the Web. A few feet away a girl about the same age was using another application to make her own manga comic. (In Japanese, *manga* means "comic," but it has come to refer to any comic bearing the characteristics of that particular aesthetic.) At any given time at least five or six of the campers were using Photoshop to alter pictures from their cell phones. When one of the older campers went to lunch, a few of his cohorts altered a photograph of him to look like a "Ballchinian," a race of aliens from the movie *Men in Black II* whose genitalia appear to fall below their, well, chin. You can imagine which part of the image they imported.

In some ways these are the kids you and I grew up with. The acne, the scatological humor, the use of pop culture to create social identity—the song remains the same. But somewhere in the past fifteen years we crossed a line after which nothing will ever be the same. We—and by that I mean everyone who still gets their news from a newspaper—watch stuff, listen to stuff, and read stuff. These kids *make* stuff. A quick, informal survey of the campers indicated that Photoshop, Flash, and various blog-authoring tools have become standard technological literacy to most middle-class American kids. "Flash is really expensive," explains Josh Moran, one of the younger campers at Adelphi. "But most kids just download it off the Internet," which is to say, get it illegally using one of the file-sharing networks.

Kids are beginning to entertain themselves in a completely new way, in an emergence of what's been called "participatory culture." Henry Jenkins, the head of MIT's Comparitive Media Studies program and author of the book *Convergence Culture: Where Old and New Media Collide*, writes,

> A participatory culture [has] relatively low barriers to artistic expression and civic engagement, strong support for creating and sharing one's creations, and some type of informal mentorship whereby what is known by the most experienced is passed along to novices. [It] is also one in which members believe their contributions matter, and feel some degree of social connection with one another.

In other words, "they care what other people think about what they have created." Creative collaboration is a robust feature of the culture of many online communities, but the disparity in Pew's numbers highlights the extent to which teens exhibit this communal impulse. A full 33 percent of online teens work on other people's websites, as compared to only 13 percent of adults. Teens are more likely to help others build a blog or website than they are to create their own.

The Berkeley researcher danah boyd (her spelling) gives a telling example of this tendency to share—or, to put a fine point on it, distribute without expectation of compensation—this kind of technical knowledge. When the social networking site MySpace first began gaining popularity in 2005, early adopters noticed that unlike its predecessor, Friendster, MySpace had neglected to close a security loophole that allowed users to customize their sites by adding HTML, CSS, and JavaScript. The result is that rather than standardized profile pages, teens could create the riot of color and noise that once decorated school lockers and notebooks, but is now recognized as the MySpace aesthetic. Rather than close the loophole, the company neither encouraged nor discouraged the practice. As boyd writes, "A copy/paste culture emerged, as teens began trafficking in knowledge of how to pimp out their profiles. . . . In the early days of their infatuation, teens spent innumerable hours tracking down codes, trading tips, and setting up a slick profile."

"Through this process," boyd notes, "they learn both technological *and* social codes." The italics in the sentence are mine, because it's important to emphasize that this tendency to work well not only with others, but for the sake of others, is emblematic of crowdsourcing culture. This kind of reciprocity echoes the sorts of behavior we see in other crowdsourcing communities, where money generally ranks low on the list of motivations, below community reputation and the opportunity to learn and teach in turn. Even more than the stunning technological fluency digital natives demonstrate is their adoption of social behaviors—collaboration, free sharing, promiscuous creativity—that powers crowdsourcing. The fact that so many more kids than adults exhibit this tendency indicates that the younger generation will not only be prepared to take an active role in the sorts of online communities that form the crowdsourced workplace, but will thrive there and create an even more tightly woven community fabric.

Young people are sharing more than mere tips and tricks. Some 9 million teens share artwork, stories, or videos—a significant increase from Pew's previous study. A remarkable one in seven have posted their own videos.

In other words, millions of kids are making their own clips and posting them to the Internet. Teens also display a marked tendency to remix the content they find on the Internet. Just as hardcore gamers are inclined to approach their video games as malleable, something to be shaped according to their creative fancy, teens creating artistic works in other media are also inclined to create pastiches, homages, or parodies of the videos, photographs, artworks, or stories they encounter. Some 26 percent of Pew's respondents said that they had taken content off the Web and remixed it to create their own work.

All of this is a testament not only to Jenkins's observation that participatory culture features "low barriers to artistic expression" (enabled, in large part, by the proliferation of cheap, easy-to-use tools), but also to the overwhelming belief that their "contributions matter."

Undoubtedly their contributions do matter, but to whom is a subject of much debate. As the Pew study makes clear, most of this creative efflorescence we're witnessing takes place on sites like MySpace and Facebook. Well over half of all American teens have a profile on a social networking site, and three-quarters of those users are actively writing stories, sharing photos and videos, and otherwise engaging in acts of creation.

Social network sites thrive by making such tasks exceedingly simple, but it's hard to know what to make of the mass visual and verbal expression that has resulted. On one hand teens are creating media on a public platform. But as researcher danah boyd points out, this requires that we redefine our concept of "public." It would be unwise to assume that their intended audience, for the most part, extends beyond an immediate circle of acquaintances. This calls to mind the updated twist on Andy Warhol's maxim: In the future everyone will be famous to fifteen people.

Pew didn't ask their respondents whether they considered social networking sites to be communication tools or spaces to exhibit premeditated, creative works, but it would have been interesting to know the response. Is the prolific creativity that MySpace inspires best viewed as the stirrings of the artistic impulse or as an act of expression more analagous to passing notes in class? For anyone concerned about the future of American literacy, a tour through random MySpace sites can be a depressing experience. Most blog entries are rife with grammatical errors (intended and otherwise), spelling errors (ditto), and the sort of inane sentimentalism that make high school English teachers cringe. But then, kids aren't going on MySpace to impress their English teachers. In the words of Tiffany, a MySpace user from Houston, "Im jus on this myspace thang to have fun and meet as many cool people as I can."

For most of these young people, sites like MySpace have become an integral element in creating an identity and communicating with their peers. In other words, teens haven't changed, but their technology has. "If you look at MySpace, what kids are doing in terms of cutting and pasting and linking and forwarding is very interesting from a creative perspective," says Mimi Ito, an anthropologist whose research focuses on how children interact with new media. "But I don't think kids who participate at that level see themselves as media producers. This is simply how they hang out."

Point well taken. But while they might be "just hanging out," teens are developing radically new social behaviors and cognitive abilities. These will surely create wholesale changes to the workplace when they enter the labor force in, say, five to ten years. Most of what they make may be of little interest—or merit—to anyone outside their peer circle. But that doesn't change the fact that a legion of kids is absorbing the fundamentals of videography, among other skills. As they get older, they'll become even more adept, and the tools will continue to become cheaper and easier to use. In 2007, iStockphoto launched a separate service that applies its secret sauce to videography. Unsurprisingly, it's doing exceptionally well, earning $12 million in revenues in its first year alone. Further, to believe that as much as technology changes, people stay the same, dismisses the full social, cultural, and psychological effects of that technology, especially on those who've grown up in the networked, always-on era.

The writer and game designer Marc Prensky goes so far as to claim that digital natives have developed, as a result of near-constant exposure to digital media, a different neurological makeup than that possessed by digital immigrants. I took an informal survey during my visits to two separate Cybercamps, asking each camper when he or she had first used a computer. The kids older than fifteen generally answered that they had been four or five years old. The younger kids, however, looked at me as if I'd asked them if they remembered their first meal. None could recall their first experience using a computer, or even being on the Internet. The computer and the Internet had always been around, as much a fixture of daily life as telephones are to the rest of us.

What happens when the Adelphi teens enter the workforce? For starters, they'll help accelerate the obsolescence of such standard corporate fixtures as the management hierarchy and the nine-to-five workday. As Thomas Malone, an MIT professor and author of *The Future of Work* points out, these conventions are artifacts of an earlier age when information was scarce and all decisions, for the sake of efficiency, trickled down from on high. Information is now available to anyone with an

Internet connection. The result, Malone says, "is that decision making has been decentralized." Cybercamp's Josh Block points out that the high school students he teaches during the school year "expect to be able to do their homework together, on a wiki." They'll undoubtedly carry such habits into the workplace. Even the kids who do wind up working from the proverbial cubicle will fully expect to tap their peers on the other end of the fiber-optic cable for help. Wikis don't respect corporate firewalls (or national borders), and neither will their users.

But even this considerable shift understates the transformative effects in store. Crowdsourcing has already wreaked upheaval in a few select fields like stock photography. This is because the crowd has made a once scarce resource abundant. As digital natives continue to acquire the skills it takes to build, design, and create, the scarcity of many other commodities will also decline, posing great challenges to the companies that traffic in them. "Obsolescence itself isn't a new phenomenon," Malone points out. "Kids who grew up with running water wouldn't know how to work a hand-pump, and in this new world we're entering, a lot of what's familiar will go the way of the hand-pump."

11

CONCLUSION

The Rules of Crowdsourcing

In May 2008, a small Canadian company named Cambrian House announced the sale of much of its assets to the New York–based venture capital company Spencer Trask. While Cambrian House will carry on as a purveyor of crowdsourcing software, its existence as a crowdsourcing community had come to a close. This news didn't exactly make international headlines, but it had a considerable impact among the academics, bloggers, and companies that have closely followed the evolution of crowdsourcing. Cambrian House was the first firm to explicitly call itself a crowdsourcing company. When it launched in the spring of 2006, thousands of people were drawn to answer its call of "You think it; Crowds test it; Crowds build it; You sell it." What couldn't the crowd do? As it turned out, the crowd was great at thinking and testing, but less interested at the building component of Cambrian House's model. "The wisdom-of-crowds part of Cambrian House worked great," noted founder Michael Sikorsky at the time of the sale. "It was the participation of the crowds that we couldn't get nailed."

As this book goes to press there's much discussion about whether the failure of Cambrian House signifies the failure of crowdsourcing. I think it's a fair question, for which I have a one-word response: Google. Not only does Google's search engine essentially use a form of crowdsouring to organize its results, but the company has come to rely on the crowd's input for everything from its Google Earth program to the categorization of visual images. And when the software giant wanted to develop applications for Android, its open source cell-phone operating system, it went to the crowd, announcing it would provide $10 million in awards to the developers with the best ideas. The crowd, as is its wont, responded in great volume. Developers from over seventy countries submitted 1,788 entries. Clearly, Google isn't questioning crowdsourcing's efficiency.

But this doesn't mean crowdsourcing is easy. It constitutes a radical new approach to making stuff, and the phenomenon is still in its infancy. I wasn't surprised when Cambrian House shifted its focus away from asking the crowd to create software products, and while scores of crowdsourcing companies have launched during the writing of this book, I won't be surprised to see many of them fail too. Any journalist who covered the tech boom of the late 1990s will recall the tremendous rate of attrition that followed.

I've generally approached crowdsourcing as a journalist rather than an advocate. However, in the course of two years of research, several basic principles have emerged. I've boiled these down into ten rules of crowdsourcing. They're neither comprehensive nor fireproof, but they do provide a rough road map to help you navigate this new terrain.

1. Pick the Right Model

Crowdsourcing isn't a single strategy. It's an umbrella term for a highly varied group of approaches that share one obvious attribute in common: they all depend on some contribution from the crowd. But the nature of those contributions can differ tremendously. Before launching any crowdsourcing initiative, the first step is to determine what your ultimate goal is: Do you want to draw upon your best customers to help design a new product? Are you trying to create a platform for local bloggers? Or are you trying to find an illustrator who can redesign your logo? The answer to these questions will help you decide which crowdsourcing model to employ. There are four primary categories of crowdsourcing. Section II is devoted to examining each of these in detail, but in brief they are the following:

Collective intelligence, or crowd wisdom

A central principle animating crowdsourcing is that the groups contain more knowledge than individuals. The trick lies in creating the conditions in which they'll express that knowledge. Prediction markets like the Iowa Electronic Markets and open innovation companies like InnoCentive capture this intelligence by establishing large, diverse networks of people who often possess unique knowledge that can solve difficult problems or form highly accurate predictions. An elementary form of collective intelligence is the suggestion box, which has been taken to new levels of sophistication by such companies as Dell and IBM in the form of "idea jams." (See chapters 5 and 6.)

Crowd creation

The crowd also possesses a great deal of creative energy. Companies have successfully outsourced to the crowd tasks that include the filming of TV commercials, language translation, and redesigning audio components. (See chapter 7.)

Crowd voting

This category of crowdsourcing uses the crowd's judgments to organize vast quantities of information. It's commonly used to sift through the flood of contributions that often follow crowdsourcing's open call. But the crowd needn't consciously "vote" on something to express its preference. Google uses the crowd to organize search results, and online publishers use them to indicate which articles are the most popular with readers. (See chapter 8.)

Crowdfunding

Crowdfunding taps the collective pocketbook, allowing large groups of people to replace banks and other institutions as a source of funds. The unorthodox music label SellaBand allows people to buy shares in the bands hosted on its website. When enough "believers" buy in, SellaBand produces their album. (See chapter 9.)

A few caveats: It's worth noting that successful crowdsourcing projects often use a combination of these approaches. In fact, the T-shirt company Threadless arguably uses them all. And then there are variations even within these broad categories. The actual mechanics of any individual launch needs to be fine-tuned to your particular needs.

2. Pick the Right Crowd

Here's the good news: the crowd—the number of people around the world with Internet access—consists of over 1 billion people, and it's growing fast. Alpheus Bingham, the founder of the R&D crowdsourcing company Inno-Centive, has said that the optimum size of a user-base for crowdsourcing purposes is around five thousand people. This means that if you can entice even 1 percent of 1 percent of 1 percent of the crowd, you would still have twice as many contributors as you ostensibly need. Now here's the bad news: it needs to be the right people. This principle is closely related to picking the right crowdsourcing model. If you're creating a service in which sports teams can tap the best-performing Fantasy Baseball managers for their aggregated wisdom, ten thousand scientists won't do you much good. Craft your message for your purposes and broadcast it through the right outlets.

3. Offer the Right Incentives

The crowd moves in mysterious ways, and attracting a crowd is much easier than keeping them. With few exceptions, the most important component to a successful crowdsourcing effort is a vibrant, committed community. Getting people involved requires understanding what motivates them to contribute in the first place. Personal glory, the chance to interact with like-minded peers, and the opportunity to improve their skills or simply learn something new all play a role. And don't discount the role cash plays. One theme that emerged in many of my interviews for this book is that people need to feel rewarded for their efforts, even if the money in question is just a token amount. The question of incentives also varies according to who's doing the crowdsourcing. People might freely donate their knowledge and labor to a nonprofit, but feel far more compunction about expending that energy to benefit a VC-funded start-up. In other words, if you're planning on using the crowd to make a mint, you better consider establishing some form of revenue sharing with your contributors. The crowd is savvy. If they smell snake oil, they'll abscram and never come back, blogging about their negative experience as they leave.

4. Keep the Pink Slips in the Drawer

It sounds so easy: why pay an employee to perform a job the crowd will do for free? Lots of reasons, as H. J. Heinz discovered when it "invited America to make [its] next great Heinz Ketchup commercial" in 2007. The company spent months planning its campaign, to say nothing of the considerable expense of promoting the contest. Then it had to hire an outside promotions firm just to review the flood of submissions that resulted, the vast majority of which were deemed offensive, in violation of copyright laws, or simply bad. Ironically, Heinz was badmouthed on its website forums for being lazy and just angling for cheap labor. The magazine *Budget Travel* underwent a similar experience when it filled its June 2008 issue exclusively with content contributed by its readers. "Occasionally someone would ask if we were doing a reader-generated issue because it was cheaper or easier," the magazine's editor, Erik Torkells, wrote in a subsequent blog post. "Let's be perfectly clear: Making this issue was neither cheap nor easy." That's not to say that either effort failed. The winning Heinz ads (as well as the five runners-up) were all clever and effective, and *Budget Traveler* has said it will do another user-generated issue in 2009. "Because in the future," Torkells wrote, "love it or hate it, an editor's role will be to lead a conversation, not deliver a monologue."

5. The Dumbness of Crowds, or the Benevolent Dictator Principle

When we launched our crowdsourced journalism project Assignment Zero, we figured we'd throw up our shingle and let the crowd organize itself into an efficient volunteer newsroom. Ha! People might be enthusiastic and capable of some level of self-organization according to their interests and abilities, but they also require direction and guidance and someone to answer their questions. Assignment Zero didn't achieve liftoff until we had installed a layer of administration (albeit composed of volunteers chosen from the crowd) to serve these functions.

One of the greatest misapprehensions around crowdsourcing is that the crowd works in isolation. In reality, the most successful crowdsourcing efforts are products of a robust collaboration between the crowd and the individuals guiding them, who are called "benevolent dictators" in open source software projects. Reacting to the Web 2.0 vogue for such collective efforts as Wikipedia, in 2006 the computer scientist Jaron Lanier wrote an essay for the online magazine *Edge* entitled "Digital Maoism." While I don't share his skeptical view of the crowd's abilities, he makes a few excellent points: "Every authentic example of collective intelligence that I am aware of also shows how that collective was guided or inspired by well-meaning individuals. These people focused the collective and in some cases also corrected for some of the common hive mind failure modes." In other words, someone needs to play the role of the decider, as Linus Torvalds did in the case of the open source project Linux. Communities need community leaders.

6. Keep It Simple and Break It Down

When it comes to crowdsourcing, any task worth doing is worth dividing up into its smallest possible components. In his book *The Wealth of Networks*, legal scholar and writer Yochai Benkler refers to this as "modularity," which he defines as the "property of a project that describes the extent to which it can be broken down into smaller . . . modules that can be independently produced before they are assembled into a whole." The need to do this isn't because the people in the crowd are stupid, it's because they're busy. "While creative capacity and judgment are universally distributed in a population, available time and attention are not," Benkler writes. This mimics the way people already work on the Web: a blog post, for instance, can be as short as a link or as long as a book.

This basic principle has been applied to a wide variety of crowdsourcing applications. The NASA clickworkers program has taken the job of measuring craters and made it into a five-second task. This allows contributors to analyze as many or as few craters as time and interest permits. Visitors to Threadless.com can vote on as many T-shirt designs as they like, or if time allows, create their own design. At iStockphoto, people can do as little as upload a photograph or two, or become an "inspector" that devotes up to forty hours per week examining the photos uploaded by other contributors to ensure they meet basic standards of quality and don't violate copyright.

It's also important to keep the *nature* of the tasks simple. Again, this isn't because the crowd is dense, it's because it's diverse. When Wikipedia founder Jimmy Wales was asked why his online encyclopedia had done so well, he said it was because everyone already knew what an encyclopedia entry was. By bringing clarity and simplicity to your appeal—find the best minor league pitcher, translate this paragraph into French—you greatly increase the odds that someone will want to contribute.

7. Remember Sturgeon's Law

Because of the potential size of the audience (which includes, in theory anyway, the over 1 billion people with Internet access), the response to an open call for participation can be overwhelming. Most of the resulting submissions—as Heinz, Current, or any number of the other people profiled in this book can attest—will, to put it charitably, fail to meet a desired standard of quality. Sturgeon's Law (named after the science-fiction writer Theodore Sturgeon) holds that 90 percent of everything is crap, and a number of the people I talked to for this book thought that was a lowball estimate.

I've argued that the proliferation of technology, in all its myriad forms, has led to an increase in the stock of knowledge, ability, and taste among the general population, but this welcome development will take years to fully manifest. And even then I suspect real talent will remain a rare commodity. Crowdsourcing's chief merit lies in providing a previously nonexistent outlet for this talent. The challenge lies in finding it, which is the subject of the next rule.

8. Remember the 10 Percent, the Antidote to Sturgeon's Law

Crowdsourcing presents us with two invaluable gifts: First, it provides a venue in which we can pursue pastimes for which we have no aptitude or ability. Second, it ruthlessly, and perhaps mercifully, buries the products of these adventures where few are likely to witness them. If there's any real magic in crowdsourcing, it lies in the ability of the crowd to correct its tendency to flood the networks with a glut of low-quality fare. In other words, if you find yourself inundated with submissions, don't bother sifting through them yourself. Take the expedient and democratic course of allowing the crowd to find the best and brightest diamonds in the rough.

9. The Community's Always Right

Think of this as the complement to the Benevolent Dictator Principle. Yes, communities need a decider (as well as a helping hand, a shoulder to cry on, and an occasional dean of discipline). But in the end, as Yochai Benkler noted in the context of Linus Torvalds, the dictator's authority is moral and persuasive, not absolute. You can try to guide the community, but ultimately you'll wind up following them.

10. Ask Not What the Crowd Can Do for You, but What You Can Do for the Crowd

I saved this rule for last because if I could leave you with any single thought it would be this one: crowdsourcing works best when an individual or company gives the crowd something it wants. Another way of thinking about this is that successful crowdsourcing involves satisfying the uppermost tier on Maslow's hierarchy of needs. People are drawn to participate because some psychological, social, or emotional need is being met. And when the need isn't met, they don't participate.

What this means for companies is that they must reverse the thinking that normally goes into employee relations. If iStockphoto had approached community building by trying to create a low-paid workforce of amateur photographers, it would have failed. Instead, Livingstone set out to create a home on the Web where enthusiasts could share and critique one another's work and, oh yeah, maybe make a few bucks on the side.

NOTES

INTRODUCTION

Pages 1–3: The story of how Threadless came into being originated in a series of interviews I did with Threadless Chief Creative Officer Jeffrey Kalmikoff, as well as from Threadless.com's Website (www .Threadless.com). Also see: "Threadless Puts Art Before TS," by Beth Wilson, *Women's Wear Daily,* December 27, 2007; "String of New Concepts Puts Threadless on Map," by Mary Ellen Podmolik, *Chicago Tribune,* October 29, 2007; and "Designed to Grow," by Marc Weingarten, *Fortune Small Business,* July/August 2007. Jake Nickell also wrote an informative history of Threadless (www.threadless.com/profile/1/skaw/blog/227766/Threadless_com_The_History).

Page 4: "Teen Content Creators and Consumers," by Amanda Lenhart and Mary Madden, Pew Internet & American Life Project, November 2, 2005. The report is available as a free download (www.pewinternet .org/ppf/r/166/report_display.asp). Alvin Toffler, *The Third Wave* (New York: Random House Value Publishing, 1987).

Page 6: "The Rise of Crowdsourcing," Jeff Howe, *Wired,* June 2006.

Page 8: "IBM has pumped a billion dollars into open source development." Yochai Benkler, *The Wealth of Networks: How Social Production Transforms Markets & Freedom* (New Haven and London: Yale University Press, 2006).

Pages 9–13: A. G. Lafley and Ram Charan, *The Game-Changer: How You Can Drive Revenue and Profit Growth with Innovation* (New York: Crown Business, 2008).

Pages 11–13: Information on SETI@home originated in "SETI@home: Massively Distributed Computing for SETI," by Eric Korpela et al., *Computing in Science & Engineering,* January 2001; "SETI@home: Classic: In Memoriam" (http://setiathome.berkeley.edu/classic.php); and in "Scientists, Be on Guard . . . ET Might Be a Malicious Hacker," by Ian Sample, *Guardian,* November 25, 2005.

1 • THE RISE OF THE AMATEUR

Page 27: "The IRS defines . . ." Clay Shirky, *Here Comes Everybody* (New York: Penguin, 2008, p. 75).

Page 27: The information attributed to "one study of the iStock workforce" came from an unpublished report: "Moving the Crowd at iStockphoto: The Composition of the Crowd and Motivations for Participation in Crowdsourcing Applications," by Daren Carroll Brabham, a graduate student at the University of Utah doing his master's thesis on crowdsourcing.

Page 28: Charles Leadbeater and Paul Miller, *The Pro-Am Revolution: How Enthusiasts Are Changing Our Economy and Society* (London: Demos, 2004). The book is available for download at www.demos.co .uk/publications/proameconomy.

Page 29: The data on job satisfaction rates came from a 2007 survey conducted by The Conference Board. Available at www.conference-board.org/aboutus/about.cfm.

Page 29: "By 2005, that number had jumped to 11.5 billion . . ." A. Gulli and A. Signorini, "The Indexable Web Is More Than 11.5 Billion Pages," University of Iowa Department of Computer Science, 2005.

Pages 30–31: Ornithology and birding: An interview with Pat Leonard of the Cornell Lab of Ornithology. Also "The Growing Popularity of Birding in the United States," by H. Ken Cordell, Nancy G. Herbert, and Francis Pandolfi, *Birding,* April 1999; and "Birdwatching Hobby Takes Flight," by Kristen Wyatt, *USA Today,* September 19, 2007.

Page 33: Elizabeth B. Keeney, *The Botanizers: Amateur Scientists in Nineteenth-Century America* (Chapel Hill: University of North Carolina Press, 1992).

Page 34: Francis Bacon from *The Stanford Encyclopedia of Philosophy,* available at www.plato.standord.edu.

Page 34: *Novum Organum,* by Francis Bacon, was published in 1620. The full text is available at www.constitution.org/bacon/nov_org.htm.

Pages 32–35: The Invisible College: "Comenius and the Invisible College," by Dorothy Stimson, *Isis,* September 1935. Also by Stimson: "Dr. Wilkins and the Royal Society," *Journal of Modern History,* December 1931, and "The Royal Society and the Founding of the British Association for the Advancement of Science," by L. Pearce Williams, *The Journal of Modern History,* November 1961.

Page 35: Adam Smith, *An Inquiry into the Nature and Causes of the Wealth of Nations* (London: 1776), is available online at www.econlib.org/library/Smith/smWN.html.

Page 36: Charles Babbage, *Reflections on the Decline of Science in England, and on Some of Its Causes* (London: B. Fellowes, 1830), is available online through Google Books.

Page 37: "a full 63 percent of high school graduates . . ." Tamara Henry, "Report: Greater Percentage of Americans Educated," *USA Today,* June 5, 2002.

Page 38: "The number of art degrees granted . . ." National Center for Education Statistics at www.nces.ed.gov/programs/digest/2007menu_tables.asp.

Pages 41–44: The information about Giorgia Sgargetta came from an article in the German magazine *Zeit Wissen* by Jens Uehlecke, "Will Trade Brains for Cash." General InnoCentive information came from conversations with Karim Lakhani at Harvard, InnoCentive founder Alpheus Bingham, and Chief Scientific Officer Jill Panetta.

Page 46: "Roughly 45 percent of iStockers . . ." from Daren Carroll Brabham's report.

Page 46: "One revealing MIT study . . ." from a 2007 Harvard Business School Working Paper, "The Value of Openness in Scientific Problem Solving," by Karim R. Lakhani, Lars Bo Jeppesen, Peter A. Lohse, and Jill A. Panetta.

2 ● FROM SO SIMPLE A BEGINNING

Pages 47–52: For the early history of computing and open source software I drew on three books: *Rebel Code: Inside Linux and the Open Source Revolution,* by Glyn Moody (Cambridge, Mass: Perseus Publishing, 2001); *The Success of Open Source,* by Steven Weber (Cambridge,

Mass., and London: Harvard University Press, 2004); and *Free Software Society: Selected Essays of Richard M. Stallman,* edited by Joshua Gay (Boston: Free Software Society, 2002).

Page 56: Eric S. Raymond's essay "The Cathedral and the Bazaar" first appeared in print in *The Cathedral & the Bazaar: Musings on Linux and Open Source by an Accidental Revolutionary,* by Eric S. Raymond (Sebastapol, Calif.: O'Reilly Media, 2001). The essay is available online at www.firstmonday.org/ISSUES/issue3_3/raymond/index.html.

Pages 55–60: The history of Wikipedia was informed by an interview with Larry Sanger, as well as "The Hive," by Marshall Poe, *Atlantic Monthly,* September 2006; and "The Early History of Nupedia and Wikipedia: A Memoir," by Larry Sanger, published on the website Slashdot. Sanger's memoir is available at www.features.slashdot.org/article/pl?sid=05/04/18/164213.

Pages 64–65: On IBM's patent portfolio: www.ibm.com/ibm/licensing/patents/portfolio.shtml.

Page 67: Information on the growth of patent suits from "Patents Pending: Patent Reform for the Innovation Economy," by Julie A. Hedlund, The Information & Technology Foundation, May 2007. Information on the cost of patent litigation from a 2003 Report of Economic Survey published by the American Intellectual Property Lawyers Association.

Page 67: Figures pertaining to USPTO backlog, examiners, and filings all taken from the USPTO website: www.uspto.gov. The figure of twenty hours per application: "Patently Absurd—the US Patent System Is in Disarray," by Eric Chabow, *Information Week,* February 20, 2006. Restrictions on examiners' use of the Internet and USPTO's refusal to recognize computer science training as qualifications: "Community Patent Review Project Summary," New York Law School Institute for Information Law & Policy, February 2007.

Page 71: Microsoft's patent strategy: "Why Bill Gates Wants 3,000 New Patents," by Randall Stoss, *New York Times,* July 31, 2005.

3 • FASTER, CHEAPER, SMARTER, EASIER

Page 75: British Internet ad market: "UK Web Ad Spending 'To Exceed TV in 2009,' " by Mark Sweeney, *Guardian,* January 3, 2008. In the U.S. market, the technology research firm Yankee Group estimates the online ad market will reach $50 billion by 2011, well above the projected revenues for the U.S. newspaper advertising industry.

Page 78: In October 2005, the Olympic Stylus 6 megapixel camera went on sale for just under $300. In 1991, the first digital SLR camera, the Kodak DCS-100, cost $13,000.

Pages 78–80: The passages on the birth of desktop publishing are from Pamela Pfiffner, *Inside the Publishing Revolution* (Berkeley, Calif.: Peachpit Press, 2003).

Page 84: Shirky, *Here Comes Everybody,* pp. 128–129.

Page 85: The information on amateur contributions to astronomy, as well as technological improvements to affordable telescopes, from Chris Anderson, *The Long Tail: Why the Future of Business Is Selling Less of More* (New York: Hyperion, 2005), as well as Timothy Ferris, *Seeing in the Dark: How Backyard Stargazers Are Probing Deep Space and Guarding Earth from Interplanetary Peril* (New York: Simon & Schuster, 2002).

Pages 85–90: Some of this material first appeared in *Wired* in an article I wrote about *The Burg,* "Must-Stream TV," February 2007.

Page 94: Recording industry revenues available at www.riaa.com/keystatistics.php.

Page 96: "acute combined effects" James Montgomery, "Hawthorne Heights' Casey Calvert Died of Accidental Mixture of Medications," MTV.com, December 17, 2007. The article is available at www.mtv.com/news/articles/1576570/20071217/hawthorne_heights.jhtml.

Page 96: For more on the "fab revolution" see "The Dream Factory," by Clive Thompson, *Wired,* September 2005.

4 • THE RISE AND FALL OF THE FIRM

Page 100: Robert D. Putnam, *Bowling Alone: The Collapse and Revival of American Community* (New York: Simon & Schuster, 2000).

Pages 101–09: Parts of the section on the *Cincinnati Enquirer* were previously published in "To Save Themselves, US Newspapers Put Readers to Work," by Jeff Howe, *Wired,* July 2007.

Page 110: "The Nature of the Firm," by Ronald Coase, *Economica,* Vol. 4, No. 16, November 1937, pp. 386–405. The essay is also available online at www.cerna.ensmp.fr.

Page 111: Thomas Malone, *The Future of Work: How the New Order of Business Will Shape Your Organization, Your Management Style, and Your Life* (Boston: Harvard Business School Press, 2004).

Page 112: Eric von Hippel, *Democratizing Innovation* (Cambridge, Mass.: MIT Press, 2005). The book can be also be downloaded at web.mit.edu/evhippel/www/books.htm.

Page 112: Clay Shirky, "Situated Software," first published March 30, 2004, on the "Networks, Economics, and Culture" mailing list.

Pages 114–116: Benkler, *The Wealth of Networks,* pp. 91–127.

Page 117: "The Computer as a Communication Device," by J. C. R. Licklider and Robert W. Taylor, *Science and Technology,* April 1968.

Pages 119–121: I drew most of the information about the early days of the WELL from Howard Rheingold, *The Virtual Community: Homesteading on the Electronic Frontier* (New York: HarperCollins, 1993), and from "The WELL: Small Town on the Internet Highway System," a paper presented by Cliff Figallo at a Harvard University conference in May 1993.

Page 127: "The Benefits of Facebook 'Friends': Social Capital and College Students' Use of Online Social Network Sites," by Nicole B. Ellison, Charles Steinfeld, and Cliff Lampe, *Journal of Computer-Mediated Communication,* Vol. 12, No. 4.

5 • THE MOST UNIVERSAL QUALITY

Pages 130–132: Scott Page, *The Difference: How the Power of Diversity Creates Better Groups, Firms, Schools, and Societies* (Princeton, N.J.: Princeton University Press, 2007); pp. xviiii–xxi and 133–135.

Page 134: "Works better in practice . . ." Noam Cohen, "The Latest on Virginia Tech, From Wikipedia," *New York Times,* April 23, 2007. This transposition of the familiar adage "It works in theory, but not in practice" predates Wikipedia, and has even been used by the Cornell economist Maureen O'Hara to describe the stock market.

Pages 135–138: I gleaned most of the information on the MATLAB contest from a series of interviews and e-mails with Ned Gulley. However, Gulley has written several edifying papers about the contest and its implications. "Patterns of Innovation: A Web-Based MATLAB Programming Contest" was delivered at the Conference on Human Factors in Computing Systems in 2001 and is available online at portal.acm.org/citation.cfm?id=634266; and "In Praise of Tweaking: A Wiki-like Programming Contest" (New York: Association for Computing Machinery, 2004) is available at portal.acm.org/citation.cfm?id=986253.986264.

Pages 138–140: "The Use of Knowledge in Society," by F. A. Hayek, *American Economic Review,* Vol. XXXV, No. 4; September 1945, pp. 519–530.

Page 140: Gulley presented his charts in a PowerPoint presentation, "Addictive Collaboration: Patterns of Participation in an Open Programming Contest," at the 2007 O'Reilly Media hacker confab, Foo Camp.

Page 142: James Surowiecki, *The Wisdom of Crowds: Why the Many Are Smarter Than the Few and How Collective Wisdom Shapes Business, Economies, Societies, and Nations* (New York: Doubleday, 2004), pp. xi–xiv, 3–6.

Pages 143–145: I am indebted to Scott Page for the passages explaining why the *Who Wants to Be a Millionaire* audience can beat the "experts" and why the MATLAB contest works as well as it does. He provided me with an excellent distillation of the logical truths at work in collective intelligence in *The Difference,* and he patiently explained the thornier passages to me.

6 · WHAT THE CROWD KNOWS

Pages 146, 151–152: Karim R. Lakhani et al., "The Value of Openness in Scientific Problem Solving."

Page 152: "strength of weak ties . . ." The results of Granovetter's survey were published as part of his doctoral dissertation: "Changing Jobs: Channels of Mobility Information in a Suburban Community" (Cambridge, Mass.: Harvard University, 1970) and informed Granovetter's landmark paper "The Strength of Weak Ties," *American Journal of Sociology* (Vol. 78, Issue 6, May 1973), pp. 1360–1380.

Page 154: "introduced a bill that would replace the drug monopolies . . ." from "Invent a Drug, Win $1 Million," by Catherine Rampell, *Slate* magazine, January 23, 2008.

Pages 155–157: Netflix Prize: "This Psychologist Might Outsmart the Math Brains Competing for the Netflix Prize," by Jordan Ellenberg, *Wired,* February 2008.

Pages 160–169: There's a wealth of material on prediction markets. Surowiecki wrote about them in *The Wisdom of the Crowds* (pp. 19–22 and 79–83), and he took the subject up again in two articles: "The Science of Success," *The New Yorker,* July 9, 2007; and "Crowdsourcing the Crystal Ball," *Forbes,* October 15, 2007. Scott Page explores prediction markets in *The Difference* (pp. 231–234, 320–322); and Cass R. Sunstein, a University of Chicago law professor, devotes a chapter to information markets in *Infotopia: How Many Minds Produce Knowledge* (New York and Oxford: Oxford University Press, 2006).

Pages 160–161: "Results from a Dozen Years of Election Futures Markets Research," by Joyce Berg et al., College of Business Administration, University of Iowa, November 2000.

Page 161: "While the laws of statistics . . ." from "Speculating on Politicians, Not Pork Bellies," by Mike Allen, *New York Times,* September 1, 1996.

Page 163: "Kerry's Iowa Problem," by Farhand Manjoo, *Salon,* August 16, 2004.

Pages 164–166: Robin Hanson and the Policy Analysis Market: "The Man Who Would Have Us Bet on Terrorism—Not to Mention Discard Democracy and Cryogenically Freeze Our Heads—May Have a Point (About the Betting, We Mean)," by Jeremy Kahn, *Fortune,* September 15, 2003.

Pages 166–167: Thomas Malone, *The Future of Work,* pp. 95–109.

Page 167: The Commodity Futures Trading Commission letter that excepts Iowa Electronic Markets from prohibitions on gambling can be viewed online at www.cftc.gov/files/foia/repfoia/foirf0503b002.pdf.

Page 168: The information on thin markets and Bernardo Huberman's systems of correcting for resulting biases comes from two interviews with Huberman and from an article he coauthored with Kay-Yut Chen and Leslie R. Fine, "Predicting the Future," *Information Systems Frontiers* 2003, 5:1, pp. 47–61.

7 · WHAT THE CROWD CREATES

Page 186: "They can break the story . . ." from "The Rise of the Citizen Paparazzi," by Andrew Lavallee, *Wall Street Journal,* February 26, 2008.

Page 187: "User-generated pornography . . ." from "Obscene Losses," by Claire Hoffman, *Portfolio,* November 2007.

Page 209: "User-Submitted Content: Current Versus CNN," by Caroline Palmer, *Broadcast & Cable,* January 1, 2007.

Page 213: "It's like throwing a party . . ." from "All the World's a Story," by David Carr, *New York Times,* March 19, 2007.

Pages 218–219: The WNYC Crowdsourcing: the SUV project can be viewed at www.wnyc.org/shows/bl/suv_map_07.html; and the Deli project is at http://www.wnyc.org/shows/bl/gouge_map_milk_07 .html.

Page 219: TalkingPointsMemo: See Noam Cohen, "Blogger, Sans Pajamas, Rakes Muck and a Prize," *New York Times,* February 25, 2008.

8 • WHAT THE CROWD THINKS

Page 224: " 'Idol' " Attracts More Than 32M Viewers," by David Bauder, Associated Press, January 30, 2007.

Pages 238–239: "What is the 1% rule?" by Charles Arthur, *Guardian,* July 20, 2006. Horowitz's original blog post proposing the rule, entitled "Creators, Synthesizers, and Consumers" (February 17, 2006), can be found at www.elatable.com/blog/?p=5.

Page 229: ". . . a strategy that turns market research into quick sales . . ." from "Collective Customer Commitment: Turning Market Research Expenditures into Sales," by Susumu Ogawa and Frank T. Piller, *Sloan Management Review,* Vol. 47 (Winter 2006).

Page 232: "Hardware doesn't matter at this point . . ." from "Intel Launches a Digg to Rate Software Startups," by Bryan Gardiner, Wired.com, October 8, 2007.

Pages 232–237: John Battelle, *The Search: How Google and Its Rivals Rewrote the Rules of Business and Transformed Our Culture* (New York: Penguin, 2005).

Page 237: John Riedl, Joseph Konstan, and Eric Vrooman, *Word of Mouse: The Marketing Power of Collaborative Filtering* (New York: Warner Books, 2002).

Pages 237–238: The passage about the seminal Xerox PARC collaborative filter from: "Using Collaborative Filtering to Weave an Information Tapestry," by David Goldberg et al., Communications of the ACM (Association for Computing Machinery): 35, 1992.

Page 240: "One early paper on Folksonomies . . ." from "Folk-sonomies: Cooperative Classification and Communication Through Shared Metadata," by Adam Mathes, Computer Mediated Communication, University of Illinois Urbana-Champaign, December 2004.

Page 242: Henry Wang and Famster from "The Wizards of Buzz," by Jamin Warren and John Jurgenses, *The Wall Street Journal*, February 10, 2007.

Page 244: The interview between Derek Powazek and Ragnar Danneskjold can be read online at http://zero.newassignment.net/filed/exploring_dark_side_crowdsourcing_ragnar_danneskjo.

Page 245: Andrew Keen, *The Cult of the Amateur: How Today's Internet Is Killing Our Culture* (New York: Doubleday Business, 2007).

9 • WHAT THE CROWD FUNDS

Page 247: Nicholas P. Sullivan, *You Can Hear Me Now: How Microloans and Cell Phones Are Connecting the World's Poor to the Global Economy* (San Francisco: Jossey-Bass, 2007).

Pages 247–253: The passage on Kiva was based on an interview with Matt Flannery as well as an article Matt wrote, "Kiva and the Birth of Person-to-Person Microfinance," in *Innovations* (MIT Press, Winter & Spring 2007). The information about Elizabeth Omalla is from the excellent *Frontline: World* segment entitled "Uganda: A Little Goes a Long Way." The entire segment can be viewed at www.pbs.org/frontlineworld/stories/uganda601/.

Page 255: Contributors from Assignment Zero, the crowdsourced journalism experiment I write about in Chapter 7, conducted Q&As with both William Brooks (MyFootballClub) and Matthew Hanson (A Swarm of Angels). Johannes Kuhn interviewed Brooks (zero.newassignment.net/filed/crowdsourced_soccer_uk_interview_william_brooks) and Elina Shatkin interviewed Hanson (zero.newassignment.net/filed/interview_matt_hanson_director_crowd_funded_open_s).

10 • TOMORROW'S CROWD

Page 261: Marc Prensky, *Don't Bother Me Mom—I'm Learning!* (St. Paul, Minn.: Paragon House, 2006).

Pages 262, 263: "Where Death Is Final, and Caution Is a Must," *New York Times,* by Charles Herold, January 18, 2001; and "Top Ten Reasons Half Life Is Still #1," by Kevin Bowen, GameSpy.com, February 9, 2003.

Page 266: "The tech-camp market is now worth . . ." from "At Tech Camp, Video Games, Robots—and No Lanyards," by Nelson Hernandez, *Washington Post,* July 13, 2007.

Pages 266–268: There isn't much of a literature about modding video games outside of the predictable *Half-Life 2 Mods for Dummies,* but the tech writer Wagner James Au wrote a seminal history of the art form, "Triumph of the Mod," for *Salon* (April 16, 2002).

Page 268: Gaming revenue figures from PricewaterhouseCoopers, "Global Entertainment and Media Outlook: 2007–2011: Video Games," p. 10.

Pages 266, 270: "Teen Content Creators and Consumers," by Amanda Lenhart and Mary Madden; and "Teens and Social Media," by Amanda Lenhart et al., December 19, 2007.

Page 272: Henry Jenkins, *Convergence Culture: Where Old and New Media Collide* (New York: NYU Press, 2006).

Page 273: "Copy, Paste, Remix: Profile Codes on MySpace," by danah boyd and Dan Perkel, paper presented at the annual meeting of the International Communication Association, April 8, 2008.

ACKNOWLEDGMENTS

Writing any book is, in its way, an act of crowdsourcing. This was especially true in the case of this book. While the words are mine alone, the ideas were influenced by a multitude of sources. First and foremost I would like to thank my longtime editor at *Wired* magazine, Mark Robinson. He suffers my half-baked story ideas, delivered via frequent, elliptical phone calls, with cheerful stoicism. The basic thesis behind crowdsourcing—as well as the word itself—emerged out of just such a conversation. Without his capacious intelligence the article that inspired this book would have never found its way to publication. I owe a debt as well to *Wired*'s editor in chief, Chris Anderson, who has not only given me an incomparable venue for my writing, but also offered his advice and support at every juncture. He even introduced me to his literary agent, John Brockman. John wisely rejected my first pass at a book proposal, and he performed wonders with the second.

Most authors are lucky to have one good editor on their book. I was fortunate enough to have two. John Mahaney at Crown and Nigel Wilcockson at Random House UK both made enormous contributions to the book. John was as gracious an editor as any writer could want. He gently pushed me to refine my arguments and clarify my ideas. Nigel consistently identified troubled passages and just as consistently suggested deft corrections for them. The book benefited immensely from their ministrations. In addition, Kyle Pope at *Portfolio* magazine and my colleague Frank Rose gave selflessly of their time and considerable editorial experience in agreeing to read (and reread) early drafts. Vanessa Mobley, a friend and an editor at Penguin, provided the compass that guided me through the emotional rigors of writing a book. She is adored by her authors, and now I know why.

I would be remiss if I neglected to thank the readers of the crowdsourcing blog. Alan Booker, Shazz Mack, and Daren Carroll Brabham offered astute criticism that helped shape my thinking at crucial junctures. I'd also like to thank my assistants, Suzanne Wu, Angela Watercutter, Daniella Zalcman, and, last but decidedly not least, David Cohn. They helped with much of the tedious research that is at the heart of any book. My colleagues in *Wired*'s New York offices—Mark Horowitz, Nicholas Thompson, and Daniel Roth—tolerated my constant queries with inexplicable patience. I owe thanks as well to those friends who offered encouragement and advice when I most needed it. Valerie Stivers talked me off the cliff more than once, and whatever equanimity I maintained during the long march is due to people like Brendan, Ernie, Ellen, David, Eddie, and James.

Finally, I offer my entirely inadequate gratitude to my parents and sister. They taught by example—lessons from which I draw daily. If this book exhibits a certain optimism regarding the human condition, as I'd like to think it does, this is due to my mother. Her unflagging faith in our better angels has shaped my outlook on the world. This book is, in the end, a product of a catholic curiosity, a virtue inherited from my father. He devoted his life to teaching, but in truth he best embodies the perpetual student. The fact I write at all is thanks largely to my sister, Jeanine, who filled my childhood with drama, art, and song.

Writing a book places the burden of toil on its author. But the greater burden is borne by his or her family. I spent much of the last two years sequestered in a fluorescent-lit cubicle in Midtown Manhattan. At my desk, time slowed to a crawl; outside, the rush of events continued unabated, with, or—as was too often the case—without my presence. My wife, Alysia, picked up the considerable slack during this period, taking care of one child and bearing another all while producing some of the most provocative radio on the New York City dial. Alysia—my wife, coconspirator, lover, muse, and most of all, dearest of friends—this book is yours at least as much as it is mine.

INDEX

CROWDSOURCING THE COVER

It would be convenient for me to say I crowdsourced the making of this book. And it wouldn't precisely be a lie. Regular readers of my blog made crucial contributions early in the process. But for the most part, this book was produced the old-fashioned way—through countless hours of solitary toil. However, thanks to my publisher, I have been able to pull off the neat post-modern trick of not only exploring a topic but also embodying it. In November 2007 Adam Humphrey, Random House UK's marketing manager, dropped me an email: "We've put together a unique proposal to, in essence, 'crowdsource' the jacket design of the hardback publication here in the UK." Mildly abashed for not having thought of the idea myself, I gave Adam my unqualified blessing and so Random House launched the "coversourcing" campaign.

We employed the standard-issue crowdsourcing formula: Anyone who wanted to could submit designs, and the crowd would vote on their favorites. Through that January and February nearly 400 artists uploaded designs of varying quality, while some 10,000 votes were cast. At the end, a jury composed of myself, Random House UK's art director Richard Ogle, Angus Hyland at Pentagram Design UK, and Patrick Burgoyne, the editor of *Creative Review,* chose a winner from the twenty most popular entries.

The coversourcing campaign achieved its primary goal admirably: it generated a cover that was appropriate to the contents of the book, as well as being wonderfully inventive and visually appealing. It works on multiple levels: anyone familiar with the field of collective intelligence would recognize the ants as a sly reference to that particular insect's use of distributed cognition to accomplish tasks no individual ant could hope to perform. And for the uninitiated, it's simply a cool motif through which to visually depict the phenomenon of crowdsourcing.

But coversourcing served other purposes, equally valuable. One of the central advantages of crowdsourcing is that it provides answers to questions you didn't know you were asking. Which is to say, a large number of people will generally conjure up a far more interesting set of solutions than a single employee or freelancer might. The crowd thinks different. The covers are on view at www.coversourcing.co.uk and they provide ample evidence of this. Crowdsourcing, in this sense, is a ticket out of homogeneity.